The Romanovs

HARPER & ROW, PUBLISHERS NEW YORK EVANSTON SAN FRANCISCO LONDON

The Romanovs
Virginia Cowles

With colour photographs specially taken in Russia by Victor Kennett

Design and production by George Rainbird Ltd,
Marble Arch House, 44 Edgware Road, London w 2, England

Picture research: Tony Birks and Mary Clark
Design: Trevor Vincent

Text set and colour plates printed by
Westerham Press Ltd, Kent, England
Text printed and book bound by
Jarrold & Sons Ltd, Norwich, England

Text set in Monophoto Ehrhardt Series
453-11 on 13 pt

Library of Congress Catalog Card Number: 78-156516
ISBN 06-010908-4

Printed in Great Britain for Harper & Row, Publishers, Inc.

First published 1971

Dedicated to 'J'

1

Acknowledgments

The author would like to thank Mr John Hadfield for his many helpful suggestions
and for the eagle eye which he cast over the text; also Mr Tony Birks, Mrs Mary Clark,
and Mrs Audrey Kennett for their marathon research on illustrations; and
Miss Diana Matias for the perplexing work of checking and co-ordinating the
Russian spelling.

Lastly I would like to thank Professor Douglas Johnson of University College,
London, for reading the text and making a number of valuable (and amusing)
observations, although I do not want to incriminate him in the final deed, which
remains the author's responsibility.
V.C.

Contents

Colour Plates

All colour photographs are by Victor Kennett except for pages 18 (*above*), 45, 48 (*below*), and 165 (*above*), which are by Michael Holford, and page 255, which is by William MacQuitty.

CHAPTER I

The First Romanovs

1613–1696

SEVENTEENTH-CENTURY MOSCOW was the bastard child of East and West: a bizarre mixture of chanting priests and torture chambers, of gilded icons and oriental seraglios. Although the Russians had been converted to Christianity at the end of the tenth century, the Mongolian invasion two hundred and fifty years later had turned their piety into superstition, introduced autocracy in its most despotic form, and left behind a society both savage and perverse.

The French Foreign Office issued instructions to its emissaries describing the Russian boyars as 'bearded, long-haired men dressed with barbaric and sordid magnificence, maintaining a horde of lackeys who resemble janissaries and speaking a strange tongue which no one can understand . . .' Dr Samuel Collins, a Scottish physician who attended the Tsar, declared that the Russians were 'a people who differ from all other nations in most of their notions', and proceeded to list some of their idiosyncrasies:

> They whistle not with their lips (that they count profane) but through the teeth, a strange way of whistling indeed. When they spit on anything to wipe it (as shoes etc) they do use an action not unlike sneezing. In cases of admiration or incredulity instead of a shrug they wave their heads from one shoulder to another . . .
>
> In our clock-dials the finger moves to the figure; in the Russian *e contra*, the figures move to the pointer. One Mr Holloway, a very ingenious man, contrived the first dial of that fashion; saying, because they acted contrary to all men, 'twas fitting their work should be made suitable'.
>
> Because the Roman Catholics kneel at their devotion, they will stand, for they look upon kneeling as an ignoble and barbarous gesture. Because the Poles shave their beards, they count it sinful to cut them. Because the Tartar abhores swine-flesh they eat it rather than any other flesh . . .
>
> They paint or stain their teeth black upon the same design that our ladies wear black patches; or it may be that their teeth being spoiled by mercurial painting, they make a virtue of necessity and cry up for an ornament which is really a deformity . . . They have a secret among them to stain the very balls of their eyes black . . .
>
> Narrow feet and slender waists are alike ugly in their eyes. A lean woman they account unwholesome, therefore they who are inclined to leanness, give themselves over to all manner of Epicurism, on purpose to fatten themselves, and lye a bed all day drinking Russian Brandy (which fatten extremely) then they sleep and afterwards drink again like swine designed to make bacon . . .
>
> These are their odd customs which we may justly censure as the satirist did the debauched Romans in his time saying *Dum vitant stulti vitia in contraria currunt*. And indeed to say truth their madness is so great that all the *Hellebore* in Anticyra cannot purge it away . . .[1]

Michael Feodorovich (*left*), the reluctant founder of the Romanov dynasty. He was a delicate and melancholy man who shunned power and gladly allowed his father, the Patriarch Philaret, to become the effective ruler of Russia.

Foreign emissaries dreaded nothing more than a trip to Moscow as they found the country not only exasperating but frightening. Once, when a French ambassador unwittingly annoyed Ivan the Terrible, the latter flew into such a fit of pique that he nailed the envoy's hat to his head. That sort of behaviour belonged to the past, but even in the seventeenth century no western traveller could be certain when he would see the outside world again.

Foreigners usually entered the country through Poland or Lithuania; and if they were travelling in winter mounted their carriages on skis at Vilna. When they reached the frontier they invariably met with confusion. The Russians had instructions to treat all diplomats according to rank; but as the local governor found it difficult to assess the exact importance of his guests he usually insisted on sending a courier to Moscow for instructions, which of course meant weeks of waiting. When the welcoming party finally arrived an elaborate farce was played out. The Russians were determined not to lose face by being the first to mount, dismount, bow, remove their hats or even replace them. Some diplomats, unaware of this latter quirk, could not imagine what was causing the delay as they stood bareheaded in the freezing temperature.

Baron von Mayerberg, the Austrian emissary, who was sent to Moscow in 1661 to try and restore peace between Tsar Alexis and the King of Poland, complained that the officials with whom he had to deal were vain, arrogant and impolite; and that their food and manners were beyond the pale. Although the frontier Governor entertained the large Austrian delegation at dinner the members were dismayed to find that plates, napkins and cutlery were not regarded as necessary adjuncts. All the dishes were smothered in garlic and no one was allowed to leave the dining room 'unless he be carried out dead drunk'. The Baron himself was provided with a pewter plate as a mark of distinction but unfortunately it bore the remains of a previous meal. However, von Mayerberg had plenty of time to accustom himself to Russian ways, as the Tsar considered his mission 'inopportune' and reprimanded him by refusing to allow him to return home for two years.

Other diplomats were not as fortunate as the Baron. Frequently they were 'penned up like cattle' or treated more like convicts than ambassadors. When the Danish ambassador, M. Grab, was venturesome enough to visit Novgorod in 1649 he was accused of searching for treasures 'to take out of the country', and not only beaten but robbed of everything he possessed.

The manners of the Moscow nobility were not much superior to the rough ways of peasants. The Tsar's ambassadors to the West incurred such disapproval by their rowdy behaviour that the Austrian Emperor refused to give the usual golden chains and portraits to 'such worthless dogs'; and Christian IV of Denmark said: 'If these people come again we must build them a pig-sty, for nobody can live in any house that they have occupied till six months afterwards because of the stench they leave behind them.'

The announcement in Red Square that
Michael Romanov had been elected
Tsar (*above*) was hailed as a sign that the
'Troubled Time' was over.

This, then, was the Russian world that saw the dawn of a new dynasty.
The first Romanov ruler, Michael, emerged in the angry glare of 'the
Troubled Time', a modest phrase used to describe the utter chaos that
marked the end of the Rurik line at the close of the sixteenth century.
For fourteen years usurpers and pretenders vied with one another for the
throne, plunging the whole land into anarchy.

13

Such traditional enemies as the Poles and the Swedes were quick to seize the opportunity of attacking in the west, while marauding bands of Don Cossacks and Crim Tartars galloped in from the east. The Poles captured Moscow and installed themselves in the Kremlin. The Cossacks, after pillaging all the towns along the Volga, stormed the capital and besieged the occupying Poles. The Patriarch Hermogen, a prisoner in the Kremlin, smuggled out notes appealing to the people to assert themselves.

The Patriarch's pleas were answered and the invaders were thrown out of the capital.

The Church made use of the respite to convene an assembly of representatives to elect a new ruler. The most powerful candidates were caught in a deadlock and the choice finally fell on a boy of 16 whom no one knew personally and whose whereabouts was a mystery. Nevertheless, Michael Romanov had the right credentials. He was the grandnephew of Ivan IV and his first wife; his father, Patriarch Philaret, was not too deeply compromised with the past. After some months Michael was found living with his mother, who had taken the veil, in Ipatiev Abbey near Kostromo. Three hundred and five years later another Ipatiev house – at Ekaterinburg – was destined to provide the setting for the murder of the last Romanov ruler, which marked the end of the dynasty.

Michael ascended the throne in 1613 and, after a rule of thirty-two years, dominated by the struggle to rid the country of Poles and Swedes, succeeded in restoring a semblance of order. He was followed by his son, who ruled for almost the same length of time.

Tsar Alexis was a tall, handsome man 'of good impulses'. Unfortunately, he was ineffective as a ruler and allowed his favourites to administer the country as though it were a private concession. Corruption became so rampant that whatever taxes were raised the Treasury was always empty. Russian historians, however, praise his 'gentle and amiable character'. Throughout Lent he fasted for three days each week and on the other days ate only one meal composed of cabbage or mushrooms; 'he often prayed for five or six hours at a time and was said to prostrate himself between a thousand and fifteen hundred times daily.'

Nevertheless, when Alexis was angered his wrath assumed a distinctly Tartar complexion. This happened in 1662 when the currency had become so debased that thousands of starving people decided to petition the Tsar. They forced their way into the grounds of Alexis's estate at Kolomenskoye, a few miles from Moscow, and begged the sovereign to punish the men responsible for their wretched condition. Some of the leaders even had the temerity to catch hold of the buttons on the Tsar's long coat.

Although Alexis promised to look into the people's grievance he had undoubtedly had a bad fright; and when his troops arrived from Moscow, commanded by foreign mercenaries, he ordered them to fire on the

Eudoxia Streshneva (*above*), the second wife of Michael Romanov. The Tsar had tried to break with tradition by proffering a matrimonial hand first to Denmark and then to Sweden, but he was firmly snubbed by both.

LEFT Alexis was a firm believer in the Divine Right of Kings; he was so horrified to learn of the fate of Charles I of England that he immediately broke off diplomatic relations with the 'wicked infidels'.

BELOW 'The palace is worth seeing even though it is built of wood. Its decoration, which is astonishingly executed, is so remarkable and its profusion of gilding so brilliant that it appears to have emerged from a jewel-box.' Thus a visiting foreigner described Alexis's new palace at Kolomenskoye.

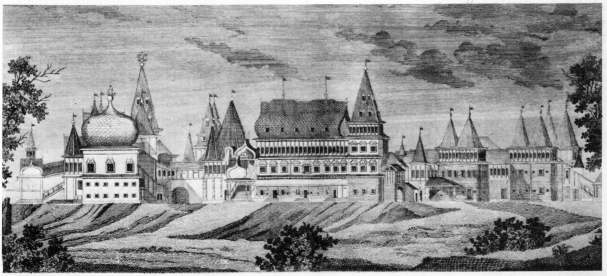

unarmed crowd. Hundreds were killed and wounded. But the matter did not end there. Although the great mass of demonstrators were village folk who had merely followed the rest through curiosity, he sentenced seven thousand people to death and ordered that another fifteen thousand should have their arms and legs cut off.

Apparently the Church found nothing to censure in this behaviour, as it continued to praise the pious Alexis for his God-fearing ways. Alexis responded by indulging the whims of the Patriarch, who believed that merriment was diabolical, and persuaded the Tsar to sign a *ukaz* proscribing musical instruments and outlawing jugglers. For superstitious reasons, not quite clear, the people were not allowed to bathe in lakes and rivers during thunderstorms, nor to gaze at the moon in the first days of the month. They were forbidden to lead about or encourage dancing bears or dogs; to sing popular 'devilish' songs or utter filthy jests; to box, or swing on swings, to leap on tables or wear masks. Church on Sunday became obligatory, soothsayers were outlawed, and cards, draughts and knucklebones declared an offence against the State. In 1660 a still fiercer *ukaz* confirmed the first edict and in 1687 the Patriarch issued an encyclical threatening persistent offenders with excommunication.

It is not surprising that drunkenness and homosexuality – two pleasures not outlawed by the Church – increased by leaps and bounds. 'In no other country in the world,' wrote the Serb traveller, M. Krifanic, 'is such disgusting drunkenness to be found . . . men, women, priests, laymen, roll about in the muddy streets and drink themselves to death.' As for unnatural vices, 'Go and learn temperance from the Turks,' he exhorted. 'These infidels are guilty of similar offences; but they have some shame . . . while in Russia people openly jest . . .'[2]

Surprisingly enough, the Tsar allowed his Chief Minister, the immensely rich and clever Artamon Matveyev, to ignore the anti-merriment law. Matveyev possessed the grandest house in Moscow and was encouraged to give concerts and theatricals for the sovereign's entertainment. His palace was furnished with all the comforts and luxuries that the West could produce, largely owing to the influence of his wife, a Miss Hamilton, from Scotland. Unlike the veiled ladies of Moscow who languished in seraglios and travelled through the streets in heavily curtained litters, Madame Matveyevna received her husband's guests and presided at his table.

The lady undoubtedly kindled the Tsar's interest in the skills and talents of the West. She persuaded Alexis to send emissaries abroad to collect as many coppersmiths and goldsmiths, bellmakers, stonemasons and agriculturalists as could be found. Soon the number of foreigners in Moscow had swollen to over a thousand families. While western envoys, dabbling in the dangerous business of politics, complained of the hazards of life in Russia, these men, many of whom had fled from persecution in their own country, enjoyed the protection of the Tsar and led reasonably secure lives.

Krutitskoye Podvore, the episcopal home of Patriarch Philaret.

Alexis was a responsive patron. He ordered upholstered carriages with glass windows, and planted the asparagus and roses introduced by a Dutchman and a Dane in his gardens at Kolomenskoye. He was delighted by the mechnical toys offered by the German craftsmen, and bought canaries that sang and dolls that walked. What pleased him most, however, were two copper lions dressed in sheepskin, which flanked his throne at Kolomenskoye. They rolled their eyes, wagged their tails, and opened ferocious jaws. Their life force was supplied by a man behind a curtain operating a pair of bellows.

The foreign quarter was situated on the river Yauza, about three miles from the Kremlin. It was known as the *Nemetskaya Sloboda* which, translated literally, meant Quarter of the Mutes – people who could not speak Russian. As, originally, Germans outnumbered other foreigners the words 'mute' and 'German' became synonymous and gradually were applied to all Westerners. Although in the seventeenth century the sector was dominated by Scots and Dutchmen it was still known as the German Quarter.

This small village with its neat houses and spotless streets offered a striking contrast to the Russian area; but the difference was most apparent in the treatment of women. Russian women were not regarded as individuals, but the property of their husbands. Men were forbidden to strike them in the eye or under the breast; otherwise they could treat them as they liked. Any woman foolish enough to rebel was punished severely; and a woman wicked enough to murder her husband was buried up to her neck and left to die.

The Tsar's sister and daughters escaped such fearful hazards by the depressing fate of spinsterhood. Too exhalted to become the property of one of the Tsar's subjects they were doomed to a life of excruciating boredom in the *terem*, or women's quarters, where they passed their lives embroidering and praying and supervising the children of their brothers. Only the Tsar's closest relations or most intimate friends entered the *terem*, lest an evil eye fell upon the inmates. Even a doctor was restricted in his movements and made to feel the pulse of his patient through a curtain.

As it was not the custom for girls to be educated, Tsar Alexis took a radical step when he allowed his precocious daughter, Sophia, to share lessons with her brother Alexis. The celebrated scholar, Simon Polotsky, taught her French, Latin and Polish, lectured her on world affairs and acquainted her with the peculiar state of Russia. The Tsar would have been appalled if he had known that one day Sophia would direct a bloody battle from the *terem* and become the first woman to rule Muscovy.

The Tsar was not quite 40 when his wife died. During twenty-one years of married life, Maria Miloslavskaya, who was a member of one of the most distinguished families in Russia, had provided him with thirteen children. But by 1670 death had taken such a severe toll that only two sons remained. The heir, Theodore, was intelligent but disfigured and

Dee Fornemsfies af Rysfe Fruentimbretz Fordenskap om Winteren, Betwander
der altydz för sina Jotter, eller Bladen spitiandes Een Knul Talersch Sklavinna på Dett att dee skelsive mage deste
Rionare Fonas.

sickly, and the second boy, Ivan, not only was defective in speech and sight but a semi-imbecile.

Alexis decided to re-marry. Although Russian nobles were not allowed to see their brides before the wedding, tsars had never adhered to this frustrating tradition. Custom decreed that two hundred of the most attractive females in the kingdom should be assembled for the sovereign's inspection.

Before the day arrived, however, Alexis had made his choice. At dinner one night Artamon Matveyev produced his very pretty ward, the 17-year-old Natalia Naryshkina, who instantly captivated the Tsar. Natalia was the daughter of Cyril Naryshkin, a petty nobleman of Tartar origin, whose brother was married to another Hamilton, a niece of Matveyev's wife.

Natalia sat at the table with the Tsar and when the latter departed he took her hand and said: 'Little pigeon, I will find thee a suitable mate'; and on his next visit he put his own ring on her hand. Matveyev, fearing the jealousy of the boyars – and the Miloslavsky family in particular – begged the Tsar to go through the ordinary motions by including Natalia in the selection panels. Matveyev's anxiety was not unfounded as Alexis's first choice of a bride, many years earlier, had been Euphemia Vsevolshka. When this girl was being dressed for her meeting with the Tsar her female attendants (said to have been bribed by the Miloslavskys) had pulled her hair so tight that she had fainted in the august presence. Alexis was told that she was suffering from epilepsy, and was so enraged that he had packed the girl and her entire family off to Siberia, and married Maria Miloslavskaya instead.

Stories soon were circulating that Matveyev had used sorcery to enable his ward, Natalia, to dazzle the Tsar. The marriage actually was postponed for half a year and when it finally took place Natalia was five months pregnant. She gave Alexis a fine, healthy son who was named Peter and later became known as Peter the Great.

The Tsar was so enamoured of his bride that he insisted on her accompanying him at all times, even when he went hawking. This suited Natalia who had been brought up by Matveyev's Hamilton wife, and entertained firm ideas about what she should be allowed to do. Soon she was driving to the country with the Tsar in an open carriage. At Preobrazhensky Palace a small theatre was built and plays were performed; and at Kolomenskoye a special cubicle was constructed in the audience chamber so that Natalia could amuse herself by watching the presentations.

The young Peter was adored by his parents and deluged with playthings, which included spears, pikes, and miniature bows and arrows. When the child was three Matveyev presented him with a tiny carriage. His mother's coach always went first, preceded by two hundred runners and twelve large snow-white horses. Then followed the tiny gold carriage of the youngest prince, drawn by four dwarf ponies. At the side rode four dwarfs on ponies.

Alexis's happiness was short-lived, for in 1676, after being married to Natalia for only six years, he died. His ailing son, Theodore, was proclaimed Tsar.

To keep Peter from the throne, Sophia urged her brother Theodore (*below*) to produce an heir. His first wife and child died, and his second bride could do little more than weep by his bedside.

Sophia's hour was approaching. Historians who never met this daughter of Alexis and Maria Miloslavskaya – a sister of the new ruler, Theodore – tell us that she was beautiful. But the French diplomat, Adrien de la Neuville, who encountered her frequently, has left a repellent portrait: 'A shapeless body, monstrously fat, a head as big as a bushel measure, hairs growing on her face, sores on her legs . . .' He goes on to add, however, that 'she is acute, subtle and shrewd in mind, as she is broad, short and coarse in person. And although she had never read Machiavelli, nor learnt anything about him, all his maxims come naturally to her.'[3]

Sophia had long foreseen that one day a battle would develop between the families of Alexis's two wives. Whichever faction succeeded in keeping a boy upon the throne would dominate the Kremlin; and Sophia decided to lead the Miloslavsky clan herself. She was at a disadvantage in having two brothers in poor health, while the Naryshkins not only possessed a robust candidate in the form of Peter, but also had the support of the powerful Matveyev, the Minister of Foreign Affairs.

However, with Theodore's accession Sophia moved into a commanding position. The new Tsar was devoted to his sister and showed his regard by summoning her to the Council Hall and inviting her to speak. The boyars were astonished that a woman should be held in such esteem; but as it gradually became apparent that Sophia was the power behind the throne, ambitious courtiers made it their business to win her favour. Prince Vasily Golitsyn made sure of it by becoming her lover.

Theodore was so fragile that no one expected him to live long; and Sophia was well aware that the real struggle would come after his death, when the choice would lie between the simple-minded Ivan and the obstreperous Peter. No chance must be lost to discredit Peter's mother and her Naryshkin relations, and the first obvious step was to bring about the downfall of their protector, Matveyev.

Sophia and Vasily Golitsyn opened their campaign by spreading rumours that Matveyev practised black magic and consorted with demons. But soon they hit upon an even better idea. Matveyev was head of the Apothecaries' Hall, which supplied the Tsar with his medicines; and it was quite obvious that the Tsar's health was not improving. Sophia succeeded in implanting such suspicions in Theodore's mind that he dismissed Matveyev as Foreign Minister and appointed him Governor of Verkhoturye in Siberia, to get him out of the way.

Matveyev put a brave face on his fall from favour and set out on his long, rough trip accompanied by his wife and son, and his son's tutor. His cortège consisted of more than a hundred servants. But when he reached the town of Kazan an official caught up with him and announced that he had been stripped of his title of boyar and all his possessions. He was to be escorted under heavy guard, like a common malefactor, to a

'A shapeless body, monstrously fat . . . hairs growing on her face, sores on her legs.' Adrien de la Neuville's contemporary account of the Tsarevna Sophia (*right*) is prejudiced, but he continues: '. . . she is acute, subtle and shrewd in mind.' Sophia was intelligent and ambitious, with a flair for government. After seven years of regency, she struggled with Peter for absolute power – and lost.

place of perpetual exile, Pustozersk, a wretched little town on the shores of the Arctic. His wife returned to Moscow, but his son, the tutor, and some fifty servants accompanied him in peasant carts across icy wastes inhabited by savage nomads, to his dismal destination.

In 1682, when Sophia was 25 years old, Theodore died and the Patriarch called an assembly which, recognizing the fact that Ivan was mentally retarded, proclaimed 10-year-old Peter the new Tsar. The time had come for the Miloslavskys and the Naryshkins to settle the issue by force. Sophia naturally wished her mother's kinsfolk – the Miloslavskys – to win. She knew that success depended on the support of the *streltsy*, the 'home guard' musketeers stationed in Moscow. For many months she had been preparing the ground, inviting the officers to the Kremlin and confiding her fears that her poor little brother, Ivan, might be deposed by the Naryshkins.

Sophia broke all tradition in her bid for power. Only the mother of the new Tsar was expected to take part in the procession. But to the

23

amazement of the crowds Sophia and all her ladies flowed out of the *terem* and followed the litter of Natalia Naryshkina and her son Peter on foot. The public had never seen these royal ladies before; their place was at home. Although their faces were veiled the daring spectacle of women marching defiantly in a public parade created a sensation.

Natalia was so angry that she left the ceremony and returned to the palace, but Sophia remained unperturbed, and when the service was over not only led her ladies across the square again but had the temerity to lament to the crowd: 'Ah, here we are, left all alone with nobody to protect us. My brother Ivan's rights had been passed over most unjustly . . . and it should be known to all in Moscow that wicked people hurried on my poor Theodore's death.'

Meanwhile poor old Matveyev had returned from his Arctic exile, summoned by the triumphant Naryshkins. He was unaware that Sophia and Prince Vasily Golitsyn were exciting the *streltsy* by their accusations. Not only did they claim that Theodore had been poisoned – this time by Dr von Gaden, the court physician, bribed, they said, by the Naryshkins – but that these same fiendish people now were plotting the death of the defenceless Ivan. The night that Matveyev arrived back in Moscow nineteen regiments of the *streltsy*, inflamed by the rumours, had come out in favour of Ivan as Tsar.

On the fifteenth of May the confrontation took place. At nine o'clock in the morning a *streltsy* officer rode through the streets of Moscow crying: 'To the Kremlin! The Naryshkins wish to kill the royal family. To arms, to save the Tsar!' Soldiers rolled up their sleeves and sharpened their spears in preparation for the bloody work before them, drums rolled, and thousands began the march to the Kremlin. For some inexplicable reason people inside the palace did not know what was happening until the *streltsy* surged into the courtyards. A frenzied mass of soldiery surrounded the palace, their spears shining in the sun, crying: 'Where is the Tsarevich Ivan? Death to the traitors!'

Matveyev and the Naryshkin family were holding a terrified council in the banqueting hall. In order to dispel the false rumours of treason it was decided that Natalia must show Ivan and Peter to the crowd. Trembling with fear she led the two boys to the balcony known as 'the Red Gate'. Matveyev accompanied her and spoke quietly to the savage sea of faces below. They had been deceived, he said; there were no traitors. He advised them to go home quietly. The men fell silent and it seemed as though Matveyev had won the day. Natalia and the princes withdrew to an inner room and the old man followed.

Unfortunately, a few minutes later Prince Michael Dolgoruky appeared on the balcony and, thinking the victory won, spoke roughly to the soldiers and ordered them out of the Kremlin precincts. His words had the effect of a charge of dynamite. The mob exploded; men climbed up to the balcony, caught the prince by the cloak and flung him to the soldiers below, who caught him on their spears and cut him to pieces.

Other soldiers swarmed into the palace, where they found Matveyev
in a room with Natalia and Peter. Despite Natalia's tears and exhorta-
tions, they took hold of the once mighty boyar and dragged him to the
Red Gate. She followed, with Peter at her heels, pleading for Matveyev's life. But when they reached the balcony they threw him, like
Dolgoruky, to the waiting spears below. The soldiers cut off his hands
and feet, then killed him.

Hundreds of soldiers were now running through the palace searching under beds, even behind altar cloths. Their prey was Dr von Gaden and anyone called Naryshkin or Matveyev. They murdered half a dozen Naryshkins and twice as many bystanders whom they mistook for the wrong people. Some historians say that Peter witnessed the butcheries; even that one of the soldiers dragged Peter's feet through Naryshkin blood to make sure he understood what was happening.

Natalia's father, and her brother Ivan, along with the 17-year-old son of Matveyev, escaped by hiding in a store-room. They left the door slightly ajar to allay suspicion. 'We had scarcely got there,' said young Matveyev, 'before several *streltsy* passed and looked around quickly. Some of them peered in through the open door, stuck their spears into the pillows saying spitefully: "It is plain our men have already been here."'

Although Natalia's father and young Matveyev remained undetected, the soldiers caught Dr von Gaden, who was hiding in the German Quarter dressed as a beggar. They tore him to pieces. Then they issued an ultimatum that unless Natalia's brother, Ivan, was delivered to them they would murder everyone in the palace. The helpless Natalia burst into tears. 'Come, come,' said Sophia brutally, 'the *streltsy* must have your brother. We cannot all perish because of him.' Ivan Naryshkin behaved with immense courage. After taking communion he walked out and surrendered himself to the soldiers, who tortured him to death.

When the slaughter finally stopped Sophia rewarded the *streltsy* with ten roubles each and the title of 'Court Infantry'. The musketeer officers presented a petition to the Assembly recommending that Ivan and Peter should reign jointly, with Sophia as Regent. The members had no option but to accede.

Peter and Ivan sat on twin thrones. Even their crowns and sceptres were identical, for Sophia found goldsmiths who managed to copy the originals, down to the smallest detail, in a few weeks' time. Poor backward Ivan always sat staring at the floor, while Peter, restless and animated, attracted all who saw him. 'His great beauty and lively manner,' wrote a German traveller, 'struck all of us so much that had he been an ordinary youth . . . we would gladly have laughed and talked with him.'

Peter was far from ordinary; he was to become probably the most boisterous, impulsive and terrifying monarch who ever sat upon a throne. Even physically he was astonishing, growing to a height of six feet eight inches. The fact that Sophia refused to allow the boy and his mother to live in the Kremlin, and banished them to Preobrazhensky on the outskirts of Moscow, was a stroke of luck for Peter. The young giant needed air and freedom. Anything that made a noise excited him: raucous laughter, the beat of a drum, the ring of a forge-hammer. He had a passion for war games, and rounded up dozens of boys of his own age – mostly sons of palace servants and junior officers – and forged them into

ABOVE Sophia is said to have prompted the young Tsars through the curtain that hung behind their twin thrones.

RIGHT Peter as a young man wearing the uniform of his own Preobrazhensky regiment, with its characteristic metal neckplate or gorget.

two opposing 'armies'. Rank meant nothing to him, and the lad who amused him most was Alexander Menshikov who sold pies in the streets of Moscow. Menshikov became Peter's inseparable companion and in later years received all the honours and riches the sovereign could heap upon him.

The Kremlin courtiers were shocked by these vulgar companions and alluded to them as 'blackguards'. Sophia, however, was thankful that the young Tsar found politics dull, and encouraged his war games, even providing him with guns and ammunition from the State arsenal.

Yet Peter's life was not all sport. Preobrazhensky was only a stone's thrown from the German Quarter, and the inhabitants soon became accustomed to the sight of the young giant striding through the streets, dropping in to the shops of stonemasons and carpenters and demanding to be taught their trades. Peter was fascinated by all the skills of the hand; he learned to use a lathe and a pile-driver, to swing an axe and to work in metal and stone. One of the Dolgoruky princes returned from Germany and brought him an astrolabe, an instrument for measuring distance. He found a Dutchman, Frans Timmerman, who taught him how to use it, schooled him in geometry and explained the theory of building fortifications. The boy Tsar put his knowledge to the test by constructing with his own hands a fort on the river Yauza, which he named 'Pressburg' in honour of one of his German helpers, and where he frequently held manoeuvres.

Yet his interests soon swung from the land to the sea. When he was 15 he chanced upon an old dilapidated English boat, locked away in a boathouse, which he was told could sail even against the wind. He became fascinated with sailing, and then with boat building. Indeed, the science of navigation, the construction of a navy, and the building of a capital on water opening out to the ocean, eventually became the dominating theme of his life.

If Peter worked hard, he played with uproarious abandon. His mother had no control over him and he disappeared for days at a time, drinking and whoring in the German Quarter. Natalia became so concerned that she found a pretty girl, Eudoxia Lopukhina, and persuaded him to marry her. Apparently Eudoxia was too tepid a character, for although she bore him a son, Alexis, he saw as little of her as possible and returned to his foreign mistresses.

But Peter's exuberance, and his wild passion for life, gave a misleading impression of his character. Far from being a tower of strength, the terrible scenes of the palace massacre had turned him into an emotional cripple. One side of his face twitched and his hand shook; he suffered from nightmares; and his temper was so appalling that it frequently brought him to the verge of convulsion.

Meanwhile Sophia was consolidating her position. In her own way she was just as startling as Peter. That a member of the despised sex could have fought her way from the shadows of the *terem* and grasped the

Miniature of a seventeenth-century smithy, from a *sinodik* or memorial book.

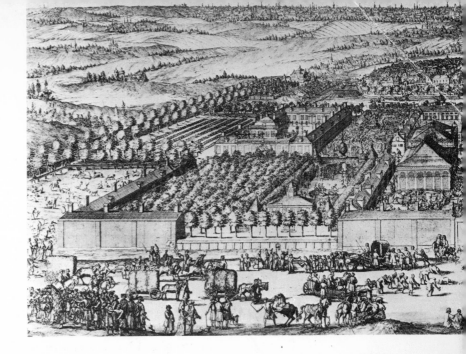

In 1652 Tsar Alexis ordered all foreigners to move from Moscow to the banks of the Yauza, where each family was allocated a plot of land. By 1660 more than a thousand Westerners had settled in this 'German Quarter'.

power of Russia was such an extraordinary feat that many people, even the officials at the Kremlin, found difficulty in reconciling themselves to the new order.

Sophia became increasingly aggressive. She refused to sit behind a screen, and occupied a throne a step lower than the two Tsars. She instructed her ambassadors to inform foreigners that Russia was ruled 'by two Tsars both handsome, intelligent, universally endowed, well-disposed toward foreigners, generous toward their subjects, and that their sister reigned with them'. In 1684 she ordered her likeness to be engraved on coins and medals; two years later she assumed the title 'Autocrat' and proclaimed the feast of St Sophia a national holiday.

Sophia even became more generous in her favours. Although she still loved Prince Vasily Golitsyn, whom she had appointed 'Grand Guardian of the Seal of State' and 'First Gentleman of the Bedchamber', she took a second lover, Theodore Shaklovity, a man who had started life as an obscure clerk in a government department. Apparently the two men felt no jealousy, for the triumvirate worked in harmony. Shaklovity delighted Sophia by having an engraving made showing her wearing the imperial cloak and crown, and holding a sceptre and orb in her hand. An inscription compared her to Elizabeth of England, Semiramis of Babylon and the Byzantine Empress Pulcheria.

Sophia's love-life was common knowledge and Natalia referred openly to her as a whore. Indeed, some people whispered that the whole *terem* had become a house of ill-repute. Sophia's sister, Martha, took a deacon called Ivan as her lover; another sister, Catherine, fell under the spell of a priest, Gregory Alexeyev, who convinced her that the stars had confided to him the burial places of inexhaustible treasure. She had hundreds of holes dug all over the capital but nothing was found except the bones of people murdered throughout the centuries.

Sophia was considered a wise and competent ruler but she longed for the accolade of a conquering sovereign. And this led to a fatal mistake. She promoted Prince Vasily Golitsyn to the rank of general and sent him to war against the Crim Tartars. The Prince had no military experience and fought two campaigns both of which ended in failure. The second excursion resulted in heavy losses, which were attributed to the Prince's ineptitude, provoking widespread anger.

Probably nothing but military incompetence could have aroused young Peter's interest. The Tsar was now 17, and in July 1689, at the Feast of Our Lady of Kazan in commemoration of the deliverance from the Polish invaders, he flung down the gauntlet to his half-sister. Although Sophia had attended this ceremony every year since she had become Regent, Peter's face grew dark when he saw her and he ordered her to return to the palace. She refused, and he lost his temper. He handed his icon to a priest, rushed out of the Kremlin, called for his horse and rode away.

Although this incident took Sophia by surprise she had always expected her power to be challenged when Peter grew up. Indeed, five years earlier Sophia had found a bride for the poor, half-witted Ivan in the hope that he might produce an heir which in some mysterious way would help her to circumvent Peter. As Ivan was almost a cabbage, sitting motionless for hours at a time, and only walking with the help of two men, no one believed him capable of consummating the marriage. When four children were born in rapid succession people whispered that Sophia had planted a strapping youth in the bride's bed. Unfortunately for the Regent all the offspring were girls.

There can be little doubt that Sophia and Theodore Shaklovity plotted to depose Peter. Sophia had placed Vasily Golitsyn's cousin, Boris, in Peter's household, but Boris had defected and now worked loyally for Peter. He infiltrated spies into Sophia's court and master-minded every move that Peter made.

Occasionally the secret agents made mistakes. Such an occasion occurred two weeks after the quarrel between Sophia and Peter in the cathedral. Peter was staying at Kolomenskoye Palace when an informer arrived in the middle of the night and told him his life was in danger. The *streltsy* were on the march. This was quite untrue, but Peter became hysterical. All the hideous scenes of his childhood flooded back to him. Still in his nightshirt he ran to the stable, leapt on his horse and rode hell for leather to Trinity Abbey, where he asked for refuge. Sobbing distractedly he told the abbot that he had escaped death by a hair's breadth. The next day Natalia joined him, and his own regiment – formerly a group of boys but now the expertly trained Preobrazhensky Guards – arrived to protect him.

Both Sophia and Peter knew that once again the *streltsy* held the key. Would these regiments who had come to Sophia's aid seven years earlier remain loyal or would they move over to Peter? Sophia had taken great care to retain their good will, even meeting an outrageous claim for thirty-five years' back pay. Yet their allegiance was no longer automatic.

For one thing the boy Tsars were young men; secondly the scandals surrounding the *terem* and Prince Golitsyn's failures had not enhanced the Regent's popularity. Sophia tried to arouse the populace, as she had done in former days, by a stirring speech outside the Kremlin; this time the impassioned words fell on deaf ears.

Prince Boris Golitsyn assessed the current accurately and advised Peter to provoke a show-down with the *streltsy*. The Tsar issued his challenge by summoning the colonels of eighteen regiments to Trinity Abbey. But as no one in seventeenth-century Russia could afford to make a mistake only a few officers accepted. On 20 August Peter sent a second summons, this one 'on pain of death'. For twenty-four hours everything hung in the balance. Then an astonishing event took place. The little men of the German Quarter – all foreigners of course – responded. Hundreds of carpenters and stonemasons and blacksmiths, who had known Peter since boyhood and who had taught him their trades, began to march to Trinity Abbey.

Their move was contagious: suddenly the Russian private musketeers joined the procession, and soon the trek became a stampede. This persuaded even the foreign mercenaries to throw in their lot with Peter. When the wavering colonels of the *streltsy* saw what was happening they dared not delay any longer. They knew they had lost a Regent and gained a Tsar.

Peter's first demand was that Sophia's lover, Theodore Shaklovity, should be handed over to him. Although this unfortunate man was tortured abominably he refused to denounce Sophia and went to his death loyal to his Regent. Prince Vasily Golitsyn was stripped of his possessions and sent into exile. And Sophia, still only 32 years old, was banished to a convent for the rest of her days, never again seeing anyone from the outside world.

Although Ivan continued to share the throne until his death in 1696, Peter's voice was the only one that counted.

The walls of the Novodevichy Convent, where Sophia was condemned to spend the rest of her life as Sister Suzanna.

CHAPTER II

Peter the Great
1696–1725

Peter the Great as a ship's carpenter in Zaandam. This portrait hints at the chronic nervous tic in Peter's left eye.

NO ONE knew what to make of the 25-year-old giant who toured western Europe in 1697, the first Tsar ever to leave his own domain. Some thought him a madman, others a genius; but everyone agreed that his like had never been seen before. He wore sailor's clothes and hobnobbed with ordinary workmen, and his manners stunned society. He did not know what to do with his table napkin; he belched and farted and picked his teeth. His temper was so alarming, arising from the most trivial incidents, that many people were afraid to meet him. One observer marvelled that 'the Providence of God . . . had raised up such a furious man to so absolute an authority over so great a part of the world.'

On the other hand, the Electress of Hanover, a granddaughter of James I of England, found Peter 'charming'. Although at first he seemed shy, hid his face in his hands and said: *Ich kann nicht sprechen*, she managed to 'tame him a little'. 'He was very gay, very talkative and we established a great friendship,' she wrote. '. . . But with all the advantages with which nature had endowed him, it could be wished that his manners were a little less rustic . . . He told us that he worked himself in building ships, showed us his hands, and made us touch the callous places that had been caused by work.'[1] He mistook the whalebones of the ladies' corsets for the real thing and showed his astonishment by saying that the German ladies had 'devilish hard bones'.

Everyone commented on the twitching face and limbs; a Swiss gentleman referred to the 'convulsions, sometimes in his eyes, sometimes in his arms, sometimes in his whole body. He at times turns his eyes so that one can see nothing but the whites.' However, the Electress's daughter, Sophia Charlotte, wrote that the grimaces were less bad than she had imagined. Bishop Burnet spoke of 'convulsive motions all over his body' but was more concerned with Peter's prodigious consumption of brandy, which 'raises his natural heat and renders him very brutal in his passions'.

Peter journeyed with a retinue of 250 people known as the Great Embassy. As he himself insisted upon travelling incognito foreigners were obliged to pay their respects to the titular head of mission, François Lefort. Lefort was one of Peter's closest friends, a Swiss adventurer who drank 'like a hero' and had been given the title Governor-General. At banquets Peter obliged Lefort to sit at head of table and frequently startled western diplomatists by standing in servant's dress behind Lefort's chair. Although the royal entourage consisted mainly of lackeys, musicians, guards, chaplains and court dwarfs, it included twenty nobles and thirty-five young men, hand-picked by the sovereign, known as 'volunteers'.

What was the purpose of the Great Embassy? Years later Voltaire wrote that the Tsar 'resolved to absent himself from his dominions in order to learn better how to govern them.' Napoleon echoed the same theme. 'He left the country to deliver himself for a while from the crown, so as to learn ordinary life.' But the Austrian agent, Pleyer, a contemporary, reported to his sovereign that it was a cloak to enable the Tsar 'to get out of his country and to divert himself a little'.

None of these explanations was correct. Peter's mind was filled with visions of creating a Black Sea fleet which he could use against the Turks. He had already opened shipyards at Voronezh on the Don, and built a fleet of war galleys which had played a crucial part in the capture of the Turkish fort at Azov. Now he dreamed of a fleet that would enable him to take possession of the Crimea. His purpose therefore was twofold: to study shipbuilding and to recruit foreign experts for service in Russia.

Although the Tsar was known as *Mynheer Peter Mikhailov*, and refused to answer if anyone addressed him as 'Sire' or 'Majesty', he nevertheless expected foreign envoys to entertain him sumptuously and to accord him special favours. When the Swedish Governor of Riga decided to observe meticulously the Tsar's incognito, and confined himself to cold formalities, Peter was so indignant that he later made it a *casus belli*.

The Great Embassy crossed the Baltic and visited the Hanseatic ports. At Mitau, the capital of the Duchy of Courland, they were welcomed with enthusiasm. 'Open tables were kept everywhere,' wrote the Austrian ambassador, Baron von Blomberg, 'with trumpets and music, attended with feasting and excessive drinking all along, as if his Czarish Majesty had been another Bacchus. I have not seen such hard drinkers; it is not possible to express it, and they boast of it as a mighty qualification.'

After visiting Königsberg, Pillau and Koppenbrugge, the Embassy proceeded to Holland. Here Peter separated from his retinue, and with only six companions, one of them Alexander Menshikov, he went to the shipbuilding centre of Zaandam, and enlisted as a ship's carpenter at the wharf of Lynst Rogge. He lived in a tiny cottage cooked his own food and took a local serving girl as his mistress. Unfortunately, word spread of the Tsar's presence and thousands of sightseers poured into the town. Although Peter wore a workman's dress and a tarpaulin hat his great height and twitching face made him easily recognizable, and after a week he moved to Amsterdam in search of greater privacy.

Here he worked for four months at the East India Company docks, with ten Russian 'volunteers' labouring alongside him. He would only answer if people addressed him as 'Carpenter Peter of Zaandam'. Nevertheless when he was walking down the street one day, eating plums, and a group of school-children began to throw stones at him for not sharing his fruit, he complained angrily to the Burgomaster; and the latter immediately issued an edict 'forbidding insults to distinguished persons who wish to remain unknown'.

Peter's curiosity was insatiable. In his free time he visited every

Portrait of Peter the Great

technical and scientific establishment in the city. He studied engineering, botany and printing. He learned to etch and even took lessons from a travelling dentist in the art of extracting teeth. And from then on, if anyone was foolish enough to complain of a toothache, he insisted on pulling out the offending molar himself. What interested him even more than teeth, however, was the dissecting rooms of a professor of medicine, Dr Ruysch. When one of his Russian companions expressed horror at the sight of the corpse he was so irritated he forced the wretched man to bite into it.

After six months in Holland Peter went to London. King William III of England thrilled him by making him a gift of his private yacht, *The Transport Royal*, which had been constructed on a new plan and was armed with twenty brass cannon. The Tsar crossed the North Sea in this vessel, transferred to a barge in the Thames, and was rowed past the Tower, under London Bridge and lodged in a house in Norfolk Street.

Three days later King William called upon him, and was received by Peter in his shirt-sleeves. Apparently the King nearly fainted from the foul air and was appalled to find that Peter was sleeping with four other people in one small room, the windows of which were tightly sealed.

Peter did the usual sightseeing: the Royal Society, the Mint, the House of Commons, the Observatory, Windsor, Hampton Court, and Oxford where he received a degree of Doctor of Law. Once again he was bothered by crowds, and he moved to Deptford where he worked all day in the docks. He lived at Sayes Court in a house belonging to John Evelyn, 'new furnished for him by the King'. However, he saw the King very rarely as he did not wish to change his singular manner of life, dining at ten o'clock in the morning, supping at six in the evening, going to bed very early, and getting up at four o'clock, which, according to the Austrian Ambassador, 'very much astonished those Englishmen who kept company with him'.

Apparently not all was hard work, however. Peter found an actress, Miss Cross, who became his mistress; and much of the night was given to wild parties. John Evelyn's servant wrote to his master that 'there is a house full of people, and right nasty'. This turned out to be something of an understatement for curtains were slashed and carpets ripped. Pictures had been used for target practice, and the great holly hedge, Evelyn's pride, had been ruined by the Tsar's enthusiasm for a wheelbarrow, which he had never seen before and which he drove backwards and forwards through the shrubbery. 'I went to Deptford to see how miserably the Czar had left my house after three months making it his court,' wrote Evelyn. 'I got Sir Christopher Wren, the King's surveyor, and Mr London, his gardner, to go and estimate the repairs, for which they allowed £150 in their report to the Lords of the Treasury....'[2]

Peter's travels came to an abrupt end in the middle of 1698 soon after his arrival in Austria. A message from Theodore Romodanovsky, a monstrous man whom he had left in charge of internal security, informed him that the obstreperous *streltsy* musketeers were rebelling once again.

The Samson Fountain in the gardens at Peterhof

The tiny house in Zaandam where Peter lived like any other shipwright. He was always happiest among the rank and file, and the motto of his Great Embassy was: 'I am among the pupils and seek those who can teach me.'

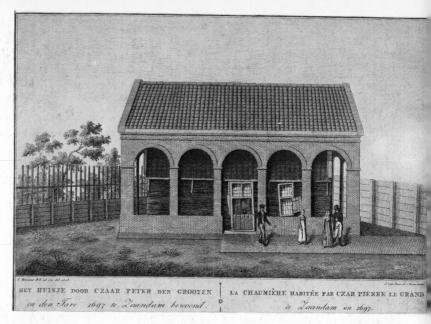

HET HUISJE DOOR CZAAR PETER DEN GROOTEN in den Jare 1697 te Zaandam bewoond. LA CHAUMIÈRE HABITÉE PAR CZAR PIERRE LE GRAND à Zaandam en 1697.

'A most beautiful place' is how Samuel Pepys described Sayes Court at Deptford, the home of the diarist Evelyn. Peter and his retinue caused havoc when they stayed here in 1698, and were described by Evelyn's servant as 'right nasty'; Peter himself ruined Evelyn's prize holly hedge with a wheelbarrow.

The Tsar sent a messenger from Vienna to Moscow acknowledging the letter 'in which your grace writes that the seed of Ivan Miloslavsky is sprouting. I beg you to be severe; in no other way is it possible to put out this flame. Although we are very sorry to give up our present profitable business yet, for the sake of this, we shall be with you sooner than you think.'[3]

Peter travelled day and night, but the revolt was extinguished by the time he reached Moscow. Several hundred *streltsy* had been executed and seventeen hundred imprisoned in monasteries. He learned that the main cause of the rebellion was the fact that hundreds of musketeers had been torn from their families and sent to fight in the Azov area; that their pay was bad, their privations great, their punishments excessive. The soldiers had heard rumours that the absent Tsar was dead and that foreigners were threatening to take over the government. They had sent three men to Sophia, still in her convent, with a petition asking her to intervene; but there was no evidence that any Miloslavsky had taken the initiative.

Nevertheless Peter was not satisfied. He was determined to uncover a deep-laid plot on the part of Sophia; and, no doubt, to revenge himself on the hated *streltsy* who had murdered his mother's relations and stamped his mind forever with nightmarish memories. He now behaved so diabolically that the events of 1682 paled into insignificance.

The imagination recoils from Peter's revenge. Fourteen torture chambers were set up on his private estate, each one in the charge of a suitably cruel subordinate. The seventeen hundred *streltsy* imprisoned in monasteries were sent to Preobrazhensky to be slowly roasted alive. Thirty furnaces were lit each day, while Peter watched the process with relish, ordering doctors to revive the men who fainted.

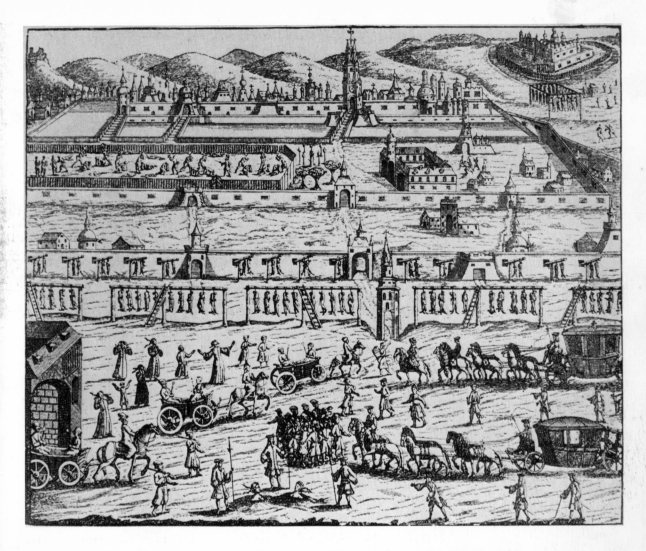

'It had come to pass that Muscovy was only to be saved by cruelty, not by pity.' Thus a contemporary diarist recorded Peter's savage and final break with the past, demonstrated by his destruction of the *streltsy*.

After torture came the executions. Finding the headsman too slow at his job, Peter picked up the axe himself and sent his subjects' heads rolling to the dust, a royal giant with contorted features, foam-flecked lips and clothes stained with his victims' blood. Peter invited the foreigners in his service to help in the inquisition but Lefort and von Blomberg declined this peculiar honour on grounds that it would be inconsistent with their national codes of behaviour.[4]

At every gate leading into the capital gibbets were erected from which bodies dangled; and even the wives of musketeers were tortured and killed. The massacre went on for six months, ending in February 1699 when 195 musketeers were hanged beneath Sophia's convent window, three of them holding in their lifeless hands a copy of the petition they had sent to her.

No one was allowed to be buried until the spring; and the sight of fleshless skulls impaled on iron spikes made it clear that the Muscovites had not yet escaped from the days of Ivan the Terrible.

Peter imposed a tax on beards. He wanted Russia to go clean-shaven '. . . to sever the people from their former Asiatic customs, and instruct them how all Christian peoples comport themselves.' The medal (*below*) is a receipt for tax paid, and had to be worn with the beard as a licence. Those opposed to Peter's new ways, like the boyar (*foot of page*), were referred to by the Tsar as 'long beards'.

Europe was horrified. Bishop Burnet, who had spent a great deal of time with Peter during his stay in England, showing him St Paul's and discussing religion, had prophesied that 'the Czar . . . will become a great person'; but now he wrote in his *History of Our Times*: 'How long he is to be the scourge of that nation, or of his neighbour, God only knows.'

Yet Peter thought of himself not as a savage but as a civilizer. At the very moment that he was planning his ghastly reprisals he set about 'modernizing' his subjects. On the day after his return from Moscow he assembled his nobles and cut off their beards with his own hands. As the beard was as sacred to a Russian as a pigtail to a Chinese the experience was nothing short of traumatic. But Peter soon hit upon the happy idea of giving a series of parties and instructing the court barber to shave all those who passed out through drink, which accounted for almost everyone.

Once Peter's will was known, anyone who persisted in wearing a beard or even Russian dress (with the exception of the clergy and peasantry) was subjected to a large fine. The 'new look' of the Russian diplomatic corps created a sensation abroad. The British Ambassador in Constantinople reported to London:

> The Moscovite Ambassador and his retinue have appeared here so different from what they always formerly wore that ye Turks cannot tell what to make of them. They are all coutred in French habit, with an abundance of gold and silver lace, long perruques and, which the Turks most wonder at, without beards. Last Sunday, being mass in Adrianople, ye Ambassador and all his company did not only keep all their hats off during ye whole ceremony, but at ye elevation, himself and all of them pulled off their wigs. It was much taken notice of and thought an unusual act of devotion.[5]

Peter's foreign policy was dedicated to expansion; and this meant gaining outlets to the sea. Although he had recruited 750 foreign shipwrights and carpenters on his western tour, most of whom were sent to Voronezh to build his Black Sea fleet, he did not attack Turkey. Instead, in 1700, he embarked on a struggle with that great power, the mistress of the Baltic, Sweden. This was destined to drag on for twenty-one years, but its ultimate success not only gave Russia the hegemony of the North but won for Peter the titles 'Father of the Fatherland, Peter the Great and Emperor of All Russia'.

The Great Northern War, as the struggle is now called, took Peter away from his capital for months, even years, at a time. When he was at home he led a life which was a mixture of asceticism and the grossest profligacy. He always rose at four in the morning and held his Council at five. Although he forced his favourites – Lefort until his death, then Alexander Menshikov – to entertain for him in their palaces, he himself had no liking for grandeur. He usually wore a rough brown uniform and was as happy sitting at dinner next to a workman as an ambassador.

He received foreign envoys without ceremony, saying that they were accredited to him and not to this hall or that palace. 'He gave his first audience to the Austrian Ambassador at five in the morning, amidst the confusion of setting to rights his cabinet of natural history. Printz, the Prussian Ambassador, had to carry his credentials on board a ship. The Czar was aloft and bawled to him to climb up into the maintop. Printz pleaded his want of practice as an excuse . . . and the Czar came down to him on the quarterdeck.'[6]

Peter's favourite amusements were burlesques of appalling coarseness. Christmastide, Twelfth Night and the carnival before Lent were celebrated each year with fantastic rites. Peter and his notables roamed the streets dressed as patriarchs and bishops (later changed to popes and cardinals) followed by a 'Drunken Synod' composed of the most dissolute men in Moscow. On other occasions the highest dignitaries were forced to don ridiculous costumes and ride in carts drawn by cows, goats, dogs, even swine. When Matthew Golovin, a man of illustrious family, 80 years of age, was ordered to take part in one of these processions dressed as a devil, he refused. At a word from Peter he was seized, stripped naked, a cap with pasteboard horns was placed upon his head and he was made to sit on the frozen Neva for an hour. He caught pneumonia and died a few days later.

For years Peter's former tutor, Zotov, was made to play the role of an inebriated Prince-Pope; and the diabolical Theodore Romodanovsky was known as the King of Pressburg (the name of Peter's fort) and addressed by Peter as 'Majesty'. Sometimes the mock Tsar was dressed in silks and satins; sometimes, like the Biblical David, he wore a bearskin and carried a lyre. On one occasion Peter placed Romodanovsky on the throne and paraded a group of astonished Swedish prisoners of war before him. Anyone who displeased Peter, and was lucky enough to escape with his life, ran the danger of being forced to wear cap and bells and act forever the part of a fool.

Everything about Peter's court was crude and coarse. He delighted in forcing his guests to do the things they most hated, whether it was eating oysters that made them ill, dressing in ludicrous clothes, or drinking until they fell down unconscious. A great bumper of brandy, taken without stopping, was the worst experience that could befall a courtier; and at every orgy a number of unfortunate people were singled out for this ordeal which frequently proved fatal.

Even foreign envoys were not spared. Juel, the Danish Minister, describes an occasion when he knelt before the Tsar and asked to be let off with one and a half pots of wine instead of the regulation couple, but that Peter only laughed and kneeling down by Juel's side, vowed he would not rise from his knees until the Dane did. The upshot was that Juel was forced to swallow half a dozen bumpers while he knelt, so that by the time he was allowed to stand up he could not keep his feet. On the way home from these banquets Juel frequently saw the icebound river and the snow-covered fields 'black with the bodies of drunken men and women sleeping off their carouse under the open sky, like the slain on the battlefield'. And many never rose again as they froze during the night.

Alexander Menshikov distinguished himself as a brave and talented commander during Peter's Swedish campaigns. The Tsar called him his 'liebste Kamerad', and rewarded him generously.

Peter not only revelled in drunkenness, but took particular pleasure in making his guests physically sick. Dr Birch, a scholar and one of the original trustees of the British Museum, who was fascinated by Russia and made a point of interviewing British diplomats upon their return from Moscow, has left a fantastic description of Peter's banquets. 'The Russian cooks,' he wrote, 'often tie eight or ten young mice in a string, and hide them under green peas, or in such soups as the Russians have the greatest appetite to, which sets them kicking and vomiting in a most beastly manner, when they come to the bottom and discover the trick; they often bake cats, wolves, ravens and the like, in their pastries, and when the company have eaten them up, they tell them what they have in their guts.'[7]

At these entertainments Peter himself was always under the influence of drink and always dangerous. He attacked the Dutch Minister with his fists, the Duke of Holstein's Minister with the flat of his sword, and frequently sent Alexander Menshikov reeling across the room. But if he liked to brawl himself, he liked even better to see his guests setting upon one another. For this reason he always invited two to three hundred people to dinner but only provided places for a hundred.

There is such scuffling and fighting for chairs that nothing more scandalous can be seen in any company, [wrote Dr Birch.] . . . Several foreign ministers have complained of this to the Czar and refuse to dine any more at court, but all the answer they got was, that it was not the Czar's business to turn master of the ceremonies, and please foreigners, nor was it his intention to abolish the freedom once introduced; this obliged strangers for the future to follow the Russian fashion in defending the possession of their chairs, by cuffing and boxing their opposer. The company thus sitting down to table without any manner of grace, they all sit crowded together, that they have much ado to lift their hands to their mouths and if a stranger happens to sit between two Russians, which is commonly the case, he is sure of losing his stomach, though he should have happened to have eat nothing for two days before. Carpenters and shipwrights sit next to the Czar; but senators, ministers, generals, priests, sailors, buffoons of all kinds, sit pell-mell, without any distinction.[8]

Peter loved commotion and the fighting for chairs was only a prelude.

As soon as one sits down [wrote Dr Birch] one is obliged to drink a cup of brandy, after which they ply you with great glasses of adulterated Tokay, and other vitiated wines, and between whiles, a bumper of the strongest English beer, by which mixture of liquors every one of the guests is fuddled before the soup is served up. The company being in this condition, make such a noise, racket, halloing, that it is impossible to hear one another, or even to hear the music, which is playing in the next room, consisting of a sort of trumpets and cornets, for the Czar hates violins, and with this revelling noise and uproar the Czar is extremely diverted, particularly if the guests fall to boxing and get bloody noses.

Formerly the company had no napkins given them, but instead of it they had a piece of very coarse linen given them by a servant, who brought in the whole piece under his arm, and cut off half an ell for every person, which they are at liberty to carry home with them, for it had been observed that those pilfering guests used sometimes to pocket the napkins; but at present two or three Russians must make shift with but one napkin, which they pull and haul for, like hungry dogs for a bone. Each person of the company has but one plate during dinner, so if some Russian does not care to mix the sauces of the different dishes together, he pours the soup that is left in his plate either into the dish or into his neighbour's plate, or even under the table after which he licks his plate clean with his fingers and, last of all wipes it with the tablecloth.[9]

A soldier with a hand-mortar from Peter's army. The first flintlocks and bayonets used by the Russian soldiers came from England, but Peter aimed at self-sufficiency for his newly constituted army, and set up cloth mills and ironworks to clothe and arm his men.

If Peter's court was fantastic, so was his personal life. He had sexual relations with his favourite, Alexander Menshikov; he married a servant girl and made her Empress; and he murdered his son and heir, Alexis.

Menshikov was a quick-witted, brilliant scoundrel who managed to retain the Tsar's affection throughout his life. Although sexually Peter preferred women to men, buggery was so widespread in seventeenth-century Russia that it was scarcely regarded as a vice; and contemporary writers claim that the Tsar alleviated the boredom of long military campaigns by his attentions to Menshikov. He addressed him in letters as 'My heart' and gave him every distinction the state had to offer, even persuading the Habsburg ruler, Charles VI, to create him a prince of the Holy Roman Empire.

Menshikov fulfilled the role of chief executive and war leader, serving both as an admiral and a general. But Peter cherished him most of all as a companion who never failed to cheer and divert. They shared the same

'The ox did not want to be an ox and so became the butcher.' This print was banned in the seventeenth century lest it should incite a revolt against the landowners. From D. A. Rovinsky, *Russian Popular Prints*, 1881.

cruel humour, the same love of carousing, even the same women. Menshikov could match the Tsar drink for drink; and when Peter beheaded his wretched musketeers Menshikov picked up an axe and worked alongside his master.

Although Peter regarded speculation as a crime, and sent more than one man to his death for corruption, his favourite amassed a fortune and was allowed to keep it. Peter was well aware of his knavery, and often struck him blows that sent him reeling, once boxing his ears until blood poured out of his nose. Frequently he imposed huge fines on him; and, when Menshikov took down the silken draperies in his palace in protest, Peter sent a message that unless the room was restored immediately to its former luxury the penalty would be doubled. 'Menshikov was conceived in iniquity, born in sin, and will end his life as a rascal and a cheat,' he once ranted bitterly, 'and if he do not reform he will lose his head.' But in the end he always forgave him, as he could not do without his undoubted charm.

The only person Peter cared more about than Menshikov was one of Menshikov's mistresses, Martha Skavronska. When Peter returned from his first tour of the West in 1698 he sent his poor wife, Eudoxia, to a convent and went back to the arms of his mistress, Anna Mons. Anna was the pretty and vivacious daughter of a German wine merchant. Peter talked about marrying her but the years passed and he never got round to it, because Eudoxia persisted in remaining alive. In 1703 Anna began to worry about her future and started a flirtation with the Prussian Minister, von Keyserling. The latter fell madly in love with her and she finally agreed to marry him. But when Keyserling asked Peter's permission the Tsar was so angry that he not only forbade the marriage but revoked the grant of Anna's estate, took back his portrait set in diamonds, and placed the whole Mons family under house arrest for two years. Even four years later, when Keyserling, still anxious to wed Anna, mentioned the name of Mons, Peter flew into a rage. 'I educated the Mons girl for myself with the sincere intention of marrying her, but since she was enticed and inveigled away by you I do not want to hear or know anything about her or her relations.'*

Peter's reaction was nothing more than wounded pride, as he had been living happily for several years with Martha Skavronska, the orphaned daughter of Lithuanian peasants. Martha had been brought to Russia as a slave. She was working as a nursery maid in the house of a Lutheran pastor, named Gluck, when the Russians attacked Marienburg. With the capture of the city the 17-year-old girl became part of the war booty, and was taken back to Moscow by General Sheremetyev as his concubine. Somehow Menshikov got hold of her; and after living with her for some months transferred her to Peter when the latter was looking for a replacement for Anna. Martha embraced the Greek

OVERLEAF
The Battle of Poltava, from the Salon of Paintings at the Catherine Palace.

*Peter did not allow Keyserling to marry Anna until 1711; and then it was too late as the bridegroom died on his honeymoon.

44

Orthodox faith, changed her name to Catherine, and bore the Tsar three children. In 1707 he overcame his scruples about Eudoxia, and secretly married her.

Catherine was not at all pretty but her plump figure obviously appealed to Muscovite taste. Peter loved her because she was vulgar and good-natured and could drink and swear like a man. She was clever enough to retain Menshikov's friendship and they helped each other in controlling Peter.

Catherine was also wise enough to throw herself into the Tsar's enthusiasms. Peter had begun the construction of a Baltic fleet; and in 1703, the year that he met Catherine, he decided to build a city on the mouth of the Neva – within reach of his shipbuilding – and to call it St Petersburg. He commandeered slave labour from all over Russia, but the marshy lands and damp climate took a fearful toll of life, and work proceeded slowly.

Although Peter ordered his nobility to build residences and to spend half the year there, they hated this 'paradise', as he insisted on calling it. Only Catherine pretended to enjoy the cold swamp in which a city was being forged. There was so little sunlight that nothing would grow except cabbages and turnips, and fruit of a poor quality. As it was forbidden to cut down trees on the islands there was no fuel and people were allowed hot water only once a week; and as there were no bridges across the swamps and waterways the inhabitants had to move about in boats, which they disliked and feared. The Tsar further increased the difficulties of the residents by forbidding them to use oars, insisting that all his subjects must learn to sail.

When Peter left his icy Eden and went off to war, Catherine went too, riding all day in the saddle and sleeping on the hard ground without complaint. Sometimes she shaved her head and wore a grenadier's cap. The troops adored her, as she always went down the lines on the eve of battle, handing them bumpers of brandy.

In 1709 Peter won a great victory over Charles XII of Sweden at Poltava which opened the way to Russia's conquest of Karelia and the Baltic provinces. It also enabled the Tsar to marry off his niece, Anna (the daughter of the imbecile Ivan who had shared his throne), to the Duke of Courland.

However, twelve months after the wedding a disaster occurred which nearly cost the Tsar everything he had gained in ten years of fighting. It came about because Charles XII hurried off to Turkey and by adroit diplomacy persuaded the Sultan to declare war on Russia. Peter countered by marching his army to the Danube, hoping to enlist the help of the Rumanian provinces of Moldavia and Wallachia, and to arouse Christian Slavs throughout the Balkans to rebel against their Moslem masters. Peter pressed forward far down the river Pruth and detached the bulk of his cavalry to raid the Turkish rear; but the Grand Vizier, at the head of a far superior army, succeeded in surrounding his forces and threatened him with total annihilation.

Peter won a great victory against
Charles XII of Sweden at Poltava
(*above*); but was beaten decisively by
the Grand Vizier of Turkey at Pruth.

Never before had Peter found himself in such a desperate position.
He had no alternative but to sue for peace; and he instructed his emissaries that he was willing to agree to everything 'except slavery'.

The Grand Vizier's terms were surprisingly mild. He demanded the
surrender of Azov, the Russian Black Sea fleet, and all that Peter had
gained from Turkey in 1700; but he did not force the Tsar to disgorge
the fruits of his Swedish victories. Some historians claim that Catherine

50

bribed the Grand Vizier with her jewels and with carts of gold collected from the troops.

Although this romantic story appears to be apocryphal, there is no doubt that Catherine's cool courage, to which Peter later paid tribute, helped him through the greatest ordeal of his life. And the following year he acknowledged his debt by marrying Catherine publicly.

Europe was agog to see the new Tsarina but Peter did not take her

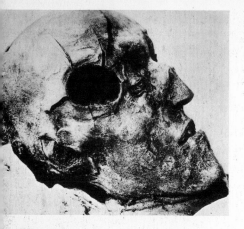

The skull of Charles XII of Sweden (*above*), killed by a cannon-shot at the siege of Fredrikshald in 1718. Voltaire compared him unfavourably with Peter the Great who, he wrote, fought for the interests of the state whereas Charles only fought for his own glory.

Catherine I (*right*). From camp-follower to Empress of Russia.

abroad for another five years. When they visited Berlin in 1717 Wilhelmina, the 8-year-old daughter of the King of Prussia, and a sister of the future Frederick the Great, was spellbound by the Imperial couple. In her copybook the child wrote:

The Czarina has a stumpy little body, very brown, and had neither air nor grace . . . with her huddle of clothes she looked for all the world like a German play actress; her dress you would have said had been bought at a second-hand shop; all was out of fashion, all was loaded with silver and greasy dirt. The front of her bodice she had ornamented with jewels in a very singular pattern: a double-eagle in embroidery, and the plumes of it set with poor little diamonds, of the smallest possible carat, and very ill-mounted. All along the facings of her gown were Orders and little things of metal; a dozen Orders and as many Portraits of saints, relics and the like, so that when she walked, it was with a jingling, as if you heard a mule with bells to its harness . . .

At table the Czar placed himself beside the Queen. It is understood this Prince was attempted with poison in his youth, and that something of it had settled on his nerves after. One thing is certain, there took him very often a sort of convulsion, like Tic or St Vitus, which it was beyond his power to control. That happened at table now. He got into contortions, gesticulations; and as the knife was in his hand, and went dancing about within arms length of the Queen it frightened her, and she motioned several times to rise. The Czar begged her not to mind, for he would do her no ill; at the same time he took her by the hand, which he grasped with such violence that the Queen was obliged to shriek out. This set him heartily laughing; saying that she had not bones of so hard a texture as his Catherine's. . . .[10]

Peter provoked further astonishment in Berlin when he fell so much in love with the figure of a heathen divinity, which he saw in an antique shop, that he forced Catherine to kiss it. In Danzig he attended divine service and, finding the church cold, snatched off the wig of the Burgomaster and put it on his own head; in Copenhagen he took a fancy to a mummy in a natural history museum and announced his decision to appropriate it. When he was refused, on grounds that there was not another like it in the world, he fell on the mummy and tore off its nose, saying: 'Now you can keep it.'

Peter sent Catherine home and journeyed alone to France. He did not like French wines and lamented in a letter: 'There is only one bottle of vodka left. I do not know what to do.' Perhaps this shortage explains why the Tsar made such a favourable impression on his new hosts. The mother of the Duc d'Orléans commented on 'his very good manners', and Saint-Simon observed that 'his whole air showed his intellect, his reflection and his greatness.'

Praise froze on French lips, however, when Peter returned to Russia and stories filtered out about his appalling treatment of his son and heir, Alexis.

Alexis was the son of Eudoxia: a frail, intelligent, sensitive dreamer

Peter the Great and his son Alexis

in his late twenties. Unlike his father, he was happier with a rosary in his hand than a sword. This infuriated Peter, who was indignant at having what he called 'a physical weakling' for a son. Furiously he tried to remould the boy in his own image. He sent him to war as a bombardier, into the dockyards to build ships, to sea on a galley. He constantly upbraided him for not taking more interest in the sciences, and forced him to study engineering and mathematics. Alexis was so terrified of his father that he often fainted when summoned to his presence. Once, when Peter asked to see a mathematics paper he had set him, he shot himself in the hand to provide an excuse for not completing it.

Peter forced Alexis to marry a German princess, Sophia Charlotte of Blankenburg-Wolfenbüttel, to whom, luckily, he became deeply attached. But the Tsar kept the bride so short of money that she lived in abject poverty. After four miserable years she gave birth to a son, Peter, and promptly died.

Although Alexis was beside himself with grief he received a heartless letter from his father on the very day of the funeral castigating him for not giving 'any attention to military affairs' and saying that if he did not change his attitude 'Be quite sure that I will deprive you of your succession; I will cut you off as though you were a gangrenous swelling.'

Alexis wanted nothing more than to be free of his terrible father; and he promptly wrote back renouncing the succession on grounds of illhealth and general incompetence. This enraged Peter still further. He wrote a second letter, now offering him the choice of 'mending his ways' or becoming a monk. 'It must be one or the other. It is impossible for you to be neither fish nor flesh for ever.' Once again, without a moment's hesitation, Alexis chose the monastery and signed his reply, 'Your slave and useless son, Alexis.'

Peter could not believe that Alexis was serious. At the end of August 1716 he despatched a third letter telling him that if he wished to remain the heir he must join him at the front without delay. Instead Alexis went to Vienna accompanied by a pretty Finnish girl, Afrosina, with whom he was now deeply in love. Hysterical with fear that his father might pursue him, he asked the Austrian Emperor (who was married to a sister of Alexis's dead wife) to grant him political asylum.

Peter was insensate with anger. He regarded the flight of the Tsarevich to a foreign potentate as nothing less than treason. He instructed his ablest diplomat, Count Peter Tolstoy, to get Alexis back at any cost. In order to make Tolstoy's task easier he handed him an autographed letter for Alexis in which he swore 'before God and his judgment seat' that if he returned to Russia he would not be punished but 'cherished like a son'. Then he departed on his western tour with Catherine.

It took Tolstoy eighteen months to persuade Alexis to do as his father wished. Every pressure was put on the terrified young man, including threats against his beloved Afrosina. However, a second letter from the Tsar assured him that he would be allowed to marry Afrosina and live quietly on his estates.

The idealized portrait of Peter on the medal (*above*) contrasts with the brutality of the man. The medal marks the end of the *streltsy* rebellion of 1698.

Peter arrived back in Russia about the same time as Alexis. What happened next was so barbarous it can only be compared with the punishment of the *streltsy*. Peter was determined to uncover a plot, and Alexis was subjected to days and weeks of interrogation, sometimes by his father, sometimes by Tolstoy. It was clear that Alexis had never lifted a finger either to depose Peter or to secure the succession; yet it was also clear that hundreds of people looked upon Alexis as their only hope. 'The clergy, the nobility, the common people,' the Hanoverian Resident, Weber, reported to his government, 'respect the Tsarevich like a God.'

It was not surprising that elements hostile to Peter should have been attracted to a son so different. The clergy saw Peter as an anti-Christ; the nobility as a man who had sold Russia's soul to foreigners. The peasantry, who represented ninety per cent of the country's twelve million people, groaned under the appalling burdens imposed on them and cried out for any relief. '. . . and of the simple people,' Alexis told his father, 'I heard from many that they loved me.'

No matter how unpalatable these revelations were, the fact remained that Alexis had done nothing treasonable. But when he was confronted by his awful father his will collapsed and he was persuaded that every mark of sympathy shown toward him, every chance encounter, every stray remark, had been a crime. He supplied a list of his friends, who subsequently were tortured and killed. Kikin, the man who had advised him to go to Vienna, was broken on the wheel. Although his mother, Eudoxia, still languished in her convent, the priests surrounding her and all those with whom she was in communication suffered the same fate. Finally, poor Afrosina was brought before the inquisitors. Under threat of punishment she incriminated Alexis by repeating all his confidences. She revealed that he hated his father, longed for his death, rejoiced when he learned of plots against him, and had pledged himself to restore Moscow as the capital.

These indiscretions sent Peter mad with fury, and he sentenced Alexis to twenty-five strokes of the knout. This terrible instrument was a whip made of parchment and hardened in milk so that it could cut to the bone with every lash. Probably Alexis was not intended to survive this punishment, as five days later he was given another fifteen lashes; but he still did not die.

Peter was not taking any more chances. That night he convened the High Court, composed of his own hand-picked creatures, and asked them to decide Alexis's fate. Servilely and without discussion, the 127 members condemned the Tsarevich to death 'for having desired the death of the sovereign, plotted the ruin of his country, of his lord and father, with the aid of foreign arms.'

As Peter had given an oath to respect the life of Alexis he could not bring himself to sign the sentence, but there were other ways. The Tsarevich was confined in the Trubetskoy bastion; and in the Day Book of the Guard an item appears on 26 June stating laconically that in the presence of the Tsar and others torture was applied. It does not say on whom. But further on another sentence records that on the same day, at six o'clock in the evening, Alexis Petrovich died.

Word was put around that Alexis had expired of apoplexy; and Peter issued an Imperial rescript describing his demise as 'an act of God'. Few people accepted it. The Austrian Resident, Pleyer, wrote to Count Schönborn that it was generally believed that Alexis had been killed by a sword or an axe; while the Dutch Resident, De Bie, reported that his veins had been opened. No one knows the truth; only that Peter visited the prison on his son's last day.

Alexis's death was of so little concern to Peter that he gave a banquet and a ball the following night in celebration of the anniversary of Poltava. It took place at Prince Menshikov's palace, the grandest house in St Petersburg. Although Peter himself lived for years in a small log cabin, composed of three rooms, he encouraged Catherine to compete

A foreign diplomat who described St Petersburg as a 'heap of villages linked together, like some plantation in the West Indies', a few years later called it 'a wonder of the world, considering its magnificent palaces'. One of the first of these residences to be built was the Menshikov Palace (*below*).

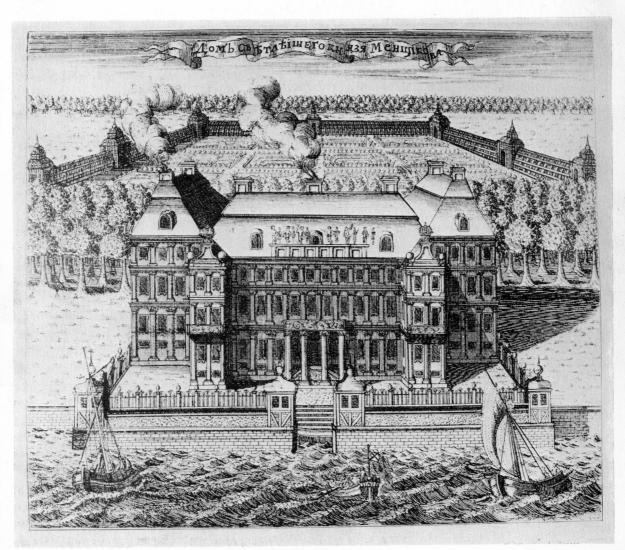

57

with Menshikov in splendour. He loaded her with jewels and dresses and was proud of the hundreds of dwarfs, lackeys, grooms, musicians, all in brilliant attire, who made up her court.

Catherine's magnificence struck a slightly incongruous note, however, against the background of a city which even now had few amenities to offer. It was still a heap of villages linked together like 'some plantation in the West Indies'. Scarcely a thoroughfare was paved because of the shortage of stone; there were no street lights; and wolves occasionally prowled into the main squares. In 1714 these animals killed two sentries outside Menshikov's palace.

An even more frightening hazard was the lawlessness of the desperate serfs used to build the city and the Baltic fleet. Conditions were appalling, and some historians claim that two hundred thousand people died in twenty years. But Peter showed no mercy.

> Edict after edict was issued drafting carpenters, stone-masons, labourers and yet more labourers from all over the Empire; Tartars, Chuvash, Cossacks; so many from Siberia, so many from Kazan, so many from each province. Wages were not paid; desertion was chronic; sickness festered; death battened, in that fir-birch-stunted delta-marsh, with the Neva constantly in flood, or arctic winter in grip, where the 'Czar-reformer' willed it that his 'paradise' should rise.[11]

Occasionally the slaves rebelled.

> The godless rabble breaks into houses both day and night [wrote the Hanoverian Resident in 1714] and perpetrates all sorts of insolent deeds ... People scarcely consider themselves safe in their houses, and at night have to use all imaginable precautions ... Prince Menshikov, two years ago, was attacked by a whole village who knew him well, and was only saved by his fleet horses. Thereupon he had all the inhabitants, as well as the priests hanged.[12]

The Swedish war came to an end in 1721; Peter styled himself Emperor, and plunged into a Persian campaign which accomplished little. Meanwhile he continued to fling himself into activities which ranged from the usual orgies and burlesques to extracting the teeth of his wretched courtiers. He hammered out sheets of iron weighing a hundred pounds and, with the anatomical instruments he had brought from Holland in 1698, performed an operation on a woman suffering from dropsy. When she died he attended her funeral as a public apology.

Above all, Peter continued with the reforms and innovations, almost all borrowed from the West, which had occupied him throughout his reign. The record for posterity was impressive. His Baltic fleet numbered 25 men-of-war, a large galley fleet, and an establishment of 16,000 men. He had built up heavy industry in the Urals, founded military and naval colleges and schools for engineers, and was in the process of inaugurating an Academy of Science. He had freed women from the subjugation of the *terem*, reformed the Civil Service, and introduced the first newspaper, the first public theatre, the first hospital.

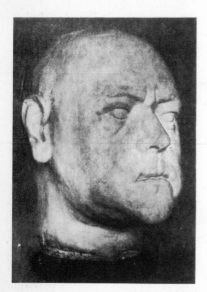

The face-mask of Peter, made in 1719 while he was alive, was by Carlo Rastrelli, sculptor father of the great architect.

Whereas during the whole of the seventeenth century only 374 books were published in Russia, in the twenty-seven years following Peter's tour of the West over seven hundred were printed.

There were some changes, however, that smacked of the East. The bonds of serfdom were tightened, and the *chin* system, or Table of Ranks, introduced to 'encourage merit and to eliminate privilege', belied its progressive ring. As 'merit' depended on the Emperor's pleasure the nobility lost its last shred of independence. All trembled before the despotic power which allowed no one to possess anything which he could call his own.

Peter had more shocks up his sleeve. Although Catherine had borne him eleven children, all had died except for two daughters, Anna and Elizabeth. The rightful heir was Alexis's son, Peter. But in order to blot out the memory of the hated Alexis and his issue, in 1722 the Emperor changed the law of succession, decreeing that in future the successor would be chosen by the Sovereign.

An even greater sensation was caused the following year when Peter lauded Catherine's 'valour and heroism' during the Battle of the Pruth, and announced that he had decided to place the Imperial crown upon her head. The nation was aghast. The coronation of a woman was unprecedented and nothing short of an outrage. But no one dared to protest. The event took place in the Cathedral of the Assumption,

In 1724 Peter crowned Catherine Empress. Although only 52 years old, he suffered from frequent bouts of illness and bad temper which only Catherine could appease, and this was her reward.

inside the Kremlin, on 7 May 1724. Catherine's crown was the most costly ever worn by a Russian sovereign. It was made in Paris on the model of the old Byzantine Imperial crown, and was studded with 2,564 precious stones. Each of the numerous pearls on it was said to be worth £500; but the most dazzling of all the jewels was a ruby as large as a pigeon's egg, placed at the apex of the crown. This incredible stone was purchased in Peking, at Menshikov's order, for 60,000 roubles, the equivalent of seven or eight thousand pounds.

Never had the consort of a Russian ruler been accorded such favour. Yet six months after Catherine's coronation, both she and Menshikov were in disgrace. Indeed, the mighty Peter was so angry with them that people feared for their necks. The breach occurred when Peter discovered that one of Catherine's courtiers – the handsome unscrupulous William Mons, a brother of Peter's former mistress, Anna – had been taking huge bribes. Peculation was something Peter had fought all his life and would not tolerate. But when he learned that Mons had been aided by Menshikov and abetted by Catherine, he flew into an insane temper. Mons was arrested and beheaded, and Menshikov stripped of his office.

Catherine was in even worse trouble for Peter accused her of having had an affair with Mons. Some historians claim that he preserved Mons's head in spirits and placed it in her bedroom. Apparently Catherine remained as icily calm as she had at Pruth. When Peter smashed a priceless vase in her apartment and observed: 'Thus, I can annihilate the most beautiful adornment in my palace,' she replied coldly: 'And have you made the Palace any more beautiful by doing so?'

In the end he forgave Menshikov, as he always did; and after a month, during which people remarked the strained relations between the imperial couple, he once again began to dine with Catherine.

Peter was now 53 years old and although his energy still appeared inexhaustible he looked an old man. At the end of January 1725 he was forced to take to his bed, suffering from a stone in the kidney. He had just arranged the betrothal of his daughter, Anna, to the Duke of Holstein but was forced to cancel his plans to travel to Riga for the wedding. He began to run a fever and at times was in such pain that he screamed and tore the bedclothes.

His mind turned to his successor. He asked for paper. He only wrote two words, 'Give all', and the pen dropped from his hand. He called for his daughter, Anna, to dictate his will, but when she arrived a few minutes later he could not speak. He sank into unconsciousness and died on 8 February 1725.

Meanwhile the Senate had assembled to decide the succession. Some members wanted to recognize Alexis's son, Peter, but the majority voted for the widowed Catherine.

The truth was that the awe and terror inspired by Peter was still too overpowering to allow them to deviate from what they believed he wanted.

Peter on his death-bed

Peter the Great raised Russia to the status of a primary power and gave her a voice in the Concert of Europe. But he bought his victory with the souls of his people. He knew nothing of human dignity and bent all Russians to the pursuit of his own conception of glory. 'They are animals,' he once remarked, 'whom I have dressed to look like men.'

This outlook provoked ironic consequences. Although Peter literally dragged his subjects into the technological age, and taught them western skills, he so debased their hearts and minds that western morality remained permanently elusive. 'The Russians as fashioned by Peter,' wrote Diderot mournfully, 'were rotten before they were ripe.'

After Peter's death a woodcut was issued which enjoyed great popularity. It was entitled 'The mice bury the cat.' But there were more cats to come.

CHAPTER III

Anna, Elizabeth and Peter III

1725–1762

ONLY THIRTY-SEVEN YEARS separate the reigns of Peter the Great and Catherine the Great; yet in this short period Russia had six sovereigns. The two who ruled the longest and made the worst and best impressions were women: Anna, the dark, ugly daughter of the half-witted Tsar Ivan who had shared the twin throne with Peter; and Elizabeth, Peter's beautiful, amorous and only surviving offspring.

Anna mounted the throne five years after Peter's death, following Peter's widow, Catherine I, and Peter's grandson – another Peter – both of whom went to their graves after ruling little more than two years. Anna, coarse-featured and bad-tempered, was 37 when she became Empress. Her sullenness was not altogether surprising as in 1710 she had married the Duke of Courland, who had expired on the honeymoon; and for nineteen years she had lived in humiliating penury in Courland, a dependency which passed from Russia to Prussia and then to Poland. She existed as best she could on lean beef and pickled cabbage and wore dresses run up by her serving women. 'She is a most venomous cicatrice and vulgar to boot,' wrote a Baltic baron to a friend in Sweden. 'She has been known to count the apples on a tree for fear that her gardener would cheat her.'

Anna soon made it plain, however, that her meanness sprang from necessity rather than parsimony. She arrived in Moscow with a very handsome and unscrupulous lover, Ernst Biren, the grandson of a stable-boy, and proceeded to load him with all the honours and riches at her command. She built him a palace in St Petersburg and gave him estates in Courland, Livonia, Silesia and the Ukraine, making him the largest landowner in Russia. Biren's passion was horses; and Anna not only constructed a huge riding-school which became the meeting place for society, but created a Department of State to look after his brood mares and stallions. 'When Monsieur de Biren speaks of horses,' observed the Austrian Minister, Ostein, 'he talks like a man; but when he speaks of men, he talks like a horse.'

Unfortunately Biren not only liked to speak of men but to terrorize them. Although he had no desire for political power and was content to leave foreign affairs in the hands of the Empress's Vice-Chancellor, Ostermann, and military affairs to Field Marshal Münnich – both protégés of Peter I – he insisted on being recognized as the first man of the Empire. Adulation was what he craved and he was not happy unless princesses of the blood and ministers were quailing before him.

He soon found a method of inducing servility. He set up an inquisitorial department, known as the Secret Chancellery. Soon the country was honeycombed with spies and informers, and anyone who made the mildest criticism of the new régime was likely to find himself in the

The Empress, with Biren at her side (wearing a hat), shooting animals in the St Petersburg game reserve. She also enjoyed shooting nightingales through the palace windows.

torture chamber. As the old Moscow nobility had opposed Anna's candidature, Biren singled out for persecution such families as the Dolgoruky, Golitsyn and Tolstoy. Some were broken on the wheel, some impaled, others flung into dungeons or banished to the Arctic. Altogether some twenty thousand Russians were exiled, a quarter of whom disappeared without trace. 'The issues of life or death,' wrote the great Russian historian Kluchevsky, 'depended on his smile or his frown. If he were pleased to be merry, everyone was boisterous with mirth; but if he raised his voice in anger his crowded antechamber emptied itself in a minute.'

Although Biren and Ostermann and Münnich all hated one another, the trio soon became known as 'the German Party' and were blamed jointly for all the misfortunes that befell the country. Biren was well aware of the growing enmity and persuaded the Empress to have 'her person guarded by retainers from Mitau and other Courland localities, and thereby caused German officials to accumulate in Moscow like chaff sprinkled from a leaky sack, so that they overran the Court, besieged the throne, and grabbed every administrative post to which any sort of salary was attached'.[1] This, of course, only increased the hatred of foreigners, and accelerated the horrible activities of the Secret Chancellery.

Yet the ugly Empress found Biren so irresistible that she could not refuse any of his demands. When she was crowned she made him her Grand Chamberlain, and a Count of the Empire. Later, she bribed the Courlanders into electing him their reigning duke, which gave him the title 'Most Serene Highness' and the right to sit with reigning princes.

Biren's passion for luxury inspired Anna to try and create the first elegant court Russia had known. Although St Petersburg was still a muddy city of wooden houses she ordered the Winter Palace to be partly rebuilt, and she designed for her servants an elaborate green livery laced with gold. She instructed the boyars that in future their oak and deal furniture would have to give way to mahogany and ebony, and their mead and vodka to champagne and burgundy. And she also let it be known that she expected everyone to equip his house with carpets, mirrors and pictures. As for herself, she ordered a dressing-table and a mirror made of solid gold; and people talked about 'baths of white wine', an easing stool of silver studded with sapphires, toothbrushes with handles embellished with rubies.

The first ball held in the new gallery of the Winter Palace, 'considerably larger than St George's Hall at Windsor', created a sensation.

Though it was very cold [wrote Lady Rondeau, wife of the British Minister] the stoves kept it warm enough, and it was decorated with orange-trees and myrtles, in full bloom; these were ranged in rows that formed a walk on each side of the hall, and only left room for dancers in the middle. The walks on each side gave the company opportunity to sit down sometimes, as they were hid from the presence of the sovereign. The beauty, fragrance, and warmth of this new formed grove, when you saw nothing but ice and snow through the windows, looked like enchantment....[2]

Peter II was 15 when he died of smallpox. He was greatly mourned by all who knew him, and even in her old age Catherine Dolgoruky, his bride-to-be, remembered him as 'my lovely eagle'.

Although Russia was rapidly heading for ruin through a combination of bad harvests and declining commerce, Anna refused to curtail her hectic entertaining. 'Your Excellency cannot imagine how magnificent this Court is since the present reign,' the British Minister wrote to Lord Harrington, 'although there is not a shilling in the Treasury and nobody is paid.' Despite the poverty, both of State and subject, the Empress frowned upon anyone who wore the same costume twice to her balls and masquerades. As a suit cost anywhere from £150 to £200 many of the foreign ministers wrote home asking for larger allowances. 'I never saw such heaps of gold and silver lace laid upon cloth,' wrote Rondeau, '... I cannot imagine that this magnificence will last many years, for if it should, it must ruin most part of the Russian nobility, for several families are obliged to sell their estates to buy fine clothes.'[3]

Everyone who attended Biren's riding school on Mondays, Thursdays and Saturdays, when the Empress was present, was obliged to wear a uniform of yellow buffalo skin embroidered with silver galloon, with a blue vest and trimmings to match. And with the new clothes came a craze for new hair styles, at least as far as the ladies were concerned. Several Parisian hairdressers set up shop in St Petersburg, but as the demand was so great before a ball many clients were forced to have their hair done three days in advance; and they passed the interval sitting upright in chairs.

Despite the Empress's extravagance her court was far from elegant. Foreign diplomats took relish in describing her vulgar preference for sky-blue or apple-green garments, and for the ugly handkerchiefs tied round her head which all her ladies were obliged to copy. No one, they reported, was well groomed. Fine materials were badly tailored, rich dresses crumpled and stained, smart uniforms topped by incongruous wigs, expensive carriages drawn by wretched hacks.

The wife of the British Minister was one of the few people who did not find the Empress repulsive to look at. Although she refers to 'an awfulness in her countenance that strikes you at first sight,' she goes on to add, 'but when she speaks she has a smile about her mouth that is inexpressibly sweet.' Yet that mouth could harden into a terrifying thin line, for Anna had a taste for cruelty. 'She knew how to mingle barbarism with extravagance so crudely as to make foreign observers absolutely gasp with amazement,' wrote Kluchevsky.

Like Peter the Great, Anna had a craze for dwarfs and jesters, and anyone who displeased her was compelled to serve in a position of degrading buffoonery. Elderly men were forced to become her pages, and run and fetch like boys; others who fell out of favour, men and women alike, were made to ape the antics of animals for the general amusement of the Court. When a member of one of the great boyar families – Nikita Volkonsky – displeased her, he was made to sit in a specially constructed basket and to cackle like a hen for hours at a time, and the distinguished general, Apraksin, who made the mistake of marrying a Roman Catholic, had to go on all fours braying like a donkey.

Anna was unpopular. Not only was she regarded as 'dull, coarse, fat, harsh and spiteful', but her reign is traditionally known in Russia as a time of government by foreigners.

Even worse befell Prince Michael Golitsyn. Like Apraksin, he also married a Roman Catholic lady, but he committed the further error of embracing the Latin heresy himself. The Empress commanded him to become her page, but this was only the beginning. She had just completed the building of an elaborate Ice Palace at a cost of £7,000 when Golitsyn's wife died and a happy idea struck her. She ordered the unfortunate widower to marry again and chose the bride herself, a hideous Kalmuck named Anna Buzheninova. She then commanded all the provincial governors to send to the capital representatives of the native races within the Empire: Lapps, Finns, Kirghiz, Bashkirs, Tartars, Cossacks, Samoyeds. These barbarous races in barbarous equipages, drawn by pigs, dogs and goats, took part in the marriage procession following the bridal pair, who travelled to church in a cage on the back of an elephant. After the ceremony a reception took place in Biren's riding school where the couple were forced to sit on a dais and watch the merry-making. When the party was over they were escorted to the Ice Palace, stripped naked and compelled to spend the night in a bedroom in which all the furniture was made entirely of ice. Guards were placed at the doors to prevent them from escaping. History does not record whether or not they survived the ordeal.

Meanwhile the policies of the German Party were creating widespread misery. Biren's intolerant reign had displaced so many people that large tracts of land were unworked, and an intolerable system of military service sent thousands more fleeing across the frontiers. The decline in commerce, caused by high taxation, and the misfortune of famine added to the bitter discontent. Yet Biren insisted that money must be found; and ordered his minions to seize goods and chattels from the poverty-stricken population, an action which can only be compared to the Tartar raids 'save for the fact that now the raiders' base of operations was the raiders' own city'.

Even the wars fought in Anna's reign were costly farces. One was fought for the Polish succession, in which the French emerged the sole victors; and the other against the Turks in the Crimea, the main result of which was to recapture Azov at the cost of thousands of dead Russians.

The smouldering hatred toward the German Party began to solidify, and the minds of many people turned to Peter the Great's daughter, Elizabeth, as their only possible saviour. Ever since the Empress Anna's accession Elizabeth had been living quietly in a country house near Moscow, at Biren's instigation. Biren did not allow her to hold court, nor encourage her to visit St Petersburg more than once or twice a year. As Elizabeth was only twenty-one, and not interested in politics, she was happy to be left alone. She adored outdoor sports, went beating, riding, sledging and skating. She hunted wolves and hyenas at Kurghanika, hawked at Alexandrovskoye, and gardened at Ismailovoye. The British Minister's wife describes her as 'fair, with light brown hair, large sprightly blue eyes, fine teeth and a pretty mouth. She is inclinable to be fat, but is very genteel and dances better than anyone I ever saw. She

Although famous for her beauty, Elizabeth's marital plans had all misfired. The Bourbons turned her down and Prince Charles of Holstein died a few days before the wedding.

66

speaks German, French and Italian, is extremely gay, and talks to everybody . . .'[4] Elizabeth's charms were universally admired for when a Chinese emissary attended Court and the Empress asked him who he considered the most beautiful woman present he pointed to Elizabeth, his only reservation being that her eyes were not small enough. '. . . He thought her the handsomest,' wrote Lady Rondeau, 'and if she had not quite such large eyes nobody could see her and live.'

Elizabeth was not only plump and pretty but very partial to the gentlemen. When she was twenty-two her eye lit on a sergeant in the Semenovsky Guards whom she took as a lover. Unfortunately, the Empress learned about the liaison; the wretched man promptly had his tongue torn out and was sent to Siberia. After several months of passionate grief Elizabeth took another lover, a handsome young Cossack shepherd, Alexis Razumovsky, who sang in the choir in the court chapel. This time she was more discreet and had him transferred to her household as a lute-player, where they were able to conduct their affair undisturbed and undetected.

Elizabeth's personality was so gay that she made friends wherever she went. The shopkeepers gave her presents and the soldiers worshipped her as the daughter of that intrepid campaigner, Catherine. As she was uninterested in power she was never in trouble and lived her feckless life without hindrance. Yet plenty of people called on her and whispered that Russia would never free itself of the German Party unless she took the lead.

The Empress Anna had decided to name her stupid, bashful niece, Anna Leopoldovna, the Duchess of Mecklenburg, as her successor, so that Biren could remain in the ascendancy. In 1739 the Empress arranged the marriage of the Duchess to Prince Anthony Ulric of Brunswick-Lüneburg; and thirteen months later Anna Leopoldovna gave birth to a son, Ivan.

Six weeks after this event, in November 1740, the Empress was seized with a fit at the dinner table and was taken to bed unconscious. It became apparent that she was dying, and Biren urged her to name the baby as Emperor and himself as Regent. Besotted though she was, Anna knew that Biren was too much hated to last long as Russia's ruler. 'Duke, Duke,' she cried, 'my heart is sad for you, for you are encompassing your own ruin!' But as she could never refuse her favourite she finally gave way, then turned her face to the wall and died.

The four-months-old Ivan VI was now Emperor of Russia. But the tiny Majesty only held the sceptre for fourteen months. Events moved with bewildering speed. Biren survived as Regent for no more than three weeks, when he was arrested in the middle of the night by Field Marshal Münnich and packed off to the Arctic. Three months later the Field Marshal was tricked into relinquishing his office as Premier Minister and the field was left to Ostermann.

As far as the Russian people were concerned, one German was as bad as another. The French Government, through its ambassador La

Anna Leopoldovna was quite incapable of ruling: she spent most of her time half-dressed, gossiping with her women friends.

Chetardie, immediately began to conspire to put Elizabeth on the throne, believing that if she became Empress she not only would alter the prevailing pro-Austrian policy, but perhaps adopt a more insular attitude which would encourage the country to slip back into the semi-barbarism whence it had come.

Elizabeth, however, was terrified of attempting a *coup d'état*. Although La Chetardie supplied her with money to be used for bribes, and many members of the Moscow nobility pledged their support, visions of failure kept rising before her eyes. The punishment would be more than she could bear: her hair would be cut off and she would be immured forever behind a convent wall.

Over a year elapsed before she gathered the courage to act. But at two o'clock on a December morning in 1741 she drove through the silent, snow-covered streets of St Petersburg to the Preobrazhensky Barracks where two hundred officers of the Guards awaited her. She wore the order of St Catherine around her neck, and as she reached the door of the barracks she snatched a pike from one of the soldiers. She stood in the dim smoke-filled room, facing the men, regal and composed. 'My children, you all know whose daughter I am. It is my resolve this night to deliver you and all Russia from our German tormentors. Will you follow me?' The men shouted their approval, and Elizabeth ordered a group of them to proceed to the homes of Ostermann and Münnich and to arrest them.

By this time men from the Semenovsky and Ismailovsky Guards had joined the Preobrazhensky. Elizabeth now rode to the Winter Palace with an escort of 400 men all of whom had their bayonets screwed on and grenades in their pockets. She went to Anna Leopoldovna's bedroom, woke her and told her that her son had been deposed. She then ordered the doors of the apartment to be locked and posted sentries outside. The following day Anna Leopoldovna, her husband and daughter were sent to Kholmogory near Archangel; but poor little Ivan VI was placed in a prison. Later he spent many years of his ghastly life in the fortress at Schlüsselburg, at the mouth of the Neva, where he grew up in solitary confinement, his speech slow and incoherent, his mind enclosed by shadows.

After achieving her dangerous *coup*, at the age of 32, the voluptuous Elizabeth showed no more interest in politics and reverted to a life of pleasure. She was the vainest sovereign in Europe, and spent hours at her dressing-table, dyeing her hair, trying on wigs, painting her face. She changed her clothes a dozen times a day, and when she died her wardrobe was said to contain fifteen thousand dresses. Foreign diplomats spoke of the 'blinding splendour' of Elizabeth's court, but the Russian historian, Kluchevsky, refers to its 'gilded squalor'. St Petersburg was still a town of wooden houses, except for the stone buildings in the Millionnaya, the Lugovaya and the Quai des Anglais. The Princess of Hesse possessed the only house in the capital with damask on the walls, the others being decorated with whitewash or wallpaper.

The coronation procession of the Empress Elizabeth

Warm-hearted, promiscuous and wildly extravagant, Elizabeth had an insatiable appetite for pleasure.

Although the Empress's palace was equipped with sumptuous salons the ordinary living-rooms to which the Court retired after its sportings were, according to Kluchevsky,

> . . . so cramped and so niggardly of fitting, and so slatternly of aspect, that their doors would not shut, their windows were draughty, water trickled down their walls so constantly as to keep the hangings in a permanent state of soddenness, the stove in the Grand Duchess Catherine's own bedroom gaped with cracks, there slept huddled into one small attic next door to her as many as seventeen servants, the furniture everywhere was scanty and rickety and broken, and, to meet requirements, mirrors, bedsteads, tables, and chairs had to be carted about between palace and palace in St Petersburg and even between the two capitals.[5]

Elizabeth's internal policy was lenient compared to that of Anna; nevertheless, like all Russian sovereigns, she knew how to be cruel. She had gusts of temper when she would slap and cuff all those about her and send offenders to the torture chamber for trifling misdemeanours. Normally, however, she retained her equable disposition and sat up all night playing cards or dancing. She chose as her Chancellor a man called Bestuzhev who, oddly enough, had been a creature of Biren. Bestuzhev remained in power for many years because of his friendship with Alexis Razumovsky, the Cossack shepherd who played the lute at Elizabeth's court. Shortly after becoming Empress, Elizabeth secretly married Razumovsky and gave him the rank of Count.

Alexis Razumovsky and his brother Cyril were extravagant, good-natured men who cared nothing for political power but a great deal for money. Alexis was the first to wear diamond buttons, buckles and epaulets; Cyril, who was appointed Grand Hetman of the Cossacks, kept a vast establishment which included half a dozen French chefs and a troupe of actors. When he ordered wine he bought a hundred thousand bottles at a time.

The white dining-room at Peterhof (*below*), a palace Elizabeth cherished for its memories of her father. As the original rooms were too small to accommodate her lavish parties, she commissioned Rastrelli to enlarge the building.

Elizabeth adored Alexis Razumovsky, and for years was never happy unless he was at her side; when he had an attack of gout she cancelled all court functions. Nevertheless, she had other lovers as well. In 1749 she took a fancy to Ivan Shuvalov, a boy young enough to be her son. Bestuzhev, who feared that the newcomer might displace Alexis Razumovsky as a favourite, promptly introduced a rival: a very handsome youth of 18 called Beketov. His move was partially successful for Beketov suddenly began to sport diamond rings and buckles. Razumovsky, who was party to the intrigue, appointed Beketov his adjutant and gave him an apartment in the palace. But instead of ousting Shuvalov, Beketov merely served as an addition, for the Empress managed to cope with all three lovers: Razumovsky and the two boys.

But now it was the Shuvalovs' turn to strike back. Ivan Shuvalov's uncle, Peter, persuaded Beketov to put a certain ointment on his face which, he said, would keep his skin young and fresh. Instead, it caused an eruption, and the Shuvalovs whispered to the Empress that the young man was suffering from a venereal disease. The horrified Elizabeth fled to Tsarskoye Selo, where she spent several days in prayer, and Beketov was banished from the Court.

Grand Duke Peter spent most of his time playing with his toy soldiers. He once court-martialled and hanged a rat which had eaten two of his sentries.

The Shuvalov uncles, Peter and Alexander, were now supreme. Peter soon controlled Russia's internal policies and put millions of money into his own pocket by introducing commercial monopolies. He established savings banks, reformed the coinage, and improved the Russian artillery. His brother Alexander served as Chief Inquisitor of the Secret Chancellery. His face twitched badly and people said that his nerves had been affected by his function as torturer. Young Ivan did better than his uncles. He was a generous patron of struggling young writers, corresponded with Voltaire, and gave the Empress the happy idea of founding the University of Moscow and the Academy of Arts in St Petersburg.

Elizabeth was not only uneducated and indolent, but firmly convinced that reading was injurious to the health. She blamed the death of her beloved sister, the Duchess of Holstein-Gottorp, on a fondness for Latin verse. One of Elizabeth's first acts upon her accession had been to send to Holstein for the Duchess's only child, Peter. Although the appearance of the 13-year-old boy came as something of a shock to the Empress she immediately pronounced him her heir. The Grand Duke Peter was a pathetic creature, pale and thin, with lank blond hair combed straight down over his collar. He held himself as erect as a guardsman and talked in a high voice of piercing intensity. Yet he had ugly grimaces and a lolling tongue. The truth was that the boy's nervous system had been permanently damaged by the cruelty of the Holstein 'governors' employed to look after him upon his father's death. Ever since his earliest days he had been beaten and tormented, sometimes being made to kneel for hours on sacks of peas until his legs were red and bruised.

Although the Empress engaged kindly tutors to educate him, they soon came to the conclusion that they were dealing with a retarded mind and reported that it was impossible to engage his attention. He played the violin a little, but what he liked best was drilling his hundreds of lead and wood soldiers. He forced all his attendants to enter into his games, and spent his days in a miniature world of battles and glory.

When Peter was 16 the Empress decided to find him a wife. She took the advice of Frederick the Great and sent for the daughter of a Prussian soldier, Prince Anhalt-Zerbst. Soon an astonishing young lady, Sophia Augusta Frederika, arrived in St Petersburg accompanied by her mother. Sophia became Catherine upon embracing the Orthodox faith, and is known in history as Catherine the Great. In her memoirs she wrote:

> I was in my fifteenth year, and he [the Grand Duke] showed himself very assiduous for the first ten days. In that short space of time I became aware that he was not greatly enamoured of the nation over which he was destined to reign; he was a convinced Lutheran, did not like his entourage, and was very childish. I kept silent and listened, which helped to gain his confidence. I remember that he told me among other things that what he liked most in me was that I was his second cousin and in that capacity, as a relative, he could talk freely to me; after this he confided that he was in love with one of the Empress' ladies-in-waiting . . . he would have liked to marry her but had resigned himself to marrying me as my aunt wished it.[6]

The nursery in the Summer Palace. On the wall are portraits of Peter and Catherine.

The Catherine Palace, from the park.

Catherine was not in the least affronted by her fiancé's bluntness. 'I did not care about Peter,' she admits, 'but I did about the Crown.' She put herself out to please the Empress, and a year and a half later she was married to the Grand Duke in a ceremony of dazzling pomp. Elizabeth was so determined to impress the onlookers with the glory of her Court that she gave all public officials a year's salary in advance and compelled them to spend a large part of it on equipment for the pageant. All those at the top of the hierarchy were ordered to have not less than eight lackeys attached to each carriage and as many more as could be afforded. Serge Naryshkin, one of the great dandies of St Petersburg, won favour by going to the wedding in a carriage which cost £7,000 and was inlaid all over, even to the wheels, with crystal mirrors. He wore:

> . . . a caftan ablaze with jewels, the back of which was made to imitate a tree, the trunk being represented by a broad golden band in the middle of his body, while the branches were indicated by lines of silver running up the sleeves to the wrists, and the roots by similar lines running down to the knees of his breeches.[7]

According to the bride her husband was unable to make himself 'aimable' to any lady, and the marriage was never consummated. After the day's functions, she wrote:

> . . . the ladies undressed me and put me to bed . . . Everybody left me and I remained alone for more than two hours, not knowing what was expected of me. Should I get up? Should I remain in bed? I truly did not know. At last Madame Krause, my new maid, came in and told me very cheerfully that the Grand Duke was waiting for his supper which would be served shortly. His Imperial Highness came to bed after supper and began to say how amused the servants would be to find us in bed together. Madame Krause questioned us the next day about our marital experiences but she was disappointed in her hopes.[8]

Catherine came to the conclusion that the Grand Duke's love affairs were no more than flirtations. 'He spent all his time playing soldiers in his room with his valets, performing military exercises and changing their uniforms twenty times a day.'

Catherine concealed her chagrin and not only kept on good terms with the Grand Duke but made a point of ingratiating herself with those she deemed important. 'I tried to be as charming as possible to everyone and studied every opportunity to win the affection of those who I suspected of being in the slightest degree ill-disposed toward me.' The sharp eyes of the Chevalier d'Éon, the secret agent of Louis XV, were quick to notice her hunger for power.

> The Grand Duchess is romantic, ardent, passionate. Her eyes are brilliant, their look fascinating and glassy – the expression of a wild beast. Her forehead is lofty, and, if I am not mistaken, a long and terrifying future is written on it. She is prepossessing and affable, but when she comes close to me I instinctively recoil, for she frightens me.[9]

Fortunately for Catherine, she did not frighten the Empress. Elizabeth loved her witty conversation and flattering remarks, and, above all, the vivacity with which the young Grand Duchess flung herself into every entertainment. Elizabeth had a passion for masquerades and, as she fancied herself in male attire, usually decreed that the men should come dressed as women and the women as men. Everyone loathed these parties as the men could not manage their whaleboned petticoats and the women were covered with shame at having to reveal their short thick legs. The Empress usually dressed as a Dutch sailor and insisted on being addressed as 'Mikhailova' in memory of her father. She had beautiful legs and feet and danced to perfection. 'At one of these balls,' wrote Catherine, 'I took the liberty to say to her that it was very fortunate for us poor women that she was not a man, as, dressed as she was then, even her portrait would be sufficient to turn all our heads. She replied in the most gracious manner in the world that if she were a man it would be to me that she would give the palm.'[10]

Catherine even managed to enter happily into the Empress's travels, which were frequent and tiring. From St Petersburg there were many excursions to Oranienbaum and to Peterhof, country residences about thirty miles from the capital. But the real trial came when the Court

When Rastrelli reconstructed Peterhof, he carefully preserved the central block which Lebland had built for Peter the Great, but added one storey so that it would remain the dominant element of the composition.

moved several hundred miles to Moscow, or all the way to Kiev, or Sophien or Reval.

> Our method of travel was neither pleasant nor comfortable, [wrote Catherine]. The post or station-houses were occupied by the Empress, while we were given tents or put into servants' quarters.
>
> I remember dressing one day on that journey in front of a stove where bread had just been baked and another time there was water above my ankles when I walked into the tent where my bed had been put up. To make matters worse, the Empress never had any fixed hours either for departures or arrivals, for meals or for rest; thus, we were all excessively harassed, both masters and domestics. At last after ten or twelve hours of travelling we arrived at the Country seat of Count Stenbock-Fermor, thirty miles from Reval. The Empress set out again from there with great ceremony, wanting to arrive at Katherinenthal by day, and I do not know how it was that the journey somehow dragged on until half-past one in the morning. The whole of Estonia was on the alert and the Empress' arrival at Katherinenthal was celebrated with great pomp between two and three in the morning in pouring rain and on such a dark night that one could not see a thing. We were all very elaborately dressed, but as far as I know no one saw us, for the wind had blown out all the torches and as soon as we alighted from our coaches everybody retired to their apartments.[11]

The first thing Peter did when he became Emperor was to stop Russia fighting his hero, Frederick the Great; and to return to Prussia all territory wrested from her.

Elizabeth found it impossible to apply her mind to serious subjects. Lord Hyndford, the British Ambassador, referred to 'this lady's mortal backwardness in all sorts of business or anything that required one moment's thought or application'. Catherine was careful to hide the excruciating boredom she felt at Court where, she tells us, half the people could not read and only a third could write. The Grand Duke Peter, however, managed to alleviate the tedium by boring holes in the floor of his apartment and peering into the Empress's private sitting-room where he could watch her making love. Elizabeth, however, was destined to leave behind one great masterpiece. In 1754 she commissioned the famous Italian architect, Rastrelli, to pull down the Winter Palace and to build her a new one made of stone.

A year after work had begun on the palace – and nine years after Catherine's marriage – Catherine gave birth to a son, Paul. In her memoirs she claims that the father was Serge Saltykov, who was placed in her entourage by the Empress for the purpose of producing an heir. If this is true, Elizabeth was the last Romanov to sit on the Russian throne. Many historians, however, doubt Catherine's veracity.

> While there is no inherent improbability in the rumour of illegitimate birth [wrote the British historian, G. P. Gooch], there is powerful argument on the other side. That Paul was to display the same mental instability as Peter might perhaps be explained away by the frustrations and anxieties arising from his mother's policy of keeping him in quarantine. Far more convincing evidence for his legitimacy is the portrait of the ugly snub-nosed man whom it is difficult to envisage as the offspring of a good-looking woman and an exceptionally handsome man.[12]

Whatever the truth of the matter, Catherine cared nothing for the boy. The Empress adopted Paul and brought him up herself.

The Grand Duke Peter is said to have been astonished at the birth of a son, and to have expressed doubts as to the child's paternity; but on the whole he was not greatly concerned. Soon afterwards he took a mistress by the name of Elizabeth Vorontsova who was ugly and stupid but very warm-hearted and whom he loved. She entered into all his games and played soldiers with him by the hour.

At this stage Peter's hero was Frederick the Great. This King of Prussia, this poet, philosopher and soldier, had already electrified Europe, and he looked as though he might do it again. By the piratical seizure of Silesia in 1740 he had started the War of the Austrian Succession. Now, in 1756, a huge European coalition, led by the Empress Maria Theresa of Austria, was forming against him. Frederick got wind of what was happening and decided to try and ward off the blow by invading Saxony. This marked the beginning of the Seven Years War in which Prussia, a tiny state of five million people, found itself facing a combined ninety million: Austria, Sweden, France, Poland, Russia and Saxony.

The Grand Duke Peter's hysterical admiration for Frederick as a fellow German and as the boldest, most breath-taking soldier in Europe is not surprising. Nevertheless, once Russia marched against Prussia the situation became acutely embarrassing. While Russian soldiers were dying on the battlefield the heir to the Russian throne was drilling his Holstein Guard and unrestrainedly cheering the victories of the great Frederick.

For once the Empress took an interest in State affairs. She was determined to prosecute the war to the bitter end, for she had no wish to see Prussia expanding into the Baltic. Besides, she hated Frederick because he made bawdy jokes about her and her lovers which were repeated all over Europe. Yet Frederick by his brilliant strategy and the miraculous spirit of his fighting men managed to hold all Europe at bay. In 1759 he felt that defeat was certain. In a battle against the Austrians two horses were killed beneath him, a bullet was deflected from his coat and he narrowly escaped capture by the Cossacks. 'Won't some accursed bullet hit me?' he cried in despair. 'I no longer have any resources,' he wrote to his minister Finckenstein, 'and to tell the truth I believe all is lost.' Yet he managed to hang on for another two and a half years, recruiting officers from university undergraduates.

At the beginning of 1762 Frederick again believed that the end had come. Nearly a third of his domains were in the hands of his enemies. The Russians had annexed East Prussia and part of Pomerania. The Austrians held the best part of Saxony, and Berlin, twice pillaged, lay in ruins. He decided to take his own life rather than sign a peace. At this moment, on 5 January 1762, he learned that his bitter enemy, the Empress Elizabeth, had died three days earlier of a haemorrhage.

The new sovereign Peter III immediately announced his intention of terminating the war. When Frederick sent an emissary, Baron von der Goltz, to St Petersburg, Peter received him enthusiastically, putting his arm around him and taking him in to dinner 'talking incessantly of the Prussian army and amazing Goltz by his intimate acquaintance with the *minutiae* of the subject.'

Frederick lost no time in writing to the new ruler.

When one behaves so nobly and with a nobility so uncommon in our days one has a right to be admired. And that is what your Imperial Majesty will find. The first acts of your Majesty's reign have drawn down upon you the benedictions of your subjects and the blessings of the sanest part of Europe.

And again:

Whilst all the rest of Europe is persecuting me, I find a friend in you. I find a friend who has a truly German heart, a friend who would never suffer Germany to become the slave of the House of Austria. In you I place all my trust, and I vow to you a loyal and eternal friendship.

Humbly, Peter replied:

Your Majesty surely laughs at me when you praise me so highly. In truth you must be amazed at my nothingness while I am amazed at your Majesty's exploits. Your qualities are extraordinary. I recognize in your Majesty one of the greatest heroes the world has ever seen.[13]

After this, Peter's infatuation for his Deity could not be contained. He talked openly of 'the King, my Master', causing the Saxon Minister to remark: 'Here at St Petersburg the King of Prussia is the Emperor.' Frederick sent a draft peace treaty to St Petersburg and Peter signed it without altering it or showing it to anyone. By a pen-stroke he returned to Prussia all the territory won from her by Russia during the past five years, and contracted a permanent alliance with his hero.

Peter celebrated the peace by a gala banquet at which he wore the Prussian Black Eagle. Afterwards a State ball was held in rooms overlooking the Neva. A display of fireworks took place which cost thousands of pounds and lasted several hours. One of the tableaux consisted of two colossal figures, Russia and Prussia, slowly approaching each other and ending in a passionate embrace.

While the new Emperor reigned as Peter III, the French Ambassador, M. Breteuil, reported to Paris that Catherine presented a mournful figure. 'The Empress is abandoned to grief and dark forebodings,' he wrote. 'Those who know her say she is scarce recognizable. She is growing thin and will soon be in her grave.' But Catherine was neither grief-stricken nor growing thin. Indeed, if anything she was becoming plumper, for she was carrying the child of Count Gregory Orlov, a dashing young Guards' officer with whom she was passionately in love, and by whom she was six months pregnant. This was by no means a unique event as she had given birth eighteen months earlier to a daughter, Anne,* fathered by a dashing Polish officer, Stanislas Poniatowski.

Peter did not seem to mind what Catherine did, as he was not only caught up in a whirl of state activity but wholly pre-occupied with his own mistress, Elizabeth Vorontsova, whose pock-marked face and shapeless figure caused general merriment, prompting Breteuil to describe her as 'a second-rate pot-house wench'. Peter did a number of praiseworthy things. He abolished the Secret Chancellery; removed the shipyards from St Petersburg to Kronstadt and ordered all future ship-building to follow English lines; and introduced a new system of police patrols and street lighting in the capital.

What alarmed Peter's subjects was the Emperor's uncouth, almost crazy, behaviour; his cavorting at the Empress Elizabeth's funeral; his appearing everywhere with a pipe in his mouth; his clownish comport-ment at banquets. When he became serious he made matters even worse, for he announced that he was going to Prussianize the Russian army. He began by discarding the red and green uniform of the Preobrazhensky

As a young girl, Princess Dashkova (*above*) adored Catherine, but was consistently rude to the Emperor.

*Anne had died a few months before Peter III ascended the throne.

Guard and donning instead the uniform of a Colonel of the Prussian Guards. He then spent hours on the parade-ground as a drill-sergeant, forcing his soldiers to learn new Prussian exercises. No officer was ever excused from attendance, and generals, and even field marshals, who had never held a demi-pike in their hands before, were obliged to turn out at the head of their regiments, whatever the weather, to their great indignation.

Although Peter introduced a number of good reforms – one of them the outlawing of the brutal knout – every innovation caused deep resentment. His appointment of Prince George of Holstein as a field marshal with a pension of £10,000 a year and precedence over all his seniors did not ease the situation; but the most unfortunate change undoubtedly was the Emperor's dismissal of the Preobrazhensky Regiment from its palace guard duties and its replacement by a regiment of Holsteiners.

He made an even more serious mistake when he moved into the magnificent new Winter Palace which stretched a quarter of a mile along the Neva. The palace had taken eight years to build and was completed in a great rush when Peter ordered thousands of workmen to proceed to the site and make it habitable within four months. He took up his new residence on 15 April 1762, accompanied by his wife, Catherine, her young son, Paul, and his mistress, Elizabeth. An imposing reception was held at which all his officers wore for the first time their dazzling new Prussian uniforms. But there was a painful omission. The open-air religious procession, usual at Easter, did not take place. As Peter only recently had told the Archbishop of Novgorod that he intended to set up a Protestant chapel in the palace, for the use of his Lutheran domestics, gossip spread like wildfire that Peter was not an orthodox believer.

The Emperor's foolish acts undoubtedly would have been overlooked if the clever, ruthless Catherine had not already been scheming to depose her husband. The French Ambassador, who a few months earlier had reported her decline, now penned dispatches in an entirely different vein. 'The Empress is putting a manly face on it,' he wrote, 'she is as much loved and respected by everyone as the Emperor is hated and despised. . . . It is impossible not to suspect (for I know her passionate audacity) that, sooner or later, she will venture on some desperate step.'[14]

Catherine not only was fortunate in having a lover, Gregory Orlov, who was an officer in the Guards, but in the fact that he had four brothers also in the army. The five Orlovs quietly began to solicit recruits for Catherine's cause, and within a few months reported that they had gained the allegiance of thirty to forty officers who in turn could command the support of ten thousand men. Other important intriguers were the 19-year-old Princess Dashkova, a sister of Peter's mistress, Elizabeth, and Nikita Panin, a distinguished diplomat who was in charge of the education of the heir to the throne, young Paul.

Peter III as heir to the throne, painted with Catherine and Paul.

As the plot developed Peter III played into the hands of the conspirators by deciding to fight the Danes over the disposal of the province of Schleswig, which, he claimed, belonged to Holstein and not to Denmark. When the Guards regiments were given their marching orders discontent spread through all ranks.

About this time Peter openly (and probably drunkenly) threatened to send Catherine to a convent, and the conspirators felt that there was no time to lose. The *coup* took place on 9 July. Catherine was sleeping in the pavilion 'Mon Plaisir' at Peterhof when she was awakened by Alexis Orlov who had driven from the capital. 'The time has come,' he said. 'All is ready for your proclamation.' Catherine dressed and climbed into a carriage with Orlov; the driver was told to head in the direction of St Petersburg.

On the outskirts of the city Catherine visited the headquarters of the Ismailovsky Guards. Soldiers ran forward and kissed the hem of her dress. She explained, with tears in her eyes, that although her life, and that of her infant son, were in danger, it was for the sake of Russia and the holy orthodox religion that she was making her dramatic move. They immediately swore an oath of allegiance to her, and led her to a neighbouring village where the same scene was enacted for the benefit of the Semenovsky Regiment.

The two divisions then escorted her into the capital to Kazan Cathedral where the Archbishop of Novgorod was waiting. With no more ado he proclaimed her Sovereign-Autocrat, and her son, the Grand Duke Paul, successor. She proceeded to the Winter Palace amid a great pealing of bells, and found the Senate and the Holy Synod in session in the Council Chamber. This convenient gathering had been arranged by Panin and enabled the assembly to draw up an Imperial Manifesto endorsing Catherine's succession.

Meanwhile Peter was drilling his Holsteiners on the parade-ground at Oranienbaum. After breakfast he drove to Peterhof, a few miles away, and was astonished to find the château deserted. He ran into all the rooms like a madman, peering under the beds and crying: 'Didn't I tell you she was capable of anything?'

A few hours later he learned what had happened, and after entertaining a number of wild ideas, returned to Oranienbaum and sent a letter to Catherine begging for his life, and offering to abdicate and leave for Holstein if Elizabeth might go with him. Catherine accepted Peter's offer but insisted in having the abdication in writing. An abject document was drawn up which the Emperor duly signed.

On 11 July the Duke of Holstein, as Peter now was called, was driven to Peterhof. Although Catherine was in residence she did not see him, and Peter was treated with scant courtesy, being stripped of his uniform and left standing in his shirt and stockings until his jailers succeeded in finding him a dressing-gown and slippers.

After a few hours he was sent to Ropsha, a country house a few miles away where he had lived as Grand Duke. Although he begged for

From Oranienbaum Peter wrote to
Catherine acknowledging defeat: 'In
the short time of my reign as self
upholder of all the Russias I have
realized only too well the strain and
burden of a task to which my powers are
not equal.' The words may not have
been his own.

Elizabeth she was not allowed to accompany him. He was transported
in a carriage with drawn blinds beside which rode Alexis Orlov, Prince
Theodore Baryatinsky and several other officers. Peter was given a
large room; and the next morning when he asked for his violin, his
poodle, his Negro servant and his German doctor the request was
granted.

What was to be done with Peter? No one could deny that if he was
imprisoned in a fortress he would remain a rallying point for an opposition; and if he was allowed to go to Holstein he would ally himself with
the King of Prussia and conspire against Russia.

Alexis Orlov knew the answer; and as Catherine's lover, Gregory,
was Alexis' brother, and as Catherine's ambition was as hard as a

diamond, there seems little doubt that she was an accessory to the crime that took place three days later. No one knows exactly what happened; some say that Peter was poisoned and then strangled with a table napkin. His dead face was black, and his body badly bruised. Alexis wrote an abject letter to Catherine saying: 'He struggled behind the table with Prince Theodore [Baryatinsky] but we succeeded in separating them, and he is no more. I myself don't remember what we did, but the whole lot of us are guilty and worthy of punishment. Have mercy upon me if only for my brother's sake. . . .'[15]

Needless to say, Catherine pardoned the assassins; then she issued a proclamation announcing to the world that the ex-Emperor had died of a violent fit of colic.

85

CHAPTER IV

Catherine the Great
1762–1796

EUROPE was scandalized by Catherine II. Her announcements of July 1762 were regarded as shockingly cynical; in one breath she informed the world that her coronation would take place in September, in the next that her husband, the deposed Peter III, had died quite suddenly of colic. No one believed this improbable tale, and the foreign embassies in St Petersburg soon were buzzing with the more likely story that Catherine had done away with her husband through the services of her lover, Gregory Orlov.

Not only was she a murderess but a usurper; not only a usurper but a whore. That a tight-lipped, German princess of petty origin should have snatched the crown first from Peter, then from Peter's son, Paul, on the grounds that Russia must be freed of foreign influence, was a paradox; and that the *coup* should have been achieved by a woman who, when her husband became Emperor, was pregnant with her lover's child, was nothing short of an outrage.

Yet Catherine appeared oblivious to the grumblings of orthodox Russia and the disapproval of the courts of Europe. On the day of her coronation she made Gregory Orlov her Adjutant-General, gave him the title of Count, and presented him with her portrait set in diamonds which he wore over his heart. She installed him in rooms in the Winter Palace which had a private staircase leading up to her own apartment. The Princess Dashkova, who took part in the conspiracy to place Catherine upon the throne, describes the favourite sprawling on a sofa in the Empress's drawing room, nonchalantly opening official communications. When Catherine arrived, and dinner was served, a table was pushed up to his couch in order that he should not be inconvenienced. 'He lacks nothing but the title of Emperor,' reported the French Chargé d'Affaires. . . . 'Scorning etiquette, he takes liberties with his sovereign in public which in polished society no self-respecting mistress permits in her lover.'

In private Orlov beat Catherine, and she fell ever more deeply in love with 'the handsomest man I have ever known'. Yet she remained strong-headed enough to resist his plea when it came to marriage, which was what he most desired. Although for a while she toyed with the idea, she heeded her Chancellor, Panin, who pointed out that an upstart like Orlov, who had fathered Catherine's child, Alexis Bobrinsky, would be seen as a threat to the legitimate heir, and as such would arouse opposition which might prove fatal. 'Madame Orlov,' he warned, 'could never remain Empress of Russia.' So she ignored her lover's tirades, wept over the infidelities with which he punished her, showered him with riches, and gloried in allowing the world to know that she was his mistress.

Catherine was 33 when she ascended the throne. 'I was very

Catherine II, Empress and Autocrat of all the Russias.

Catherine's lover Gregory Orlov had a wonderful physique but a limited mind. He studied physics and astronomy, but lacked the patience to persevere.

ABOVE Catherine commissioned Rinaldi to build the Marble Palace for Orlov.

BELOW The blue drawing-room designed by Cameron in the Catherine Palace at Tsarskoye Selo.

affectionate,' she wrote in her memoirs, 'and gifted with an appearance which was very attractive. I pleased at first glance without employing any arts or pains to that end.' Not everyone agreed with Catherine's assessment. 'Pretty rather than ugly, but not so as to inspire any violent feelings,' was the laconic verdict of her French secretary, M. Favier. 'Her figure is tall and slender but not supple; she has a noble carriage, an affected and somewhat ungraceful walk, with a narrow chest, a long face, especially about the chin, an eternal smile on her lips, a deep-set mouth, a slightly aquiline nose, small eyes, an agreeable expression, and a face marked by smallpox.'[1] As Catherine had not had smallpox the marks must have been left by chickenpox.

Catherine believed that opulence went hand in hand with power. If foreigners were impressed by the luxury of Elizabeth's reign, they were astonished by the extravagance of the new ruler. 'The richness and splendour of the Russian Court surpasses all description,' wrote the Rev. William Coxe. An immense retinue of courtiers always preceded and followed the Empress, and her bodyguard was the most 'sumptuously accoutred in Europe'. 'They wore casques, like those of the ancients, with a rich plumage of black feathers, and their whole dress was in the same style: chains and broad plates of solid silver were braided over their uniforms so as to bear the appearance of a splendid coat of mail; and their boots were richly ornamented with the same materials.'[2]

At night the men outshone the ladies in their use of precious stones. 'Many of the nobility were almost covered with diamonds; their buttons, buckles, hilts of swords, and epaulets, were composed of this valuable material; their hats were frequently embroidered, if I may use the expression, with several rows of them; and a diamond star upon the coat was scarcely a distinction.'[3] Count Orlov sported a suit in which was sewn £1,000,000 worth of diamonds, and the British Minister, Sir James Harris, described a fête at which 'the dessert at supper was set out with jewels to the amount of upwards two million sterling'. But Sir James was not impressed in the way Catherine would have wished. 'Their entertainments, their apartments and the number of their domestics is quite Asiatic,' he reported to London.

Catherine's love of grandeur, however, was not limited to personal splendour. She began to pull down the wooden houses which she considered disfiguring to St Petersburg, and she rebuilt in stone. She commissioned the Italian architect, Rastrelli, to build her a palace at Tsarskoye Selo that would outshine Versailles. The elaborate blue and white structure with two hundred rooms, known as the Catherine Palace, so delighted the Empress that she made Rastrelli a Russian Count. In St Petersburg she built a magnificent marble palace for Gregory Orlov, and added three buildings to the immense Winter Palace which already boasted 1,500 rooms. The additions, known as the Hermitage, were connected to the Palace by covered passages. Between them were courtyards, heated in winter, where rare birds flitted among

trees and shrubbery. The buildings contained splendid reception halls, rooms for cards, billiards and music, and a superb library and picture gallery which became Catherine's pride and joy. She instructed her ambassadors in Paris, Rome, Amsterdam and London to keep a sharp eye for bargains, and bought many fine pictures by Rembrandt, Rubens, Raphael, Tiepolo, Titian, Van Dyck and Reni. Near the end of her reign she commissioned Falconet to make a statue of Peter the Great. The great bronze figure, astride a horse, clad, ironically enough, in one of the long coats he refused to allow his subjects to wear, was placed on the bank of the Neva near the Senate House and across from the Academy of Arts and Sciences.

Catherine entertained in the Hermitage every Thursday evening for the chosen few of her court. Small supper tables were set up, servants excluded, and guests told to help themselves. Etiquette was in abeyance. A sign on the wall read: 'Sit down where you choose and when you please without it being repeated to you a thousand times.'

Despite these distractions Catherine flung herself into the business of ruling with an intensity that amazed even those acquainted with her boundless energy. She rose at six in the morning, rubbed her face with ice, and drank five cups of black coffee. She often worked ten hours a day. Although she surrounded herself with ministers, they were little more than cyphers appointed to carry out her orders. She attended debates in the Senate, which deliberated without power, studied the problems of schools, hospitals and local administration, probed into Treasury spending, and asked endless questions of countless State officials.

Yet all these activities were secondary compared to her main resolve; to fashion a Code of Instruction which would hold its own with the jurisprudence of the West. Catherine fancied herself as a political philosopher. During her years as Grand Duchess she had read avidly the French *philosophes*, devouring the works of Voltaire and Diderot and declaring that if she were Pope she would canonize Montesquieu.

She worked three hours a day on her 'Instructions' and finished the work five years after her accession. The opening articles rasped out the ideology of the Enlightened Autocracy.

> The Sovereign is absolute, for there is no other authority but that which centres in his single person that can act with a vigour proportionate to the extent of such a vast domain. . . . What is the true end of Monarchy? Not to deprive people of their natural liberty; but to correct their actions in order to attain the supreme good. The intention and the end of monarchy is the glory of the citizen, of the State and of the Sovereign.

Catherine wrote to Diderot that she gladly would have copied the English Constitution had it been practical; but in a state mainly composed of illiterate slaves the division of power was impossible. Diderot was not impressed. He argued that the only true sovereign was the nation, and that a good code must begin by compelling the ruler to

The Throne Room at Peterhof, with a portrait of Catherine II wearing the uniform of the Preobrazhensky Regiment.

swear by the law. 'The Empress of Russia is certainly a despot,' he commented, 'since whatever the true end of her government, it makes all liberty and property dependent on one Person.'

Catherine's Instructions contained nothing original. Indeed, many intellectuals wondered how it could have taken five years to compose, as large tracts of it were lifted from Montesquieu's *The Spirit of Laws* and Beccaria's *Crime and Punishment*. She wrote to Frederick the Great that she felt like a crow in peacock feathers; the only merit she claimed was that of arrangement, with a few lines of her own thrown in.

Nevertheless she was immensely proud of her ideas, and came increasingly to believe in their profundity. In Moscow she convened an assembly of delegates, drawn from all over the Empire, to discuss her projects. They arrived in *kibitkas*, on horseback, on foot. There were nobles dressed in lace and velvet, cut in the latest Paris fashion; Tartars and Bashkirs; merchants and military men; and a few peasants in smocks. The gathering took place in the Kremlin and the discussions dragged on for a year and a half. When Catherine returned to St Petersburg the delegates followed her in flying sledges and assembled in the Winter Palace after the Christmas festivities had taken place.

However superficial Catherine's Instructions, the fact that a Russian ruler had attempted to define autocracy in terms of reason rather than privilege was a radical move. Indeed, the Code was banned from France by Louis XV. Yet as the years progressed it became clear that what Catherine wanted was not reform but recognition of her intellectual conceptions, admiration for her liberalism. Princes do not have to search for praise. Frederick the Great made her a member of the Berlin Academy, and Voltaire wrote: 'I regard it as the finest monument of the century . . . Your genius conceived it, your pretty hand wrote it.'

If nothing else came of Catherine's work, at least it started for her a correspondence which lasted over many years with Voltaire, Diderot, d'Alembert and a frenchified German, Baron Grimm. Catherine loved to write and poured out her heart in letters and memoirs. Voltaire rewarded her with nauseating sycophancy. 'You are surely the brightest star of the North; Andromeda, Perseus and Calistro are not your equals.' 'Do you know where there is earthly paradise? I know: it is everywhere that there is Catherine II.' 'I throw myself at your feet with worship and idolatry.'

Although Catherine did not like France, she loved the French tongue, and not only used it in her private correspondence but made it the language of her Court. Society promptly aped her, and soon nothing but French was fashionable, and the acquisition of French culture became a status symbol that lasted for a century. The nobility engaged French tutors for their children, and the Russian intelligentsia worshipped at the feet of Molière and Racine, Corneille, and La Fontaine. When an Englishwoman, married to a Russian, began to study the language of her new country her husband told her it was a total waste of time 'except to speak to the servants'.

Chesme Church, built in honour of Orlov's victories over the Turks.

Soon not only the French language, not only French culture, but everything French was a craze. Two young Irish girls, Martha and Catherine Wilmot, who spent many months in Russia as the guests of the immensely rich and clever Princess Dashkova, have left us a picture of upper-class life. Martha Wilmot wrote:

> The land is overrun with French as with locusts. Milliners to the amount of some hundreds sell off ends of Gauze etc. at the most exorbitant prices because they pretend they are just arrived from Paris tho 'tis known half their goods come from the Russian shops at the other end of the Town.... Dancing masters are of course French, so are the multitudes of Physicians. In short, profession and trade of the domestic kind (I mean Tailors, Mantua-makers, Milliners, Waiting Maids, Cooks, Book-sellers etc.) swarm with French.[4]

The Russian nobles not only followed Catherine in adopting French tastes but tried to live up to the imperial standard of magnificence. Only nobles had the right to own either land or serfs; but anyone could become a noble if he served the State with distinction. The way lay through the civil administration, or court officialdom, or the army or navy. Success was achieved when the top grades of the Table of Ranks, laid down by Peter the Great, had been reached.

When Catherine ascended the throne there were half a million nobles out of a total population of some twenty million. Those whose families had been members of the nobility for some generations not only possessed huge properties but fantastic numbers of serfs. Prince Yusupov, for example, was said to own over twenty thousand serfs in fifteen provinces. He not only used them as carpenters and goldsmiths and ebony makers but formed a theatre company and a *corps de ballet*. He had his own theatre where he gave performances for his friends. Prince Kropotkin, on the other hand, had a hundred-piece orchestra in which his second butler served as a piano tuner and flutist, his tailor played the French horn, and his footman performed on the trombone or the bassoon.

Other nobles used their serfs to build houses or triumphal arches, to divert the course of a river, or for any notion that might come into their heads.

> The number of servants is dreadful [wrote Martha Wilmot]. Think of two, three and often four hundred servants to attend a small family. A Russian Lady scorns to use her two feet to go upstairs, and I do not Romance when I assure you that two powdered footmen support her [the Princess Dashkova's] lily white elbows and nearly lift her from the ground, a couple more follow with all manner of shawls, Pelisses etc. There is not a Bell in Russia except to the Churches, but if a fair-one gently calls, four or five footmen are ready in any antechamber to obey her summons....[5]

Often the ladies were the harshest masters. One Russian countess forced her serfs to read her to sleep; and to continue reading throughout

'Petro Primo Catharina Secunda' is inscribed on Falconet's statue of Peter the Great erected in 1782 at Catherine's command.

the night, as she complained that she always woke up when they closed the book. Another lady had a serf who was trained in the art of hair-dressing. As she wore a wig and did not want the world to know about it, she kept the wretched youth in a cage in her bedroom.

> The poor fellow had a bit of bread, a pitcher of water, a little stool and a chamberpot in his box [wrote Charles Masson, the French tutor at the Saltykov house]. He never saw daylight but while he was dressing the periwig on the bald pate of his old keeper. The portable prison was kept close at her bed's head, and carried with her into the country. And her husband permitted this abomination! . . . He spent three years in this *gehenna*; and when he made his reappearance he was frightful to look at, pale, bent and withered like an old man.[6]

When Catherine published her Code of Instructions in 1767 many people hoped that during her reign she would alleviate the wretched-ness of her serfs. Instead the reverse happened. She not only increased the master's right to punish them, but over the years turned over nearly a million free peasants to private proprietors. Apart from enslaving the Ukrainians, she could not resist making lavish gifts to her favourites; and the most coveted gift was the acquisition of serfs. She gave General Rumyantsov five thousand serfs after his victory over the Turks, to correspond with the number of enemy slain; and to her favourites anywhere from seven to ten thousand each.

Nevertheless, Catherine continued to think of herself as a 'liberal' until 1773, when her 'enlightened autocracy' received its first great shock. At that time Russia was engaged in a long and costly war with Turkey. Suddenly news reached St Petersburg that a revolt had broken out in the Urals, led by a Don Cossack, Emelyan Pugachev. Pugachev was a swashbuckling soldier with a black beard, a gold-embroidered caftan and a fur cap covered in medallions. He claimed to be Peter III, and roamed the countryside at the head of an army of Cossacks and Kirghiz tribesmen, calling on the people to free themselves from their slavery. He created his own court, christening his chief officers with such names as Panin and Orlov, and assigning ladies-in-waiting to his Cossack wife. This strange army of bearded men with sabres flashing and banners flying gained the sympathies of the populations along the Caspian and Lower Volga; and as they moved westward the revolt turned into a popular uprising. Pugachev promised to abolish serfdom and distribute the land to the peasants. He exhorted the people to murder their masters and burn down the estates of the nobles.

Whole districts flocked to his banner, landowners were flayed or torn to pieces by screaming mobs. All those who could escape fled to Moscow, with appalling tales of atrocity. In the winter of 1773/4 Pugachev's army, now fifteen thousand strong, came within 120 miles of Moscow, and people whispered that Catherine might do well to abdicate in favour of her son, Paul.

But Catherine remained calm. She referred to the 'Marquis de

Pugachev in a cage. Drawing by Surikov.

Pugachev' contemptuously, and gave orders that her generals were to make whatever peace they could with the Turks. In fact, the peace was more than favourable, for Russia won a great victory on the Danube, and when the treaty was signed in July 1774 Catherine gained the northern Caucasus and access to the Black Sea, and independence for the Crimea.

With General Suvorov's armies free to attack the Cossack bands the Pugachev revolt was brought speedily to an end. The false Peter III was betrayed by his own lieutenants, who secretly negotiated with Catherine in return for a pardon. He was handed over to General Panin, a brother of the Empress's minister, in October 1774, and carried to Moscow in a cage.

> He could neither read nor write [wrote Catherine to Voltaire] but he was an extremely bold and determined man. So far there is not the least indication that he was the tool of some foreign power. . . . It is to be supposed that M. Pugachev is simply a robber baron, and not the servant of any living soul. No one has done more harm than he has. He hopes for clemency because of his courage. If he had offended only myself his reasoning would be just, and I should pardon him, but this cause is the Empire's and that has its own laws.[7]

Pugachev was not tortured, as this form of punishment had been outlawed, but he was put to death. And Catherine's long arm reached out to punish all the peasants who had taken a leading part in the revolt. Although General Bibikov, who had been ordered to put down the insurrection in 1773, wrote: 'What matters is not Pugachev, but the general state of discontent,' Catherine ordered that scaffolds should be erected in the main square of every village, and the persecutions continued for over a year.

Meanwhile Catherine's personal life was almost as fevered as the pattern of wars and revolts. In 1772 she decided to replace Gregory Orlov as her lover. Before he departed for Fokshani to make peace with the Turks she discovered that he was having an affair with Princess Golitsyna and concluded that the time had come to end her own liaison.

> This one would have remained for ever [she wrote some years later] had he not been the first to tire; I learned this on the day of his departure to the Congress from Tsarskoye Selo and simply decided that I could no longer trust him, a thought that hurt me cruelly and forced me, from desperation, to take a step which I deplore to this day more than I can say, *especially at the moment when other people usually feel happy*.[8]

Catherine picked out a tall, handsome young man, Alexander Vasilchikov, and installed him in Orlov's apartments. She made him an aide-de-camp and presented him with 100,000 roubles. But Vasilchikov was dull and moody and a bad lover. He disliked the union almost as much as Catherine and complained bitterly that he was

> . . . nothing more than a kept woman and was treated as such. I was not allowed to receive guests or go out. If I made a request for anyone else, I

Pugachev issued a manifesto promising to 'free Russia from the yoke of servile toil'. After four years he was caught and executed.

received no answer. If I spoke for myself, it was the same. When I wished to have the Order of St Anne I spoke to the Empress about it. The next day I found a 30,000 rouble banknote in my pocket. In this way they always stopped my mouth and sent me to my room.[9]

Catherine, meanwhile, was almost hysterical in her longing for Orlov. 'All caresses provoke nothing in me but tears, so that I believe I have never cried since my birth as I have in these eighteen months. I thought at first that I would get accustomed to the situation but things grew worse and worse . . .'[10]

However, Catherine was determined not to have her old lover back. When Orlov learned that someone else was living in his apartment he was wild with rage and set out for St Petersburg without a moment's delay. On the Empress's orders he was stopped and confined to his palace at Gatchina, some distance outside the capital. Catherine was so frightened of him that she changed all the locks on the palace doors and kept an armed guard outside her rooms. 'You don't know him,' she wailed. 'He is capable of killing me and of killing the Grand Duke.'

In the end Orlov regained his composure and was allowed to return, not only to St Petersburg, but to the Winter Palace. Catherine loaded him with gifts: six thousand serfs, a salary of 150,000 roubles, a service of Sèvres china, porcelain worth 250,000 roubles. But in return he gave Catherine a superb solitaire diamond which cost him 460,000 roubles and is known as the Orlov diamond, probably the most beautiful single gem in the world.* Catherine had it set in the Russian Imperial sceptre under a jewelled eagle.

Orlov's life ended miserably. For the next few years he trailed disconsolately from country to country, finally marrying his second cousin, Catherine Zinovieva. She died within four years, and in 1781, after being widowed a year, he began to display symptoms of madness, believing that he was haunted by the blood-stained ghost of Peter III. He died in 1783 at the age of forty-six leaving his immense fortune to Count Alexis Bobrinsky, the son Catherine had borne him.

No one was more delighted to see the last of Gregory Orlov than Catherine's legitimate son, the 18-year-old Paul. This boy scarcely knew his mother, as he had been snatched away from her side within an hour of his birth by the Empress Elizabeth, who took him to her apartments and brought him up as her own child.

Catherine did not seem to mind. Although she was only permitted to visit her son every few months, she showed no interest in him, which convinced more than one courtier that he was not the offspring of Count Saltykov (as she claimed in her memoirs) but that of her murdered husband, Peter III.

Yet Catherine did not hesitate to make political capital out of the neglected Paul. On the night of her *coup d'état* in 1762, the 7-year-old

*In Catherine's reign 5 roubles equalled £1.

The Orlov diamond, originally known
as the Nadir-Shah, travelled from Persia
to Russia stitched into the thigh of an
Armenian smuggler.

By mounting the Orlov diamond in her
sceptre, Catherine was perhaps
reminding herself that she owed her
throne to the Orlovs.

boy was aroused from his slumbers and taken to the Winter Palace to
appear on the balcony before excited crowds at the side of his mother.
That night he learned of his father's death from 'colic'; but before long
he learned the story of the murder. No one knows who imparted the
information, but the horrific tale shattered the equilibrium of the highly-
strung child. For years he suffered from nightmares in which he pictured
his father being beaten and strangled by the Orlov giants. From then
onwards he never referred to either brother except as 'that butcher'.

Paul was an intelligent boy and when he appeared in public at the age of nine he heard several soldiers cry: 'Long live the Emperor, Paul Petrovich!' Many people believed that another *coup* might be on its way; and Paul learned that in the eyes of many people he, and not his mother, was the rightful occupant of the throne.

He began to realize, and exaggerate, the danger of his position when another claimant, Ivan VI, was brutally murdered in his prison cell in 1764 at Catherine's instigation. Ivan was the baby emperor whom the Empress Elizabeth had deposed and imprisoned. In 1764 he was 23 years old, a savage creature who could neither read nor write, having spent his whole life in solitary confinement, pacing up and down his cell like a wild animal. Catherine was well aware that as a German-born princess she was a usurper, and was on her guard against rebellion. She gave instructions to the warders at Schlüsselburg that if any attempt at insurrection took place 'the nameless prisoner', as Ivan was known, was to be killed. No one knows whether the minor rebellion that took place was provoked by Catherine; at any rate poor Ivan was stabbed to death. And the 10-year-old Paul was now the only being around whom opposition to Catherine could form.

Paul's nervous disorders grew worse. He lived in a world of haunting fears.

Ivan VI, great-great-grandson of Tsar Alexis. When Catherine heard of his murder she exclaimed 'the ways of God are wonderful and beyond prediction.'

> His highness has that most detestable habit of doing everything in haste [wrote his tutor]. He is in a hurry to get up, to eat, to go to bed. Responsive and affectionate, he forms an attachment very quickly, but the object of his affection has to exert himself to retain it at the same level, otherwise the whole thing is very soon forgotten.[11]

When the Empress decided to dispense with Gregory Orlov in 1772 she made a point of trying to win Paul's affection so that her ex-lover would not be able to revenge himself by supporting the son against the mother. 'I return to town on Tuesday with my son, who does not want to leave my side,' she wrote to a friend, 'and whom I have the honour to please so well that he sometimes changes his place at the table to sit next to me.' The Prussian Envoy watched the little game that was being played and reported that Paul was well aware of what was going on.

As soon as Orlov had accepted defeat, Catherine dropped her efforts to please Paul. Once again she became a stranger to him, while he, in turn, looked on his mother with aversion and dread. When he was 19 he found pieces of glass in his food. Apparently a bottle had broken and a negligent servant had not picked out all the pieces. Paul ran to his mother in hysterics and accused her of trying to murder him.

Soon after Paul reached his majority he was married to a Hessian princess who died within four years; then to a Württemberg princess who was to give him four sons and six daughters. Although Paul was an ugly youth, ungainly, with bulging eyes and a grotesquely snubbed nose, the new Grand Duchess, Marie Feodorovna, fell madly in love with him, referring to him as her *prince adorable*. 'He is an angel, the pearl of husbands,' she confided to a friend. 'She deserves his affection,' reported the British Ambassador, 'and he is very fond of her.'

When Paul visited Moscow in 1775 the Austrian Envoy described him as 'the idol of the nation'. The Grand Duke received such acclaim from the crowds that Count Razumovsky turned to him and said: 'You see how popular you are, Prince – if you wished.' But Paul lacked the spirit to rebel. His mother refused him a seat on her Council and watched his growing popularity with narrowed eyes.

Shortly before the Pugachev uprising Catherine pensioned off her unsatisfactory paramour, Alexander Vasilchikov, and took a new lover who was to mean more to her than any other man in her life.

Catherine had met the tall, dark, surly Potemkin shortly after the *coup d'état* of 1762, when she was reviewing her officers dressed in the uniform of an officer of the Guards. She noticed that the knot of her sword was missing, and a young man rode out from the ranks and presented her with his own. According to legend, that was the moment when young Potemkin fell madly in love with the Empress. He had taken part in the conspiracy against Peter III, and after Catherine's coronation was promoted to the rank of lieutenant and presented with 400 serfs and 10,000 roubles.

The Prince de Ligne, who knew everyone in Europe, declared that Potemkin was the most extraordinary man he had ever met. A Ukrainian by birth, he was sometimes morose, sometimes fiery and excitable; his hair was dirty and he bit his fingernails. Yet he had wit and intelligence and a strong, saturnine face that compelled attention. The Orlov brothers brought him into Catherine's life as they thought she would be amused by his gift of mimicry. When she asked him to perform, he gave an imitation of her own guttural German. Despite the horrified faces around her, she burst out laughing, and for many months Potemkin was a regular visitor at the Hermitage where Catherine entertained her friends.

Potemkin's appearance was not enhanced by losing an eye. Some historians blame the Orlov brothers, claiming that, stung by jealousy, they picked a quarrel with Potemkin and beat him up; others insist that the misfortune was caused by an abscess. Whatever the truth, he was known at Court as 'Cyclops'.

Potemkin left the capital in 1769 and joined the army to fight against the Turks, where he served as an aide to the Commander-in-Chief, Rumyantsov. In December 1773, when the war had come to a close, he received a summons from Catherine that was clearly a declaration of love. 'As I desire to keep men about me who are zealous, brave, intelligent and discriminating, I beg you do not waste time wondering to what end this has been written. I can answer you that it is to give you some confirmation of my regard for you, since I am, as always, your well-wisher, Catherine.'

The Empress kept Potemkin dangling for another year, and in a rage

Gilded statues in a fountain court at Peterhof

OVERLEAF The main room in Katalnaya Gorka, a pleasure pavilion built for Catherine II by Rinaldi at Oranienbaum

of despair he entered a monastery, where visitors found him alternating between melancholy and exaltation. One of the ladies-in-waiting, the Countess Bruce, was sent by Catherine to fetch him back, with the promise of 'the greatest favours'.

The Empress was now 44, Potemkin 34; yet Catherine looked the younger of the two. Potemkin's face was ravaged and his body bloated. 'He is of gigantic height and ungainly proportions,' wrote the British Ambassador, Sir Robert Gunning, 'and his appearance in general is far from pleasing.' Catherine thought otherwise. She installed him in the favourite's apartment and laughed to see the amazement provoked by his Asiatic habits. Slovenly and indolent, he would stride into Catherine's apartment half naked, and lie for hours on the couch. The French Minister called him 'a Tartar' as no one but an Oriental would loll about in a bright dressing-gown, playing with a handful of uncut jewels while someone read aloud from Plutarch's *Lives*.

Yet Catherine forgave him everything, as he was the first and only one of her lovers who had a mind as appealing to her as his huge body. 'What a marvellous head he has,' she wrote to Baron Grimm. 'He has done more than anyone to end the Turkish war and is as amusing as the Devil.'

Potemkin occasionally composed music and ballads. The song he wrote when he was at the Turkish War, pining for Catherine, became a legend.

As soon as I beheld thee
I thought of thee alone
Thy lovely eyes captivated me
Yet I trembled to say I loved
To thee, love subjects every heart
And enchains them with the same garlands
But, ah heaven, what a torment to love one
To whom I dare not declare it :
One who can never be mine.
Cruel Gods, why have you given her such charms?
Or why did you exhalt her so high?
Why did you destine me to love her and her alone
The one whose sacred name will never pass my lips
Whose charming image will never quit my heart.

Catherine's 357 surviving letters to Potemkin reveal her as a tremulous, love-smitten maiden, frightened of losing her lover, pathetically anxious to please, never too proud to abase herself.

A flood of ridiculous words gushes from my head. I can't understand how you can bear a woman with such incoherent ideas. Oh! Monsieur Potemkin, what sorry miracle you have wrought in deranging a head commonly regarded as one of the best in Europe! It is high time for reason to assert its sway. What disgrace! What sin! Catherine II a prey to this crazy passion! You will disgust him with your folly, I say to myself. . . .

Or in another mood:

Portrait of Catherine II in old age in the dressing-room at Peterhof

Among Catherine's lovers, Potemkin stands out. Catherine wrote that he was 'one of the greatest, the most strange, and the most amusing eccentrics of this iron age.'

Chéri, what funny things you told me! I am still laughing over them. What happy moments I pass with you! We spend four hours together without a moment of *ennui* and it is a wrench to leave you. My beloved little pigeon, I love you greatly; you are handsome, intelligent, amusing. In your company I forget the whole world. Never have I been so happy. I often try to hide my feelings, but my heart betrays my passion....[12]

More than one Russian historian in fact believes that Catherine secretly married Potemkin at the close of 1774 in the church of St Samson on the outskirts of the capital. This claim is supported by Catherine's terms of endearment, for in no less than twenty-three letters she addresses him as 'dear husband', 'my beloved husband' and alludes to herself as 'your wife'.

Whatever the truth, the ties of matrimony could not tame a love affair so stormy and unpredictable. Potemkin was torn in two by the conflicting desires of the flesh and a longing for mysticism. His wish to annihilate himself in God frequently produced a terrible despair that led to quarrels. But when he asked for forgiveness he always received it. One of the letters that has survived is a sheet of paper containing a declaration of their feelings in parallel columns.[13]

In Potemkin's hand	*In Catherine's hand*
Mon âme chérie	Je sais
Tu sais que je suis à toi	Je ne l'ignore pas
Je n'ai que toi dans ce monde	C'est vrai
Je te suis fidèle jusqu'à la mort	Sans doute
Par conséquent, tes intérêts me sont très chers	Je te crois
La chose qui m'est le plus agréable c'est de te servir et d'être utilisé par toi.	

Although the Empress consulted Potemkin on every official matter, although she showered riches upon him and persuaded the Austrian Emperor to make him a Prince of the Holy Roman Empire, although she loved him to distraction, Potemkin was too restless for captivity. After two years of life in the Winter Palace he once again had a craving for travel and began to wander across the Russian plains. He now was a prince and a general, and when he went to Novgorod or, later, to the Turkish wars (as Commander-in-Chief) he travelled in the greatest style.

Before Potemkin departed he provided Catherine with a lover, the 25-year-old Zavadovsky, who had been serving as her secretary. And this started the long chain of lovers which won for the Empress the title 'Messalina of the North'. No one knows how many young men she slept with. The tallest and handsomest soldiers were always picked for the Guard outside her apartments. But those installed in the favourite's quarters were: Zavadovsky, Zorich, Korsakov, Lanskoy, Yermolov, Mamonov and finally Zubov. All of them, except the last, were chosen by Potemkin. As Catherine had a horror of venereal disease she insisted that each should submit himself to a physical examination by her doctor,

Rogerson; and it is said that she used her two ladies-in-waiting, Countess Bruce and Countess Protasova, as official 'testers'. They were known throughout Europe as *les Éprouveuses*.

None of these young men, all tall and all in their twenties, lasted more than two years. Selected by Potemkin, they were also dismissed by him whenever he chose to come home. All of them left the Palace with a fortune. Indeed, the British Ambassador, Sir James Harris, estimated that the Empress spent a total of 250,000,000 roubles (the equivalent, then, of £50,000,000) on her lovers.

Catherine's debauchery shocked orthodox Russia, and her son Paul alluded to her as a whore. Yet by the mid-1770s her position was too secure, her prestige too high, for criticism to worry her. In 1769 she had occupied Jassy and Bucharest, and moved into the principalities of Moldavia and Wallachia; in 1772 she had partitioned Poland in conjunction with Prussia and Austria, seizing the White Russian area of Polotsky, Vitebsk, and Mogilev, a total of 36,000 square miles with a population of one and three-quarter million. The peace treaty with Turkey in 1774 had not only wrested the Crimea from the Sultan, and turned it into an independent state, but given Russia a firm hold on the

'The Cake of Kings'; Catherine was not allowed to devour all of Poland herself. Joseph II of Austria and Frederick the Great of Prussia helped themselves to generous slices.

northern shore of the Black Sea, and a foothold on the eastern shore, which marked the northern Caucasus. The great Polish patriot, Prince Adam Czartoryski, wrote bitterly that the 'prosperous reign of Catherine had confirmed the Russians in their servility . . .' 'Thus,' he continues, 'the whole nation was in no way scandalized at the depravity, the crimes and murders committed by their sovereign. Everything was permitted. No one dreamed of criticizing her debauchery. It was thus that the pagans respected the crimes and obscenities of the Gods of Olympus and of the Caesars of Rome.'[14]

Indeed, Catherine had become so vain that the foreign ambassadors found her difficult to handle. '. . . she expects to be approached with all the reverence due to a divinity,' wrote Sir James Harris. 'She is spoiled by flattery and success. Levity and want of precision in her ideas are the weak side of her character, and these increase as she gets older.'

'Vanity is her idol,' declared the Austrian Emperor in 1780. 'Luck and exaggerated compliments have spoiled her. Now we must bay with the wolves.'

Although Catherine still rose early in the morning and spent hours at her desk all the exciting new ideas of her youth, even her insistence on competent administration, had gone by the board. Masson, the French tutor living in St Petersburg, wrote:

> . . . the monuments of her reign resemble already so many wrecks and dilapidations.
>
> Codes, colonies, education, establishments, manufactures, edifices, hospitals, canals, towns, fortresses, everything had been begun, and everything given up before it was finished. As soon as a project entered her head, all preceding ones gave place, and her thoughts were fixed on that alone, till a new idea arose to draw off her attention.[15]

However, by the 1780s only two things mattered to Catherine. Her own security, which was based on an alliance between autocracy and nobility; and the joy of adding thousands of new miles of territory to the Russian Empire. In 1783 Russia annexed the Crimea; and in 1785 Catherine gave her nobles a charter which not only recognized the nobility as a separate estate with particular rights and privileges, but made it an hereditary institution, free from military service and the necessity of paying taxes.

Paul watched his mother's mounting prestige with unconcealed distaste. If he had disliked and feared her in the 1770s he now loathed her with all the passion of his soul. She refused to allow him to play any part in State affairs and encouraged him to travel abroad and stay away for months at a time. During one of these trips, in the winter of 1781, he was dangerously indiscreet. At Vienna he exclaimed angrily that he would dismiss his mother's counsellors when he came to power; in Naples he criticized his mother for 'trampling on the laws' in order to keep her throne; in Paris he observed bitterly that if he possessed a faithful dog his mother would have it drowned.

On first acquaintance many people were impressed by Paul and his Grand Duchess; but they became uneasy as time wore on and they caught glimpses of the heir's excitability.

> No private family did the honours of the house with more ease and grace [wrote the French Ambassador, Comte de Ségur, in 1784]. . . . The Grand Duchess . . . pretty without coquetry . . . created an impression of virtue without pose. Paul sought to please and was well-informed. One was struck by his great vivacity and nobility of character. These, however, were only first impressions. Soon one noticed, above all when he spoke of his personal impressions and future, a disquiet, a mistrust, an extreme susceptibility, in fact, oddities which were to cause his faults, his injustices and his misfortunes. . . .[16]

What made the situation more galling than ever for Paul was the fact that Catherine, like Elizabeth before her, had appropriated his two eldest boys and was bringing them up as her own children. She adored her eldest grandson, the handsome, gifted Alexander, and the 7-year-old prince seemed to respond to her affection. 'He is the delight of everyone, especially myself. I can do what I like with him . . . the child loves me instinctively. . . .'

Paul gave this portrait of his eldest son Alexander to the King of Naples after his visit to Western Europe in 1782.

Although Paul loathed Potemkin, nothing angered him more than Catherine's refusal to allow him to accompany her on an epoch-making tour of the Crimea, stage-managed by Prince Potemkin. The journey took place in 1787 so that Catherine could see the work that Potemkin had carried out as a colonizer and an administrator.

Leaving St Petersburg in January the Empress drove fifty miles a day to Kiev, in a huge retinue which included the ambassadors of Britain, France and Austria. After some weeks at Kiev the party proceeded down the Dnieper in a flotilla of eighty ships with Potemkin as Master of Ceremonies. The Empress's cabins were hung with Chinese silk and furnished with chairs and settees imported from France. On board the ships were musicians and dancers, not to mention the best French chefs and hundreds of lackeys.

At every stopping place Potemkin had a surprise for his Empress; in the wilderness of Kremenchuk he had built a palace for her, complete with an English garden; at Kaidak the Holy Roman Emperor, Joseph II, was awaiting Catherine, and the two sovereigns visited the lonely house of a Cossack; at Ekaterinoslav Potemkin showed her the foundations of a new city to be built in Catherine's honour. But both the French ambassador and the Austrian Emperor had their reservations. 'Potemkin soon abandons tasks which he begins with such enthusiasm,' the Comte de Ségur wrote. 'At Ekaterinoslav he has laid the foundation of a capital he will never inhabit, and of a church as large as St Peter's in Rome in which, I dare say, no Mass will ever be said.' The Emperor Joseph and Catherine both laid stones to commemorate a new building, and the former reported laconically: 'The Empress laid the first stone and I laid the last.'[17]

They visited Cherson, where Potemkin had commissioned a throne for the Empress at a cost of 40,000 roubles; Bakhchiserai, the capital of the Crimea, where Catherine sat on the throne vacated by the Khan and which now belonged to her. They visited Inkerman and drove through solitary tracts of land from which the Tartar tribes had been driven, and at night the Empress slept in enormous silken tents. But the highlight of the trip was the inauguration of the port of Sebastopol, with a Russian fleet passing before them, colours dipped. Perhaps what pleased Catherine most, however, was the great triumphal arch at the mouth of the Bug: 'Here lies the way to Constantinople.' For this alone Potemkin deserved the title Prince of Taurus.

'I have come back to life like a frozen fly,' Catherine wrote to Potemkin two years later in 1789. 'I am gay and well.' The reason was not hard to find: she had a new lover, the 22-year-old Platon Zubov. Catherine was 61. She had lost her teeth, and all the powder and rouge in Russia could not conceal the fact that her face was a ruin. Her body had run to fat, and her legs had become so swollen that she could scarcely walk, and soon would be obliged to move about her palace in a wheel-chair.

Yet her sexual appetite was as strong as ever. She was so fearful of losing her delightful new companion that once again she asked the long-suffering Emperor Joseph II to make her lover a prince of the Holy Roman Empire; and was even more extravagant than usual in loading the favourite with gifts.

Catherine's heart sang despite the fact that Russia was fighting two wars, with Turkey in the south and Sweden in the north. Added to this, 1789 had peculiar anxieties of its own. The fall of the Bastille marked the beginning of the popular revolt which swelled into the French Revolution. And the French Revolution struck terror into Catherine's soul. It ended forever her flirtation with the *philosophes*, and any pretension to liberalism. When the French Ambassador took his leave that autumn Catherine remarked that he would do better to remain in Russia and not expose himself 'to the tempests'. 'Your *penchant* for the new philosophy and for liberty will probably lead you to support the popular cause. I shall be sorry. I shall remain an aristocrat; that is my *métier*,' she told him majestically.

During the next few years Catherine followed every happening in France with fascinated horror. In 1790 she ordered all Russians residing in France to return home, so that the deadly infection would not spread. When Louis XVI and Marie Antoinette perished on the scaffold she broke off diplomatic relations and imposed six weeks of Court mourning. She then commanded that all Frenchmen residing in Russia should swear 'not to adhere to the impious and seditious principles now followed in France', and take an oath of loyalty to the Russian crown. Ships flying French flags were banned from Russian ports, and Russian subjects were forbidden to import French newspapers and even French products.

Meanwhile she had dealt harshly with Alexander Radishchev, a

For Catherine's celebrated journey to the Crimea, Potemkin is said to have lined her route with apparently prosperous 'cardboard' villages.

The Catherine Hall in the Tauride
Palace, designed by Starov.

member of a landed family and Chief of the St Petersburg Custom
House, who in 1790 published a book entitled *A Journey from St
Petersburg to Moscow*. Radishchev described the wretched condition of
the peasants, and warned his fellow serf-owners that a far more terrible
rebellion awaited them if nothing was done to alleviate the misery.
Catherine flew into a rage and called him 'a rebel worse than Pugachev
... tainted with French madness'. He was accused of trying to harm the
sovereign's health, and of mutinously attacking military installations
(for which there was no evidence), and sentenced to death by the High
Criminal Court; the sentence was commuted to ten years in Siberia.

Catherine even set up a Secret Chancellery under the direction of a
man named Sheshkovsky. Although torture had been abolished by the
Empress there was nothing to prevent the Inquisitor from knocking out
the teeth of a suspect at the beginning of an interview. Sheshkovsky had
a clear directive: to pursue all those 'poisoned with the pernicious venom
of liberal thought'.

In 1791 Prince Potemkin returned to St Petersburg and for a short
time managed to distract Catherine's mind from the outrages of the
French Revolution. Potemkin resided in a vast marble palace on the
Neva, which Catherine had built for him, known as the Tauride
Palace; and now the Prince gave a ball for the Empress to which three
thousand people were invited. No one had ever seen anything quite like
it. The candles alone had cost 70,000 roubles (£17,000), and the rooms
blazed and sparkled with the glow. An artificial elephant studded with
precious stones stood in the theatre, where curtains rose on an orchestra
of three hundred musicians. There were quadrilles and tableaux, and
finally supper where the guests ate off gold plates and drank from
Persian goblets. Among the delicacies provided by Potemkin was
sterlet from the Volga, oysters from Riga, veal from Archangel, mutton
from Astrakhan, beef from the Ukraine, pheasants from Hungary and
Bohemia, and grapes from the Crimea.

Catherine remained at the party until two in the morning. 'He has
come back to us,' she reported to the Prince de Ligne, 'as beautiful as the
day, gay as a lark, shining like a star, wittier than ever.' Then Potemkin
returned to the south, and six months later died of a heart-attack by the
roadside, 'worn out by loose living and gluttony at the age of 56'.
Catherine's secretary made notes in his diary, describing his mistress's
reaction. 'Tears and despair.' 'Tears.' 'Wept.' 'Now I have no one left
on whom I can rely,' she moaned. 'I regarded him as a very great man,'
she wrote to Baron Grimm.

Despite her grief Catherine continued to make the most of her
opportunities. In the following year, 1792, she advanced the Russian
frontier to the coastal territory between the Dnieper and the Bug; and
here the great port of Odessa began to develop. And in 1793 and 1795
she took part in a second and third partition of Poland which gave
Russia Lithuania, part of the Polish Ukraine, the Duchy of Courland
and Vilna.

During the year 1796 Catherine decided to discard her son Paul, and to appoint as her heir her eldest grandson, the entrancing, 19-year-old Alexander. Peter the Great's Succession Act of 1722 gave Catherine the right to name whom she chose. It was not only that Paul hated his mother and railed against her policies, but during the past decade Paul's courtiers frequently whispered that he was going mad, and Catherine had heard what they said.

The frightened middle-aged Grand Duke could not conquer the fear of murder that had haunted him since childhood. Always searching for tranquillity by finding the security that Catherine had denied him, he had spent four years fortifying his residence at Gatchina. This immense estate, once the property of Count Orlov, was situated forty miles from the capital. When the Empress gave it to Paul in 1783 he immediately wrote to Berlin for architects, engineers, experts in ballistics and hydraulics. Like his father, Peter III, he was a fevered admirer of the Prussian Army. And after building an enormous barracks adjoining his palace, he placed Baron Steinwehr, an officer who had been cashiered from the Prussian Army for drunkenness, in charge of five companies known as His Imperial Highness' Battalion. The men were dressed in Prussian uniforms and Paul drilled them daily.

As the years progressed the Grand Duke inveighed against his mother with increasing bitterness. 'Land! Land! Why do we want more land?' He denounced every aspect of her foreign policy and proclaimed fitfully that when he came to the throne he would reverse everything she had done. Occasionally he turned on his own sons, Alexander and Constantine, and accused them of plotting his downfall. He still woke up in the middle of the night screaming. Sometimes he told his wife, Marie, his eyes wild, about the terrible end of his father, sometimes about Alexis, the murdered son of Peter the Great, or Ivan VI, or even Julius Caesar. On one occasion he confided to his wife that Peter the Great had followed him through the streets of St Petersburg on a moonlit, summer night. 'I tell you it was Peter the Great. I was so frightened that I shook from head to foot, and it fell on a warm night and I was frozen. Then he spoke to me.'

'What did he say?' Marie asked gently.

'Nothing but three words: "Paul poor Paul."' And with this the Grand Duke began to sob.

In the summer of 1796 Catherine is believed to have confided her succession plans to Alexander; and in October she summoned Marie and asked her to sign a paper demanding that Paul should renounce his right to the throne. The Grand Duchess, although well aware of her husband's unfitness to rule, refused indignantly.

She did not tell Paul about the interview, yet he seemed to sense it, for he suddenly became deeply fearful for his life. One night he woke up sobbing and told Marie that he had had a nightmare. He had re-lived the summer day when he was a boy and Panin had driven him to the palace in his nightshirt to receive the acclamation of the crowd at the

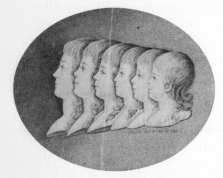

The six children of Paul and Marie Feodorovna. From left to right: Alexander, Constantine, Alexandra, Helene, Marie and Catherine.

side of his mother. But in this terrible dream the carriage never reached the Winter Palace. Instead, it took him to Senate Square where he was led up the steps to a scaffold. 'And they all shouted that I must die,' he wept. Marie comforted him until he fell asleep of sheer exhaustion.

Before Catherine got round to putting her wishes in writing, she was struck down. On 6 November 1796, she arose at her usual hour of six, bathed her face in ice water, and drank five cups of coffee. After receiving her lover, and her secretaries, she retired to her dressing-room. When she failed to re-appear her attendants entered. They found her lying on the floor paralysed. The following evening she died.

Voltaire had named Catherine 'the Great'. Although the Empress's secret wish had been the conquest of Constantinople, with her second grandson, Constantine, sitting on the throne and reviving the glories of Byzantium, her acquisitions had been impressive. If eighteenth-century rulers are to be judged in terms of expansion Catherine deserved Voltaire's accolade. Since the death of Peter the Great in 1725 the Russian Empire had annexed the Crimea, the northern Caucasus, the Ukraine, Poland and Courland; and most of the work was Catherine's. The population had increased from 18,000,000 to nearly 30,000,000.

Catherine had prepared an inscription which she wished placed on her tombstone.

> Here lies Catherine II, born at Stettin the 21/22 April/May 1729. She went to Russia in 1744 to marry Peter III. At the age of 14 she made the triple resolution to please her husband, Elizabeth, and the nation. She neglected nothing in trying to achieve this. Eighteen years of ennui and solitude gave her the opportunity to read many books. Enthroned in Russia she desired nothing but the best for her country and tried to procure for her subjects happiness, liberty, and wealth.
>
> She forgave easily and hated no one. Tolerant, undemanding, of a gay disposition, she had a republican spirit and a kind heart. She made good friends.[18]

But not everyone saw Catherine's personality or reign in the same light. The witty French ambassador, the Comte de Ségur, declared:

> Catherine's imagination was never able to rest; moreover her plans were more precipitous than mature; it was evident that this precipitation stifled at birth part of the creations of her genius.
>
> She wanted at one and the same time to form a third estate, attract foreign trade, establish manufactures, extend agriculture, found credit, increase paper money, raise the rate of exchange, lower the interest on money, build towns, create academicians, people the deserts, cover the Black Sea with manifold squadrons, annihilate the Tartars, invade Persia, continue her progressive conquests of the Turks, enchain Poland, and extend her influence all over Europe.
>
> This was a great deal to undertake [the Ambassador concluded] and although there was more to be done in a country so new to civilization, it is certain that more success would have been obtained if fewer objects had been embraced at the same time.[19]

Gatchina, once the country seat of Gregory Orlov, was given to Paul by his mother.

CHAPTER V
Paul I and Alexander I
1796–1825

WHEN NICHOLAS ZUBOV, the brother of Catherine the Great's favourite, hurried to Gatchina, Paul's vast estate fifty miles from St Petersburg, to impart the news that the Empress was dying, the Grand Duke misunderstood his visitor's intention, and cried to his wife, 'We are lost!' He thought that his mother had sent Zubov to arrest him. Instead, within twenty-four hours he was Emperor of Russia.

The shock turned yet another screw in Paul's disordered brain. Hysterical and revengeful, he opened his reign with a macabre attempt to diminish Catherine II by recalling the image of Peter III, a father he had scarcely known.

Within forty-eight hours of the Empress's death Paul summoned the abbot and monks of the Convent of Alexander Nevsky, where Catherine's murdered husband had been buried. He told them to move the coffin from the vault and bring it into the church. He then appointed an Imperial Commission to arrange a ceremonial 'for the joint funeral of Their Imperial Majesties'. This was followed by an announcement that national mourning for 'the late Emperor and Empress' would last twelve months.

The Russian public, accustomed as it was to bizarre events, was astonished to be asked to mourn for a man who had been dead for thirty-four years. But Paul believed that by honouring the memory of his father he would induce people to share his contempt for his mother.

On 19 November he had Peter III's embalmed body removed from its lead coffin and laid in a casket of gold and brocade. He sent for the Imperial crown, lifted it toward the High Altar and himself placed it on Peter's head. A few days later heralds in brilliant clothes rode through the streets of the capital with the news that 'the translation of the august remains' from the abbey would take place the following day.

Paul had another surprise in store for the public. He decided that those who had taken part in his father's murder should bear the regalia and decorations through the streets. Count Alexis Orlov was ordered to carry the crown. Soon Peter lay in state next to Catherine in the Cathedral of St Peter and St Paul. The priests censed the two bodies together; and together put them to rest in a single grave. The inscription Catherine had prepared for posterity was not placed on her tomb.

Paul was determined to reverse everything his mother had done. He stopped the war with Persia; and apologized to the Poles for Catherine's partitions, although he added that it was too late to rectify the crime. He made an alliance with Turkey at Austria's expense and offended the King of Prussia by betraying his confidence. Finally, to everyone's amazement, he imagined he had a lien on Malta, which had surrendered to the French, by becoming Grand Master of the Knights of Malta, an

Paul (*right*) who once said of himself: 'My advisers want to lead me by the nose, but unfortunately I have not got one.'

Paul wears the Cross of St John at his investiture as Grand Master of the Knights of Malta (*below*).

THE LATE EMPEROR PAUL

S. Majestät der Kaiser aller Reussen Paul I. wurde durch eine Heil. und Feyerliche Verbindung der Maltheser Ritter zu Petersburg zum Groß-Meister des Maltheser Ordens erklährt. am 10. Decemb. 1798.

1. Kaiser Paul I. 2. Krone des Groß Meisters des Ordens 3. Das große Siegel desselben. 4. das Schwerd des Glaubens. 5. sämtliche Maltheser Ritter grüssen den Monarchen mit dem Knie und ihren ...

office usually filled by a celibate, and under the jurisdiction of the Pope. The only one of his mother's predelictions that he appeared to share was Catherine's hostility toward Republican France, for he sent Russian soldiers to Italy to support the Austrians against Napoleon.

Even this policy was soon reversed, for Paul's instability made him an easy prey to adventurers. A Swiss gentleman, Gruber, rumoured to be in the pay of Bonaparte, convinced him that the monarchy was about to be restored in France. Not the Bourbons, of course, but a new line chosen by the First Consul. Paul immediately withdrew his troops from Italy, and when Napoleon's enemy, England, seized Malta, used it as a pretext for breaking off relations with Britain. Louis XVIII, who had been given a castle in Courland, and a handsome pension, was turned out overnight; and the French royalist refugees in Russia, befriended by Catherine, were imprisoned as undesirable aliens.

Paul's madness seemed to increase daily. His outbursts of temper were terrifying, for they were provoked by such petty annoyances as a courier's hurried step or a coachman's slow pace. Sometimes he would shout at the offender and stamp his foot; at other times he would attack him with a whip or a cane or even with his bare fists. 'The fact is . . . that the Emperor is literally not in his senses,' the British Ambassador reported to London.

During the first twenty-four hours of his reign Paul sat up all night dictating *ukazy* which put an end to one liberty after another. He forbade the wearing of waistcoats, branding them as 'French revolutionaries' dress'; he determined the shape of hats, the cut of collars, the depths of a curtsey, even the number of people to be invited to a party. He prohibited the import of foreign books because of 'likely injurious consequences to the national morale', and instructed the libraries not to lend out foreign editions.

'You must understand, sir,' he told one of his nobles, 'that the only important person in my Empire is the person to whom I happen to be speaking . . .' Even ladies in carriages were required to stop and curtsey to him, disobedience being punished by a birching. All foreign journeys were prohibited, and the censorship of letters became so strict that allusions to the latest fashions in Paris were interpreted as 'signs of culpable discontent'. He even sent a harsh reprimand to the historian, Karamzin, who had just translated Cicero into Russian, reminding him that 'Cicero and many others were on the proscribed list because they were republicans and their writings could be of no value to the Empire'.

Overnight Paul turned the Winter Palace into a barracks. Sentry boxes were placed every few yards outside the building, guarded by battalions from Gatchina, dressed in Prussian uniforms. Anyone who offended him was sent into exile, or, at best, ordered to leave the capital. Soon the numbers had leapt from the hundreds to the thousands. Some unfortunate people were punished for wearing too much or too little powder on their hair; others for disobeying fresh orders unknown to any except the Emperor's secretaries and the police.

Although Paul I abolished Peter the Great's Act of Succession, whereby the sovereign could name his own successor, and decreed that sovereignty should pass through the eldest living son, he treated his heir with surprising harshness. One by one he dismissed from court all of Alexander's close friends: Count Golovin and his wife, Peter Tolstoy, Victor Kochubey, Prince Volkonsky, Alexander Golitsyn, Paul Strogonov, Novosiltsov, and the Czartoryski brothers, Adam and Constantine. Not only that, but he reduced Alexander to the status of a simple soldier, occupying him from morning to night with military duties of the most trivial character.

Alexander's chief comfort during these difficult years was his wife Elizabeth, a princess of Baden. Although Elizabeth was regarded as a beauty she did not attract her husband physically. He had married her at his grandmother's behest when she was fourteen and he not more than a year older. Nevertheless he drew close to her as he saw his mother, always eager to ingratiate herself with her mad husband, subject the poor girl to endless humiliations. On the occasion of Paul's coronation in 1797 the Grand Duchess Elizabeth 'decided to pin some lovely pale pink rosebuds to the diamond buckles of her sash'. But when she went to the Empress for approval the latter looked at her stonily, and without saying a word pulled roughly at the roses and threw them to the floor, 'Cela ne convient pas,' she remarked acidly.

Despite the Empress's attempts to retain some control over Paul she failed utterly, due to the malign influence of a favourite, Kutajsov, a Turkish prisoner-of-war who served as Paul's barber. This ambitious man succeeded in so poisoning the Emperor's mind that he suddenly became jealous of the respect accorded to his wife; and soon this resentment had spread to his mistress of many years, Catherine Nelidova. Overnight Paul flatly refused to speak to either of them. Nelidova departed from the capital while the Empress followed her husband around the palace with a tear-stained face, listening to him making arrangements to install a pretty new mistress in sumptuous apartments.

By 1800 Alexander and his brother, Constantine, were in despair. 'My father has declared war on common-sense with a firm resolve of never concluding a truce,' the latter confided to a friend; and Alexander smuggled out a letter to his tutor La Harpe, who was living in Switzerland, telling him that unhappy Russia was in a state of chaos, and he himself relegated to duties 'which might just as easily be discharged by any sergeant'. 'If and when my own turn comes,' he continued, 'I shall have to dedicate myself to my country and never let it become again a toy in a madman's hands....'

Worse was to come. Paul's rage against England increased until finally, at the end of 1800, he decided to conquer India. He sent instructions to General Orlov, the hetman of the Don Cossacks: 'I know that the British are going to attack us . . . Therefore they must be attacked from the least expected point . . . India is our best objective.' A second message reminded Orlov 'that your business is solely against the British

The majority of his subjects knew nothing of Paul's madness and sadism. He was their 'little golden heart' and they prayed for him fervently.

and . . . you must assure [the natives] of Russia's friendly disposition toward them . . . Make straight for the Indus and the Ganges. . . .'[1]

Although General Orlov followed the sovereign's orders and departed from the Don with twenty thousand Cossacks, forty thousand horses and twenty-four guns, he did not get very far. Spring floods coupled with the lack of any proper victualling arrangements brought the expedition to an end. Very few Cossacks saw their native land again.

Meanwhile Paul had moved into a new residence built on the site of the old Summer Palace. He loathed the Winter Palace because of its association with his mother, and was delighted with the monstrous edifice designed for him, known as St Michael's Palace. It had a deep moat around it, and five drawbridges which were manned day and night by men from his Gatchina Regiment.

When he commissioned Brenna to build St Michael's Palace, Paul said: 'On that spot was I born and there I wish to die.' He did die there, three weeks after moving in.

Paul was right to take precautions, as a conspiracy was already forming against him, led by Count Pahlen, the Governor-General of St Petersburg. Its declared aim was to force Paul to abdicate in favour of his son, Alexander. Pahlen was in charge of the police and Paul trusted him implicitly. 'I know I can rely on you absolutely,' he frequently told him.

Pahlen did not have much difficulty in persuading young Alexander that his father must relinquish the throne. 'But can you swear that my father's life will be spared?' Alexander is said to have asked, to which Pahlen replied in the affirmative.

Pahlen then set about collecting conspirators, all of whom were chosen from the Semenovsky Guards, a regiment deeply loyal to Alexander. The Emperor had made the same mistake as some of his unfortunate predecessors. Although he had tried to alleviate the lot of the peasants by limiting their working week to six days, he had overlooked the dangers of alienating the upper classes from which his regimental officers were chosen. He had cancelled their immunity from corporal punishment, taxed their estates and forbidden them to withdraw from government service. Furthermore, he had particularly offended the Guards Regiments by refusing to allow them to serve as a bodyguard; he sneered at their colours which, he said, reminded him of his mother's petticoats.

Statue of Paul in Prussian uniform in the courtyard at Pavlovsk. In 1800 the Emperor invited the rulers of Europe to St Petersburg to decide international differences in open combat.

Pahlen recruited sixty officers. As he was responsible for protecting St Michael's Palace he planned to put the Semenovsky battalion on duty in place of the Gatchina Regiment when the right moment arrived. However, a few days before the climax, Paul summoned Pahlen and asked him bluntly if a conspiracy was forming against him. Pahlen was quick-witted enough to realize that someone had informed on him. 'It is perfectly true, sir,' he replied blandly, 'and I have joined the ranks of the conspirators in order to winkle out every last one of them, and to expose them.'

Paul screamed that he must have the names, but Pahlen begged him to wait forty-eight hours until he had a complete list. The Emperor then asked if his two eldest sons were involved. Pahlen shook his head, but Paul did not believe him, and the following night both Alexander and Constantine were placed under house arrest.

That same evening the seven leading members of the conspiracy dined together to give themselves courage for the work that lay before them. The group consisted of Platon Zubov (Catherine's last favourite), Benningsen, Skaryatin, Gordanov, Tatarinov, and two princes, Yashvili and Vyazemsky. While they were toasting each other in excited tones, the Emperor noticed that the Semenovsky Regiment had taken over the Palace Guard. He sent for Pahlen and told him angrily that the officers of this particular regiment were all revolutionaries at heart. 'See that they are on the march by six in the morning,' he barked, 'and that the guard is changed by four.'

About midnight the seven men set out for the Palace. Zubov and Benningsen decided that their five companions were so drunk that it was best to leave them at the drawbridge and continue alone. They knew the way to the secret staircase leading to the Emperor's bedroom. They overpowered two sentries, and a valet in the passage, crossed the library which was blazing with candlelight, and opened the bedroom door. Paul had heard the scuffle and leapt out of bed. He stood near the desk, his feet bare, a night-cap on his head, his eyes glazed with terror. Benningsen did not mention abdication. He merely said that he was arresting Paul in the name of 'the Emperor Alexander'. Paul stood motionless. The ghastly moment he had dreaded all his life had become a reality.

Zubov heard a noise and left the room. Suddenly the door burst open and the five drunken conspirators rushed in and moved toward Paul. He began to run around the writing table, but he tripped, and all were upon him. One of them grabbed a scarf and tried to strangle him but the cloth broke. Another picked up the malachite paperweight on the desk. 'Gentlemen, in heaven's name spare me . . . Give me time to say my prayers. . . .'

But the paperweight was pressed hard against Paul's neck; harder and harder until the twitches and gasps had stopped.

In the morning the Russian people were told that the Emperor Paul I had died of apoplexy in the forty-seventh year of his life.

124

'If and when my own turn comes, I shall have to dedicate myself to my country and never let it become again a toy in a madman's hands.' Alexander (*left*) wrote to La Harpe.

When the tall, fair-haired, 24-year-old Alexander I rode to his coronation at the end of 1801, a wit remarked that he was preceded by the men who had murdered his grandfather, escorted by the men who had murdered his father, and followed by the men who would not think twice about murdering him.

In 1801 most Europeans looked upon the Russian Government as 'an absolute monarchy tempered by assassination'. Although the happenings on the night of Paul's death were hidden beneath a rigid censorship, no one outside Russia believed that Paul had died of apoplexy any more than that Peter III had died of colic. Accounts of the murder began to appear in foreign newspapers during the first year of the new reign; and almost all the reports incriminated the handsome Alexander, who seemed to possess all the graces of western civilization.

Later a number of Russian historians tried to absolve Alexander on the grounds that he had sought nothing more than his father's abdication. The Countess Golovina wrote in her journal that when Alexander learned of Paul's cruel death he burst into tears. 'I cannot go on with it,' he sobbed to his wife. 'I have no strength to reign. Let someone else take my place.' Yet in attempting to establish Alexander's innocence an awkward question remained unanswered: what would have happened to Paul if he had refused to abdicate at his heir's insistence? And an equally stubborn fact projected itself: as no adult Russian sovereign had ever been deposed and allowed to live, would it have been possible to make an exception in the case of Paul? Contemporary observers took the view that Alexander's emotional breakdown sprang from guilt rather than shock. Even the great poet, Pushkin, who contemplated writing the monarch's biography, left notes revealing that he, for one, was unable to free his hero of complicity.

There is no doubt that the vision of Paul's battered body haunted Alexander all his life. His coronation was so painful to him that his friends were perturbed. 'The brilliant pageant of supreme power,' wrote Adam Czartoryski, 'instead of awakening Alexander's ambition, flattering his vanity and distracting him, merely aggravated his inner agony. Never in his life, I think, was he more unhappy.' His depression continued for many weeks and when Czartoryski tried to comfort him his answer was always the same: 'No, no, my friend. You cannot help me. There is no cure for such a case as mine. I have to suffer. How is it possible that I should not suffer? Things will never change.'[2]

Alexander was the first and only Romanov to dispense with royal pomp. He had no suite, wore no jewelry, and refused to allow people to dismount when they met him on the quai. The Imperial fêtes were as splendid as ever, but they no longer took place every night as in Catherine's reign, but only on special occasions. Alexander liked to wander among his guests and patterned his behaviour on that of an ordinary gentleman, using such phrases as 'Will you permit', 'I beg to be excused', and 'Please do me the honour'. 'Unfortunately all this,' wrote the Sardinian Ambassador, Count de Maistre, in 1803, 'which is good for Southern eyes who can read majesty across simplicity, does not appear to have the same effect on Russian organs, and the respect for him personally has diminished. . . .'[3]

Although by this time Alexander had fallen deeply in love with a dashing Polish lady, Madame Naryshkina, who bore him two children and tormented him by her infidelity, he took great pains to pay public deference to his wife, the Empress Elizabeth. 'There certainly does not exist so handsome a couple in Europe,' continued Count de Maistre. 'The affability of these two persons is beyond all expression. They please themselves in forgetting their grandeur and wearying no one.' However, the Irish visitor, Martha Wilmot, had reservations about the Empress's good looks. 'He is a tall fair handsomish looking Young Man — she tall, fair, and would be very pretty, only for a dreadful scurvy she has in her face . . .'

Elizabeth Feodorovna, Alexander's wife

Michael Speransky

Alexander moved through the first years of his reign as a shadowy, indecisive figure. Although he repealed the grotesque laws introduced by his father, abolished the security police, and once again allowed his subjects to travel freely and to read foreign books, he seemed to be a man looking for a mission. He summoned from Switzerland his republican tutor, La Harpe, and recalled from exile the young friends his father had persecuted. With these companions he formed a secret committee, dubbed by the cynics 'the Committee of Public Safety', which met every day to discuss the problems of Russia and mankind. They talked about freeing the serfs and introducing Parliamentary Government but whenever they tried to work out practical proposals the obstacles seemed too great to overcome. Alexander finally charged Michael Speransky, the son of a village priest, to draw up a scheme for improving the Government of the Empire; but even this came to very little, for, by the time the paper was completed, in 1809, he was too pre-occupied to make real use of it. The only idea he adopted was Speransky's proposal for a Council of State, composed of eminent men appointed by the sovereign, which would give advice when asked for it.

By 1803 Alexander's attention was absorbed by Napoleon Bonaparte, whose astonishing military successes had thrown the whole of Europe into turmoil. Alexander could not make up his mind whether to join a coalition against the First Consul, or to continue his father's policy of friendship. Napoleon had suggested to Paul that France and Russia partition the world; but this grandiose idea did not appeal to the modest Alexander. When Bonaparte trampled down the terms of the Treaty of Amiens the Russian sovereign wrote to La Harpe that he seemed to be 'one of the most infamous tyrants that history has produced'.

Yet Alexander shrank from war. 'His soul has not yet acquired any definite colour,' wrote Adam Czartoryski. 'It is all the colours of the rainbow with a misty grey predominating. The idea of war weighs upon his mind and torments him.' Within a few months, however, an event took place that had a profound effect on Alexander. A Bourbon prince, the Duc d'Enghien, was unfairly accused of plotting against Napoleon. He was kidnapped from his house in the Grand Duchy of Baden where he was living temporarily, peacefully carrying on a love affair. He was transported to France and promptly shot.

This barbaric episode provoked a storm in all the countries of Europe. The Russian Chargé d'Affaires in Paris was instructed to deliver an indignant protest to Napoleon. But Talleyrand, the French Foreign Minister, sent back a tart reply, reminding Alexander of the comments which an unfriendly Power might have made on the mysterious circumstances surrounding the death of Paul. This insult stung Alexander to the depths of his being. He broke off diplomatic relations with France, and instructed his officials that although Napoleon had now assumed the title of Emperor they were to continue to address him as General Bonaparte.

During the twelve months between November 1804 and 1805 Russia made alliances with Great Britain, Austria, Sweden and Prussia. But Napoleon did not wait for the treaties to be hammered out. He fell upon Austria at Ulm before Russian troops had arrived to stave off defeat; and he gave battle to the Russians at Austerlitz before Prussian troops appeared on the scene.

Austerlitz was a disaster for the 28-year-old Alexander. Supported by the Austrian cavalry, he led his army as Commander-in-Chief. But he refused to follow the advice of an experienced general, Kutuzov, who urged him to fall back and lure the French still farther from their base of supplies. The battle which began at nine in the morning lasted only two hours and ended in a complete rout. Kutuzov was wounded, and both the Russian and Austrian Emperors had to flee for their lives. Alexander was cut off from his staff officers and rode away from the battlefield alone. Unfortunately he was a poor horseman and could not persuade his mount to take a wide ditch. After considerable delay he finally forced the beast to obey him, and crossed safely. He dismounted and collapsed under an apple tree where he wept convulsively.

For once Alexander's gallantry deserted him, and in a letter to the Empress (which was made public) he blamed his defeat on the Austrians, describing them as 'cowards, traitors and fools whom everyone with a heart in his breast will look upon with execration'. The Russian people were only too eager to accept the Emperor's verdict, and when he returned to St Petersburg he was acclaimed there as a great leader who had been betrayed. Unfortunately, this was not the end of the story, for the Russian Army suffered another disastrous defeat when they fought with their Prussian allies at Friedland.

Much to the amazement of the Russian people, Alexander now decided to abandon his allies and sue for an armistice. He met Napoleon on a sumptuously appointed raft in the middle of the Niemen, in June 1807. The Russian officers who accompanied him to Tilsit were instructed 'to be civil to the French', to remember Napoleon's imperial title, and not to refer to him as 'Bonaparte'. The regimental chaplains, however, had in their pockets copies of the Synod proclamation describing Bonaparte as 'the Servant of Satan and the worshipper of whores and idols'.

A treaty of friendship was signed between Napoleon and Alexander in which Russia promised to take part in the continental blockade against England.

'We came out of the struggle with a sort of lustre,' Alexander wrote to his wife. 'God has saved us.'

Alexander I was more unpopular between the years 1807 and 1811 than at any time in his life. The Russian people had become accustomed to Catherine's great victories and could not adjust themselves to ignominious defeats, which they blamed on Alexander's rashness and ineptitude. Furthermore, they resented the peace treaty with France which virtually bound Russia into an alliance. Although French culture still remained a status symbol, the Emperor of the French was looked

State bedroom of the Empress Marie Feodorovna at Pavlovsk

upon as an upstart and a bounder. 'Everything is shocking for dinner that is not dress'd by a French Cook,' wrote Catherine Wilmot, 'every dress inelegant that is not Parisien . . . yet there is no one who does not blaspheme against Buonaparte and lament Lord Nelson!'[4]

By 1811 Alexander had taken the cue from his subjects. He refused to send soldiers to fight with the French and made no effort to uphold the continental blockade. Although he still professed his friendship for France, his young friends – not his ministers – were secretly trying to win Poland from France by promising the Poles that Alexander would revive their kingdom as a constitutional monarchy; to win over Austria by offering territory in the Danubian provinces; to win over Prussia by persuading her to strike a blow for her emancipation.

By 1811 the rift between the two countries was so wide that war seemed inevitable. Yet many people believed that Russia would prove a poor match for the Grand Army. Dr Clarke, an Englishman who visited the Tula arms factory in 1810, was appalled by the general incompetence.

> The machinery is ill constructed and worse preserved. Everything seemed out of order. Workmen, with long beards, stood staring at each other, wondering what was to be done next; while their intendants or directors were drunk or asleep. Notwithstanding all this, they pretended to issue from the manufactory . . . thirteen hundred muskets in a week. But the name musket is almost all that connects the appearance with the reality. It is wonderful any troops can use them; besides being clumsy and heavy, they missfire five times out of six, and are liable to burst whenever discharged.[5]

No doubt Napoleon entertained the same impressions as Dr Clarke, for in June 1812 he began his famous invasion of Russia. His Grande Armée was 600,000 strong and immensely imposing; yet over a third of his men were unwilling German conscripts, drawn from subject territories. Napoleon crossed the Niemen in three days and rolled over the plains of Lithuania to Vilna, which he occupied on the 28th. Meanwhile Alexander I was having second thoughts. He had never imagined that Napoleon would attempt a march to Moscow, and the thought of the carnage appalled him. He sent a message to Vilna assuring Napoleon that it was not too late to maintain peace, even now, if the Emperor would take his army back again across the Niemen. 'Even God could not now undo what has been started,' Napoleon pronounced. When Alexander received the reply he remarked: 'At least now Europe will know that we are not beginning this slaughter.'

Each day Napoleon, who was heading for Smolensk, drove farther into the heart of Russia. Count Rostopchin, the Governor of Moscow, wrote to Alexander that he was confident that the size of Russia would triumph over the invaders in the end. 'Your Empire, Sire, has two powerful defenders – its vast space and its climate. The Emperor of all the Russias will be formidable at Moscow, terrible at Kazan, and invincible at Tobolsk.' Alexander led his armies as their nominal

St Michael's Palace was handed over by Alexander I to the School of Engineers.

At Tilsit, Napoleon and Alexander swore eternal friendship on a raft.

Commander-in-Chief but when Smolensk finally fell, his young sister, Catherine, begged him in the bluntest terms to find a professional Commander-in-Chief. The sovereign's record as a military leader had been so disastrous that now every setback was attributed to his influence. 'For God's sake do not decide to assume command yourself . . . ,' she wrote. 'There is no time to lose to give the armies a chief in whom the men would have confidence. As for you, you cannot inspire them with any.'

Alexander heeded her pleas and quit the army. He travelled to Moscow, then on to St Petersburg. Everywhere he heard criticism of the High Command; and everywhere he heard the name Kutuzov, the veteran soldier whose advice the Emperor had ignored to his cost at Austerlitz, and whose name spelled magic to the people. This 67-year-old general was lazy, licentious, and knew nothing of scientific warfare.

Kutuzov refused to engage the enemy;
Alexander was greatly irritated.

Fat, somnolent, having only one eye, the other torn by an enemy bullet, he
had difficulty in mounting a horse and once in the saddle could not remain
in it very long. He usually spent days on a divan, his one eye half closed by a
heavy eyelid, inert and panting, changing his position only in order to go to
bed.[6]

Alexander himself had no faith in Kutuzov. He felt he was a figure
from another century; yet he decided to bow to popular demand saying
rather foolishly: 'The public want him. I have appointed him. As for me,
I wash my hands of the affair.' What the sovereign did not appreciate
was the fact that Kutuzov, despite all his shortcomings, had the common sense born of long years of experience. He was slow but tenacious;
lazy but discerning; impassive but cunning.

Those people, however, who expected the tide automatically to turn
with Kutuzov's appointment, were shocked to find that Napoleon's

advance toward Moscow continued. Panic swept the city and thousands of people packed up their belongings and began to leave. Then rumours spread that Napoleon was planning a diversion in the direction of St Petersburg, and the Government began the evacuation of valuables.

Alexander spent bitter hours pacing up and down his study. The only news he was given was bad; and even the gossip that seeped through to him was unpleasant. He was told that his life-long friend, Prince Alexander Golitsyn, was a traitor, and at that very moment was constructing an impressive new palace in which he could entertain Napoleon. The Emperor laughed at this wild tale; nevertheless he visited Golitsyn and asked why he had chosen to build in such troubled times. Golitsyn replied that he did not fear the invader because he had confidence in Divine Providence. He then reached up to one of his bookshelves to take down a heavy volume of the Bible. The book slipped and fell to the floor, open at a page on which was Psalm 41. '. . . I will say of the Lord, He is my refuge and fortress: my God: in Him will I trust.' Golitsyn insisted that the opening of the book at this place was not a coincidence but a message from the Almighty, and Alexander was deeply impressed. 'I simply devoured the Bible,' he wrote in later years, 'finding that its words poured an unknown peace into my heart and quenched the thirst of my soul.'

While Alexander passed his days reading the Bible, and meditating deeply on God and Mankind, Napoleon approached Moscow. Kutuzov suddenly halted the Russian retreat, and ordered his army to dig itself in along a vast field near the village of Borodino. On the night of 6 September the two armies faced each other across a broad expanse, the flickering lights of camp-fires throwing up eerie shadows in the darkness. When Napoleon inspected his troops the Russian officers could hear cries of 'Vive l'Empereur' as he passed down the lines.

The battle began at dawn and lasted for fifteen hours. At the end, eighty thousand men from both sides lay on the field. Kutuzov had intended to resume the fighting the next day; but when he learned the magnitude of his losses he decided to continue the retreat and abandon Moscow to the enemy. Although each side claimed Borodino as a brilliant victory, Napoleon marched into Moscow exactly one week later.

Never had Alexander I been so uncertain of himself. Although he swore 'to retreat to the Kazan', 'to fight on the shores of the Volga', 'to let my beard grow and eat potatoes like the poorest peasant' rather than sign a peace, he prayed to God to tell him what to do. When he attended a Te Deum in the cathedral of Our Lady of Kazan, on the anniversary of his coronation, the crowds maintained a hostile silence. 'One could have heard a pin drop,' wrote his wife, the Empress Elizabeth, 'and I am sure that a single spark would have put this crowd aflame.' The Sardinian Ambassador wrote to his King that 'nothing but a miracle can now save Russia', and Metternich declared that Russia 'had ceased to exist as a European power'. Even Count Rostopchin gave way to a burst of despair and cried that Russia was now 'lost for ever'.

Meanwhile Moscow was burning. The city with its thousands of wooden buildings had always been a fire hazard, and no one knows to this day whether the raging inferno was deliberate or accidental. Sir Robert Wilson, the British general attached to the Russian army, believed it was intentional. He wrote in his diary on 14 September:

> The Russians resolved on inflicting a species of vengeance more disastrous in its consequences than the slaughter of the sword. All the houses of the nobility, all the warehouses of the merchants, all the shops, etc, were fired; and, notwithstanding every effort of the enemy, the conflagration raged and rendered Moscow one flaming pile; so that, as the enemy stated themselves, they occupied only the site where the city stood, and their embarrassments were increased by an erroneous calculation that their needs would be supplied by the resources of Moscow.[7]

Wilson was an eye-witness on 1 October, when Count Rostopchin, the Governor of Moscow, set fire to his own magnificent palace and all the surrounding premises.

> Certainly the property destroyed could not be replaced for a hundred thousand pounds . . . the firing of Woronowo ought to insure, and will insure, a lasting record of Russian patriotism.[8]

The burning of Moscow had a traumatic effect on the Russian people. For once the yawning gap between noble and peasant was closed. The flames seemed to revive ancient memories of Mongols, Tartars, Poles and Swedes, arousing in the entire population a frenzied hatred of all foreigners. Napoleon, who had hoped to quarter his troops in comfort, suddenly found himself in possession of a heap of smouldering ruins. He decided that the time had come for an armistice. But this time, however, the vacillating Alexander had been transformed into a man fortified by a deep religious fervour. He replied that he would not negotiate with France while 'one enemy soldier remains on Russian soil'.

Alexander was expressing the mood of the country. 'The Russians are a terrible people,' General Benningsen told Prince Murat, 'and would kill any man instantly who even talked of peace.' The truth was that the Russian staff knew it had beaten Napoleon.

> We are now in a commanding position [Wilson wrote in his diary]. Our main army is as numerous as that of the enemy – I believe, even stronger . . . We have our supplies; he wants them. We are habituated to the climate; he has everything to fear from it. It is a great moment – an awful epoch! . . .[9]

After five weeks of occupation, and many abortive efforts to secure an armistice, Napoleon had no option but to withdraw his army from Moscow and to begin the long trek home. But he had left it too late. On 4 November the snow began to fall, and on 6 November a razor-sharp wind lowered the temperature many degrees below freezing. Now was the moment for Kutuzov to pursue the enemy, cut off the retreat, and capture Napoleon.

OVERLEAF When Alexander heard Moscow was burning he wrote to Bernadotte: 'More than ever before my people and I stand together . . . determined to perish under the ruins rather than make peace with the Attila of our days.'

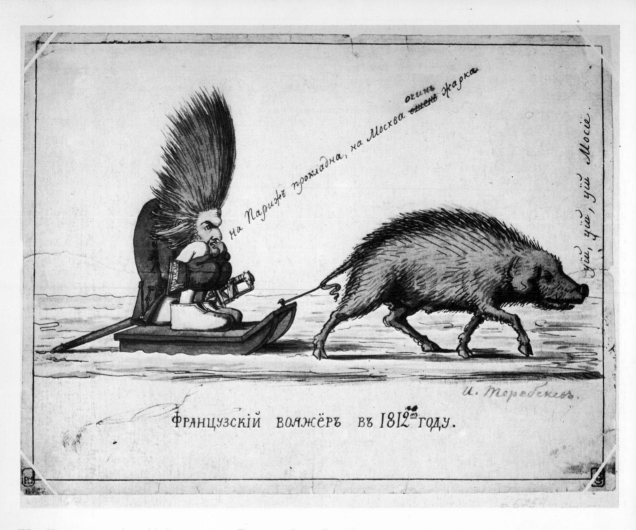

на Парижъ прохладна, на Москва очинь очень Жарка.

ую, ую, ую Мосіе.

И. Теребеневъ.

ФРАНЦУЗСКІЙ ВОЯЖЁРЪ ВЪ 1812ᵐ ГОДУ.

When Kutuzov was woken with the news that Napoleon was fleeing Moscow (*above*) he is said to have made the sign of the Cross and gone back to sleep. Caricature by Terebenev.

But, much to the disgust both of the Emperor Alexander and Sir Robert Wilson, the old soldier – now a Prince and a Marshal – refused to mount any large-scale battles. He argued that the Russian soldier had suffered enough; and that it was not a primary Russian interest to destroy totally the French army. He told an English general:

> I don't care for your objections. I prefer giving my enemy a *pont d'or* as you call it, to receiving a *coup de collier*; besides I will say again, as I have told you before, that I am by no means sure that the total destruction of the Emperor Napoleon and his army would be such a benefit to the world; his succession would not fall to Russia or to any other continental power, but to that which already commands the seas, and whose dominion would then be intolerable.

Sir Robert Wilson wrote angrily in his diary: 'If the French army is not wrecked before it reaches the frontier, the Marshal, old and infirm as he is, ought to be shot.'[10]

Wilson need not have worried, for the bitter weather, the lack of food and clothing, and the savagery of the Russian peasants, produced enough misery to satisfy the most rapacious enemy. The roads were strewn with guns, men and horses. Unwilling conscripts, and French

138

The Plumb-pudding in danger :— or State Epicures taking un Petit Souper.
— *'the great Globe itself, and all which it inherit', is too small to satisfy such insatiable Appetites.*

Pitt and Napoleon dividing the world

soldiers, tore away the clothing of wounded companions, and turned their arms against one another rather than share their food. And those who did not die of the cold, or from the knives of peasants, died of dysentery brought on by eating horseflesh. On 13 November Wilson described 'a scene as probably never was witnessed to such an extent in the history of the world'.

> The naked masses of dead and dying men; the mangled carcasses of ten thousand horses, which had in some cases been cut for food before life had ceased, the craving of famine at other points forming groups of *cannibals*; the air enveloped in flame and smoke; the prayers of hundreds of naked wretches, flying from the peasantry, whose shouts of vengeance echo incessantly through the woods; the wrecks of cannon, powder-wagons; military stores of all descriptions, and every ordinary as well as extra-ordinary ill of war combined with the asperity of the climate....[11]

Alexander I was furious with Kutuzov for not being more aggressive. 'All he did against the enemy was what he could not possibly avoid doing,' he fumed to Sir Robert Wilson. 'He won victories in spite of himself.' But as he himself had heaped the old Marshal with honours he scarcely could dismiss him. Yet he knew that Kutuzov was stubbornly opposed to continuing the war now the enemy was in full retreat, while he, Alexander, was determined to pursue Napoleon across Europe. The dilemma seemed insoluble; then Kutuzov suddenly died, an act which the Emperor interpreted as the direct intervention of Providence.

On New Year's Day 1813 Alexander inaugurated his campaign for the liberation of Europe by leading his troops across the Niemen. Many battles were fought during the next twelve months. By now Prussia and Austria had allied themselves to Russia; and on 16 October the Battle of the Nations was fought at Leipzig, which cost nearly a hundred thousand lives but freed Prussia from the French yoke. Napoleon was hurled back into France to fight, not for the preservation of his empire, but for his very existence.

Alexander's gaze was now on Paris. 'I shall not make peace until Napoleon is dethroned,' he said stubbornly. On 25 March the Russians fought their last battle and scored their last victory against the French. A few days later armistice terms were signed at the Port de St Denis; and on 6 April, at Fontainebleau, Napoleon abdicated. He was exiled to the island of Elba. Louis XVIII, who had taken refuge in England, returned to France after an absence of twenty years.

The Paris crowds went wild over the Russian Emperor, who announced that he had come as a friend, not as an enemy. He rode into Paris on a light grey horse, preceded by red-coated Cossacks, fifteen abreast; then the Cuirassier and Hussar Regiments of the Prussian Guard, then the Lancers and Hussars of his own bodyguard. With Prince Schwarzenberg representing the Austrian Emperor on his right, and the King of Prussia on his left, he was accompanied by a thousand officers of the allied general staff. The white flags of the Royalists appeared on hundreds of balconies; men sported white cockades in their hats, ladies waved white handkerchiefs and danced in the streets. When Alexander reviewed his troops on the Champs-Elysées the crowd was so dense the Prince Eugène of Württemberg feared for the Emperor's safety. People tried to touch his coat, his boots, his spurs, even the tail of his horse. 'The crowds' joyous voices were everywhere,' he wrote to Prince Alexander Golitsyn. 'But my soul was experiencing a wholly different joy . . . My soul was almost dissolved in gratitude to God . . . I was hungry for solitude so that I could pour out my heart to Him. . . .'[12] Although the people of Paris hailed Alexander as 'the new Agamemnon', his own country begged him to accept the title 'Alexander the Blessed'.

The Congress of Vienna met in September 1814 to provide a blueprint for Europe. Alexander believed that God had given him his victory, and that God now wished him 'to return to every nation the possibility of enjoying its rights and institutions' and to lead them like a flock of sheep to the true faith. 'Divine Providence has put us on the path which points directly to our goal,' he wrote to La Harpe. 'We have attained part of it. The other part is still surrounded with difficulties. It is imperative that we should overcome them.'

For years Alexander had mulled over the idea of a league of nations. Indeed, early in his reign he had sent an emissary to London with remarkable proposals for a peace treaty.

> Might one not include in it the undertaking and obligation never to begin a war without having first exhausted all the means of settling the dispute which arbitration can provide? And might one not proceed from this principle to the pacification of the world and create a League whose creed would constitute, so to say, a new code of international law, which would easily become the directing guide of cabinets – especially as those who ventured to infringe them would take the risk of finding themselves attacked by the combined forces of the League.[13]

Once again the Russian Emperor was groping for a solution which would prove durable. But his voice struck a sombre note in the festive but greedy atmosphere of Vienna, where the great men of Europe dined and danced every night and tried to pick each others' pockets every day. Instead of greeting each other as friends, the representatives of Britain, Austria, Prussia and Russia viewed one another with deep suspicion. Only in the ballroom did the delegates relax, dancing hectically to the strains of waltz music, the newest craze. '*Le Congrès ne marche pas,*' sighed the aged Prince de Ligne, '*mais il danse.*'

Soon such bitterness had developed that Britain, Austria and France signed a secret treaty and even contemplated war against Russia. Then on 7 March came the bombshell. Napoleon had escaped from Elba and was heading for Paris. The futile Louis XVIII fled to Lille, leaving on his desk the secret treaty against Russia. Napoleon found the document and sent it to Alexander, hoping that the Russian Emperor would withdraw in anger from the anti-Bonaparte coalition. But Alexander was still as firmly resolved to destroy Napoleon as he had ever been. He summoned Metternich, the brilliant Austrian statesman, showed him the paper, and flung it into the fire. 'Napoleon has returned; therefore our alliance must be stronger than ever,' he said dryly.

While Russian troops marched from the borders of Prussia, hoping to take part in the confrontation with Napoleon destined to go down in history as the Battle of Waterloo,* Alexander moved from Vienna to the small German town of Heilbronn which had been chosen as head-quarters for the Russian army. 'My first action was to open the Holy Book which I have always with me,' he wrote to his friend, Countess Edling, 'but my mind could not grasp the sense of what I was reading.'

The Emperor's aide, Prince Volkonsky, interrupted him and told him that a woman was at the door, insisting on an audience. Her name was Madame de Krüdener. Alexander leapt up and ordered that the lady be admitted. Countess Edling had often talked of Madame de Krüdener as a deeply religious woman, and he felt that she might give him the spiritual comfort that he needed.

---

*They did not arrive in time.

Madame de Krüdener was 50 years old and had once been beautiful. Her talk with Alexander lasted three hours. She is said to have told him that he was 'living in sin' and must 'seek his salvation at the foot of the Cross'. Alexander wept, and begged her to come again.

Meanwhile Waterloo was fought, and Napoleon defeated. This time he was sent to St Helena, and once again Alexander repaired to Paris, taking Madame de Krüdener with him. The Russian Emperor was installed in the Elysée Bourbon, and Madame de Krüdener in the Hôtel Montchenu, which had a convenient garden door opening on to the Champs-Elysées. Alexander saw her every day; and when he reviewed some 150,000 Russian troops early in September 1815, Madame de Krüdener stood beside him. 'Not even the homage which Louis XIV paid to Madame de Maintenon at the camp of Compiègne exceeded the veneration which the conqueror displayed toward Madame de Krüdener,' wrote Sainte-Beuve. 'She figured as a new Peter the Hermit in the presence of the kneeling soldiers.'[14]

The outcome of this extraordinary friendship was the Treaty of the Holy Alliance which Alexander asked the states of Europe to sign. The Preamble invited the contracting powers to base their conduct on 'the sublime truths contained in the eternal religion of Christ our Saviour'. In Article I they were to pledge themselves to 'true and insoluble brotherhood'; in Article III to recognize that 'the Christian nation of which they and their people form a part has really no other Sovereign than Him to whom alone supreme power belongs'. But there were more earthly clauses as well.[15]

Metternich called the document 'a piece of sublime mysticism and nonsense', but both Austria and Prussia signed if only to please Alexander. Castlereagh wrote to Lord Liverpool, however, that both the Emperor of Austria and the King of Prussia had given their signatures with reluctance, believing it to be the work of a lunatic. 'The Duke of Wellington happened to be with me when the Emperor called with the document and it was not without difficulty that we went through the interview with becoming gravity,' he reported. The British did not sign, expressing the regret that British constitutional practice made participation impossible.

In the late autumn of 1815 the Allies signed a political Treaty of Alliance. All allusions to the precepts of the Holy Alliance were carefully avoided; but the echoes of Alexander's idea continued to resound through Europe until 1918, when the League of Nations came into being.

'The great soul,' the Sardinian Ambassador reported to his King, 'has now re-entered its great body.' Alexander had returned to St Petersburg convinced that his mission in life was to strengthen the Holy Alliance by 'fighting the spirit of evil which threatens to overcome the good'.

Unfortunately Alexander began to identify 'evil' with change. This gave Metternich the idea of exploiting the Holy Alliance for the purpose of suppressing constitutionalism and reasserting the rôle of autocracy.

When he met the Russian Emperor at the Congresses of Aix-la-Chapelle and Troppau he used his silver tongue to indoctrinate, and finally persuaded him to put his signature to a resolution which astonished almost every country in Europe. The paragraph declared that States in which constitutional changes were brought about by revolt should cease to be members of the Holy Alliance; but that their former partners would have the right to restore the *status quo* of the erring Power by 'corrective acts of force'. The British House of Commons mocked the Emperor with speeches describing Cossacks, fifteen abreast, galloping down the Mall; while Lord Byron wrote a verse about

> *The coxcomb Czar*
> *The Autocrat of waltzes and of war*
> *With no objection to true liberty*
> *Except that it would make men free.*

It was plain that Alexander's passion for freedom no longer burned brightly where his own subjects were concerned. Soon after he returned to Russia he became increasingly dependent on the sinister Arakcheyev,

Arakcheyev, the arch-policeman who dominated the Emperor and the Empire after Speransky's fall.
Pushkin called him the Black Angel of Alexander's reign.

Вид. Италіанскаго Фонтана в нижнем Сад. Монарса.

Его Императорскому Величеству
АЛЕКСАНДРУ I.
Государю Императору и Самодержцу Всероссійскому.

Vue d'une fontaine Italienne dans le Jardin Imperial de Peterhoff.

Dédié à sa Majesté Imperiale
ALEXANDRE I.
EMPEREUR ET AUTOCRATEUR DE TOUTES LES RUSSIES.

144

An Italian fountain (*left*) at Peterhof dedicated to Alexander I

who had once served his father, Paul, and who for the last few years had served Alexander as a military secretary. 'He was a man of little culture, reeking of malice and spitefulness,' wrote Alexander Turgenev. 'No one except the vilest toadies could ever tolerate him ... Among the common people, and indeed, in all classes of society, he was known as the vampire.'[16]

No one could understand the Emperor's attachment. The only plausible explanation was the story that Arakcheyev, who had been in the palace on the night of Paul's murder, poured balm on Alexander's troubled soul by absolving him of all blame for his father's death.

In 1816 Alexander gave his approval to a scheme, supposedly drawn up by Arakcheyev, whereby soldiers could be called upon to work as agricultural labourers. Military colonies would be set up all over Russia where soldiers would live with their families. Alexander was so convinced of the worthiness of the plan, which would unite soldiers with wives and children and help Russia at the same time, that he was prepared, he said, 'to cover the whole road from St Petersburg to Moscow with corpses in order to enforce obedience to his will'.

Arakcheyev was merciless as an administrator. Families were forced to live in barracks so overcrowded that privacy was impossible. And they were worked so hard that hundreds of families deserted and hid in the swamps where most of them died of hunger and cold. By 1825 the various colonies contained 142,697 soldiers of the line; 93,365 cadets (under 17 years of age); 7,628 pensioners; and 50,695 children in military orphanages. A report states that 'after eight years work and an incalculable outlay the colonies presented a distressing spectacle'.

Nevertheless Alexander continued to believe that his actions were directed by God. The only innovation he produced was a Ministry of Spiritual Affairs which his more sceptic subjects dubbed the Ministry of Eclipse. Meanwhile Russia continued to groan with misery. Apart from the abominable colonies, taxes were rising and corruption seeping into every government department. Although Alexander had long ago

A detail from part of the Chinese village (*right*) in the grounds of Alexander's Palace at Tsarskoye Selo, designed for Catherine II who had wanted a Russian 'Petit Trianon'.

forbidden the sale of serfs without land, the law was flaunted from one end of the country to the other. 'Just imagine,' Prince Kochubey told Alexander Turgenev, 'the Emperor is convinced that serfs have not been sold separately ever since his accession.' 'What was there for me to say,' Turgenev observed, 'when both of us knew that within a stone's throw of the Winter Palace, at the City Hall, human flesh was being put up for sale with full permission of the authorities . . . children wrenched away from parents and husbands from wives. . . .'[17]

Hundreds of young Russian army officers, who had ridden into Paris with Alexander the Blessed, watched the reactionary tide with bitter dismay. Nothing was omitted, not even the security police and a rigid censorship. Soon these young scions of the nobility were organizing secret societies and pledging themselves to radical reforms. The Northern Secret Society, led by Muraviev-Apostol a deeply religious soldier, and the poet, Ryleyev, championed constitutional government; while the Southern Society, headed by Paul Pestel, the intellectual colonel, the most eminent of all the rebels, favoured a republic. One of the leaders, Bestuzhev, later wrote that 'free thinking' began with Napoleon's invasion of Russia. When the Russian people became aware of their power a longing for independence sprang up in their hearts.

> The Government itself spoke such words as 'Liberty, Emancipation!' [he continued]. It had itself sown the idea of abuses resulting from the unlimited power of Napoleon, and the appeal of the Russian Monarch resounded on the banks of the Rhine and the Seine. The war was still on when the soldiers, upon their return home, for the first time disseminated grumbling among the masses. 'We shed blood,' they would say, 'and then we are again forced to sweat under feudal obligations. We freed the Fatherland from the tyrant, and now we ourselves are tyrannized over by the ruling class.' The army, from general to privates, upon its return, did nothing but discuss how good it is in foreign lands. A comparison with our own country naturally brought up the question, Why should it not be so in our own lands?[18]

Meanwhile the Emperor was talking about abdicating and giving himself up to a life of meditation. The Empress Elizabeth had borne him two daughters, but both had died, and the next in line of succession was Alexander's brother, Constantine. This young man was unpopular in all classes of society. Prince Czartoryski believed he had inherited a strain of madness from his father. 'Woe to his friends, and to his enemies, and woe to his subjects should he ever have any.' When Constantine accompanied Alexander into Paris in 1814 a page at the French court wrote that 'his face was hardly human. He wore spectacles, and when he looked at anything contracted his eyes very disagreeably: his voice is rude, his manner brusque and military.'

Fortunately, Constantine had no wish to rule. As Viceroy of Poland, he resided in Warsaw, where he lived an agreeable and dissipated life. In 1819 his marriage to Princess Julie of Coburg was annulled: and he took as his second wife his mistress, Joanna Grudzinska. Although he

The Military Gallery in the Winter Palace. Alexander I is surrounded by portraits of the generals who fought Napoleon.

still bore the title Tsarevich it was unthinkable that a monarch married to a commoner could reign. People therefore regarded the next brother, Nicholas, eleven years younger than Alexander, as the likely successor.

Nicholas was remarkably good-looking and almost as remarkably unimaginative. A conscientious soldier, he was prudish and stern. In 1817, aged 20, he married Charlotte, the beautiful daughter of the King of Prussia and the famous Queen Louise. It was not a *mariage de convenance*, for the young couple had fallen deeply in love in 1814 when Nicholas had led his Guards regiment into Berlin. The following year he returned to the capital for his betrothal. 'Monseigneur,' said Charlotte, 'you have come just in time to settle a grave question. The clocks of St Petersburg are three-quarters of an hour ahead of those of Berlin, does time go quicker with you than with us?' 'I think,' said Nicholas, 'that time passes nowhere as fast as with you.'[19]

Charlotte took the name Alexandra upon marriage. She kept a diary during her first years in Russia and relates how, in the summer of 1819, the Emperor told Nicholas that he looked upon him as the person who would replace him, and that this would happen while Alexander was still alive.

> We sat there like two statues, open-eyed and dumb. The Emperor went on: You seem astonished, but let me tell you that my brother, Constantine, who has never bothered about the throne, is more than ever determined to renounce it formally and to pass on his rights to his brother Nicholas and descendants. As for myself, I have decided to free myself of my functions and to retire from the world . . . Seeing us on the verge of tears he tried to comfort us and reassured us by saying that this was not going to happen at once . . . , then he left us alone, and it can be imagined in what sort of state of mind we were.[20]

Alexander's favourite proverb was: 'One scarcely ever repents of having waited.' Perhaps this was why he refused to state publicly that Nicholas, not Constantine, would succeed him. Both brothers found the situation intolerable, and Constantine finally prevailed on Alexander at least to allow him to clarify his position in writing. After consulting Prince Alexander Golitsyn, the Emperor sent for the Archbishop of Tver and drew up a document in which Constantine formally renounced the throne. But he still insisted on secrecy. No clerk was allowed to handle the paper, and Golitsyn made four copies in his own hand. The Synod, the Senate and the Council of the Empire each received sealed envelopes, as did the church of the Assumption in Moscow. On each the Emperor wrote: *Guardez jusqu'à ma réclamation, mais dans le cas ou je viendrai mourir ouvrez ce paquet en séance extraordinaire de procéder à tout autre acte.*

The years from 1817 to 1825 are known as Alexander's twilight. The youthful dreams of public service had vanished long ago; and in their place was an all-absorbing search for personal salvation. So engrossed was the Emperor that he scarcely seemed to notice that under his aegis Russia had been caught once again in the grip of repression.

ABOVE 'The French are hungry rats.'
BELOW 'The journey of a great traveller.'
Copies of Terebenev caricatures of the French flight from Moscow, by an unknown artist.

Alexander visiting the artist George
Daw in his studio in the Winter Palace

Pushkin among the Decembrists. 'In
those days his poems circulated
everywhere, were copied and recopied,
committed to memory, and read aloud.'

Yet the darkening gloom was alleviated by the flashing genius of an 18-year-old poet, Pushkin, whose verses were passed from hand to hand, and learned by heart from one end of Russia to the other. Pushkin had many friends in the secret societies. He took up their cry for freedom and crystallized their hopes in immortal lines. He lashed out against Arakcheyev as 'the oppressor of all Russia . . . the friend and brother of the Tsar'; against the Archimandrite Photius 'whose chief spiritual instrument is the knout'; against Alexander I 'a dashing captain who ran away at Austerlitz and shook with fear in 1812'. In the political satire, *Fairy Tales*, which he wrote in 1818 after Alexander I had returned from Aachen (Aix-la-Chapelle) where he had pledged himself to preserve the *status quo*, he continued his attack on the sovereign: 'Hurrah, the wandering despot has galloped back to Russia.'

No doubt it was inevitable that Pushkin should come unstuck. In 1820 he wrote an *Ode to Liberty*, describing the assassination of Paul I and warning autocrats that unless they 'bow their heads under the safe protection of the law' nothing can save them:

> *O tyrants of the world, beware!*
> *And you, good men, take heart and dare*
> *Arise, fallen slaves.*

Alexander forgave the incitement to rebellion but he was so incensed by the veiled references to his part in the murder of his father that he exiled Pushkin to the south of Russia. And in 1823, when the poet wrote two irreligious lines in one of his verses, the period of banishment was extended still further.

In the summer of 1825 the Empress Elizabeth was in poor health and Alexander decided to accompany her to a warmer climate. They chose Taganrog on the Azov sea. The Empress improved slightly, but in November Alexander fell ill and died.

It took nearly two weeks for the news to reach St Petersburg and many people refused to believe what they heard. They remembered how often Alexander had talked of abdicating and soon stories were spreading that he had retreated to a monastery. Years later a mysterious hermit, Feodor Kuzmich, who lived in Siberia, was said to be the Emperor. Many books have been written in support of this romantic story; but the scholars regretfully dismiss it as a pretty legend.

View of the Winter Palace – through the General Staff arch

CHAPTER VI
Nicholas I
1825–1855

'THE RUSSIAN EMPIRE,' reported the correspondent of the London *Times* in November 1825, a few days after the death of Alexander I, 'is in the strange position of having two self-denying Emperors and no active ruler.'

The situation was unparalleled in the history of nations. The Russian throne remained empty for three weeks while the dead sovereign's two brothers, the Grand Duke Constantine and the Grand Duke Nicholas, each insisted that the other must wear the crown. The courtiers were astonished by this unexpected *pas de deux*, as Constantine long ago had made it plain that he did not wish to reign. Not only was he satisfied with his job as Viceroy of Poland, but determined to continue living in Warsaw with his Polish wife. Nicholas, on the other hand, was both willing and eager to rule.

Prince Golitsyn, who had helped Alexander I to draw up the document in which Constantine renounced the throne, found Nicholas's behaviour nothing short of lunatic. The 29-year-old Grand Duke was attending a Te Deum in the Winter Palace when a messenger from far-away Taganrod brought him news of the Emperor's death. Without a moment's hesitation he slipped out and ordered the soldiers at the Palace to take the oath of allegiance to Constantine. Even when Golitsyn called an Imperial Council and showed them the letter in which Constantine repudiated the crown, Nicholas refused to accept the succession. He waived the rights conferred upon him and requested that copies of the Emperor's letter should remain unopened. Next day pictures of Constantine appeared in the newspapers as 'Emperor and Autocrat of all the Russias'.

A week later Nicholas's younger brother, Michael, arrived hot-foot from Warsaw with a letter from Constantine acknowledging Nicholas as Emperor. By this time the courtiers were beginning to laugh. But Nicholas still was not satisfied and sent Michael back to Warsaw for further corroboration. Countess Nesselrode, the Empress's lady-in-waiting, wrote to Count Guriev that the two brothers were playing with the crown of Russia 'throwing it back and forth as though it were an india rubber ball'.

Nicholas, however, was not as irrational as some people supposed. He was wise enough to know that the Guards divisions had a long tradition of deciding the succession to the throne; he also knew that the army loathed him because of his passion for discipline. 'I hope military service will not make you adopt a brutal, harsh and imperious manner,' his mother had warned him many years earlier. 'It is sad that Nicholas is so wrong in his behaviour,' wrote Countess Nesselrode, 'making himself loathed and detested by the troops; they say he flies into rages and is severe, vindictive and mean.' 'His habitual expression has something

'I have three sons,' wrote the Dowager Empress, 'Alexander is an idealist and he is charming. Constantine (*above*) is hot tempered and out of all control but he can be sweet. . . . As for Nicholas (*right*) he has but one ambition – to reign.'

severe and misanthropic which makes one feel uneasy,' declared the Russian Ambassador at Stuttgart.

Although the Grand Duke Constantine was widely disliked by the nobility he had the support of the Guards regiments whom he had led through the Napoleonic campaigns. Nicholas therefore decided to prevaricate until the officers had become fully aware of Constantine's implacable stand, and were willing to pledge him their unequivocal support. 'Everyone told him he had a right to the throne and he must accept it,' his wife wrote in her diary on 27 November. 'But as Constantine had never spoken to him and never written, he decided to act as his conscience and duty dictated; he refused this honour and this burden, which surely after all will fall on him in a few days. . . .'[1]

Nevertheless the long delay had unsuspected dangers of its own. While Nicholas was waiting for opinion to harden behind him, the monarchy itself was threatened. A serious conspiracy was building up, led by army officers who had tasted the heady wine of freedom when they had accompanied Alexander I to Paris. All were members of the Northern and Southern secret societies, pledged to Constitutionalism, some even to Republicanism.

Nicholas got wind of the subversion on the very day that he received a second letter from Constantine again refusing the crown. He now realized that there was no time to lose and at midnight appeared before the Imperial Council and formally accepted the succession. At the same hour the conspirators – almost all aristocrats – were holding their last meeting in the house of Conrad Ryleyev, an employee of the Russian-American Company and a romantic poet in his spare time. Among those present were Prince Trubetskoy, designated as the future leader of the 'democracy', Prince Obolensky, Prince Odoevsky, Prince Volkonsky, the Bestuzhev brothers and a madman called Kakhovsky who had sworn to murder Nicholas and any officials who got in his way.

The plan of campaign worked out by the rebels was tragically amateurish. Instead of rallying the regiments and the populace with the cry of 'liberty' they decided to challenge the new sovereign's legality by clamouring for the Grand Duke Constantine. As no one had yet taken the oath to Nicholas, they believed that they could create enough dissension to have their demands for a National Assembly fulfilled. And once the Assembly was sitting it would dismiss the question of succession and proclaim a Constitutional government.

That was the plan. Not only did the conspirators fail to realize that cheers for Constantine were unlikely to arouse any strong emotion, but they overlooked the necessity of organizing substantial support. None of the officers seemed to know how many soldiers would follow them; none had worked out how many guns or rounds of ammunition would be needed. All was left in the hands of Providence.

Nicholas, on the other hand, was far from idle. He asked the august bodies of the State to give him their allegiance before dawn ushered in the fateful day of 14 December. The Senate and the Holy Synod took

P.M.

the oath by candlelight in the early morning hours; so did the Horse Guards, assembled in the freezing temperature of the Riding School.

The first conspirators who gathered in the huge, snow-covered Senate Square, flanked at one end by Catherine's statue of Peter the Great, were forty or fifty officers without any troops. An hour later seven hundred soldiers from the Moscow Regiment, in full-dress uniform, led by Prince Shchepin-Rostovsky and one of the Bestuzhev brothers, came marching to join them. Although the men were disconcerted to learn that the Senate already had taken the oath to Nicholas they could think of no alternative except to continue shouting for Constantine.

The labourers who were building St Isaac's Cathedral, across the square, downed tools and joined the rebels, while passers-by began to gather to watch the fun. Ryleyev, the spiritual leader of the movement, appeared in the square but departed almost at once, having decided, at this late hour, that he must gather cavalry and artillery. Trubetskoy, the appointed Prime Minister, was missing, and no one knew where to find him. But Kakhovsky was very much in evidence; armed with two pistols and a dagger he swaggered around looking for someone to kill.

Suddenly Count Miloradovich, a famous soldier and Governor of St Petersburg, came galloping up to the rebels and implored them to accept the fact that Constantine had renounced the throne. 'I have seen his abdication with my own eyes,' he told them. At that point Kakhovsky fired at him and shot him through the head. The Count's horse loped away with the lifeless body hanging across the saddle.

It was now nearly midday and exaggerated stories began to sweep the Winter Palace. In her diary the Empress wrote:

> I was alone when Nicholas came to my room saying, 'I must go.' From his voice I could tell that the news was bad. I knew he had not intended to leave the Palace. It gave me a shock. I went on with the business of dressing, for at two o'clock we had to be ready for the State procession of the Te Deum. Suddenly the door opened and the Dowager Empress appeared; her face was haggard. 'Darling,' she said to me, 'things are going very badly. There is rioting.' Pale as death, unable to say a word, I threw a garment – the first to hand – over my shoulders, and went with the Dowager Empress to her small study. From there we could see that the whole square in front of the Palace and as far as the Senate was full of people. We knew nothing: all we had heard was that the Moscow Regiment had rebelled.[2]

Some of Nicholas's high officials tried to persuade him not to face the mob, telling him that as many as a thousand officers were involved in the mutiny. 'If I am only to be Emperor for a day,' he replied, 'I will prove to the world that I am worthy.' His figure was majestic as he rode into the square, wearing the dress uniform of the Ismailovsky Regiment, white breeches, green tunic laced with gold, and a plumed hat. He made his entrance at the opposite end to where the insurgents were thronged and addressed the crowd as 'my children'. Then he dismounted and embraced those nearest to him.

ABOVE 'Sire,' said General Toll to Nicholas I, 'sweep the square with gunfire or abdicate.'

BELOW The army swearing allegiance to the new Tsar. Nicholas personally interrogated those who had joined the ranks of the Decembrists.

When the rebels saw what was happening they shouted 'Long Live Constantine' until the noise became a frenzy. Ryleyev, who had returned to the scene with the promise of cavalry but no artillery, could no longer contain himself. 'Long Live the Constitution,' he yelled. 'And who is Constitution?' asked someone in the crowd. 'It must be the wife of Constantine,' came the reply.

Nicholas was heartened to see the first battalions of the Preobrazhensky Guard and the Horse Guards advancing toward him, led by loyal generals. An hour later the *Chevalier Gardes* in silver-breasted uniforms, with snowflakes falling on their plumed helmets, took their stand beside him. But at the same time a thousand Naval Guards debouched into the square and joined the rebels. Then the Grand Duke Michael arrived with detachments from the Pavlovsky Regiment; but this was countered by companies from the Grenadier Guards who went to the opposing side.

Meanwhile the dense throng remained in a bantering mood. Most of them did not seem to understand what the conflict was about. They opened their ranks respectfully to allow carriages filled with beribboned dignitaries to pass to the Winter Palace for the Te Deum.

Yet the feeling was almost unbearably tense. A few shots in the air, the bold cry of a leader, and there might be, in the words of Pushkin, 'a real Russian riot without reason or pity'. Kakhovsky, who had sworn to kill Nicholas, could not get close enough to take aim; another assassin, who was only a few feet away, lost his nerve when he gazed upon the Emperor's fine Roman head, with its chiselled features and expressionless, wintry eyes. Nicholas had been in the saddle for two hours. He was pale, but a contemporary account declares that 'not a muscle in his face moved as death prowled around him'. 'This prince showed a composure and presence of mind and a courage that struck the spectators with profound admiration,' the Austrian ambassador wrote to Metternich.

Nicholas's cavalry tried to encircle the insurgents but they retreated when two volleys were fired into their flanks. Then the Horse Guards launched an attack, but their horses slipped and fell, and the crowd began to pelt the unseated riders with snowballs. The insurgents were not strong enough to overcome the Emperor's troops; and the Emperor's troops could not put down the insurgents, so the two sides simply stared and jeered at one another.

It was growing dark now, and Nicholas's generals urged him to allow a battery of four guns to be brought into the square. He murmured that he did not wish to begin his reign with bloodshed, but finally he nodded his head. What was curious was the fact that even when the crowd saw the guns being dragged into the square they continued to laugh and hurl insults and cry 'Long Live Constantine'. 'You will be taught to acknowledge Nicholas,' murmured the Commander of Artillery as he supervised the placing of the guns. Nicholas hesitated to give the final order. 'Sire,' said General Toll sternly, 'sweep the square with gun-fire or abdicate.'

The guns belched, and a moment later spectators and insurgents were in full rout. Sixty people lay dead upon the snow; several hundred more were injured in the stampede. At the first volley Nicholas reined up, turned his horse and galloped back to the Winter Palace. 'God, how my heart beat when I heard his voice,' wrote his wife. 'I saw before me a man completely transformed.'

The change went unnoted, for most people had always regarded Nicholas as a man of steel. Five leaders of the rebellion were sentenced to death: Ryleyev, Pestel, one of the Bestuzhev brothers, Muraviev-Apostol and Kakhovsky. Two hundred and eighty others were exiled to Siberia for life.

Nicholas astonished the public by holding a religious service in Senate Square to commemorate the executions. In the evening Prince Kochubey gave a ball to which the whole of St Petersburg society was invited. As the coaches of the guests turned on to Fontanka Quai they heard bells ringing. A procession of carts, escorted by gendarmes, filled with the friends, cousins and companions of the revellers, was beginning the long trek to Siberia. Many of the princely exiles were accompanied by their wives who, as a gesture of defiance, wore evening gowns to match the dress uniforms which their husbands had donned for the uprising and were still wearing. As they passed the palace the lights from the ballroom illuminated their ribbons and jewels, their pale faces and chains. Their pathetic incompetence has been erased by the passage of time, and in history they are known as the Decembrists, immortalized by the poems of Nekrasov and Pushkin.

The feast given to the people by Nicholas at his coronation

Nicholas I wasted no time in turning his vast Empire into a barracks. To him sovereignty was merely an extension of army discipline. 'I am,' he confided to the Austrian ambassador, 'a sentry at outpost to see all and observe all.' Although God may have recognized Nicholas as a humble soldier the Russian people saw him as a merciless drill sergeant who dragooned his fifty million subjects with passionate attention to detail. 'I cannot permit that one single person should dare to defy my wishes the moment he has been made exactly aware of them,' he wrote on the margin of a report in 1826.

His wishes were eccentric, to say the least. He imposed the wearing of uniforms on professors, students, engineers, members of the civil service, and finally, in 1831, on all nobles. Only the army had the right to wear mustaches, and all mustaches had to be black, dyed if necessary. Smoking was forbidden in the streets as the Empress Alexandra did not like it. No one could visit the Hermitage picture gallery, even in the morning, without wearing evening clothes. Grey top hats were forbidden as being 'Jewish', dress coats as being 'revolutionary'. All officers of the Household Guard were instructed to wear Nicholas's initials, embroidered in silver, on their epaulets.

Nicholas undoubtedly was the most alarming sovereign in Europe. His ice-cold gaze struck such terror into the hearts of his courtiers that one of them, Prince Lubomirski, confessed that even after the Emperor's death he kept his portrait turned to the wall. 'I had such a fear of the original,' he explained, 'that even a copy, with those terrible eyes fixed on me, frightens and embarrasses me.' When Nicholas visited Windsor Castle in 1841 Queen Victoria fathomed the secret of his awesome appearance by discovering that his left eye was slightly asymmetrical 'like a nail at white heat'. 'He is certainly a *very striking* man,' she wrote, 'still very handsome, his profile is *beautiful*, and his manners most dignified and graceful . . . but the expression of the *eyes* is formidable and unlike anything I ever saw before . . .' The Queen was disappointed to find that military matters consumed so much of his thought, felt that his education had been 'neglected' and came to the conclusion that he was 'not very clever'. 'His mind,' she wrote, 'is an uncivilized one.'[3]

Although Count Zichy, the Austrian Ambassador, reported that Nicholas spent three-quarters of his day drilling his troops and organizing massed cavalry charges, he managed nevertheless to interfere in every branch of life. If the St Petersburg firebells rang he ran out and told the firemen what to do. He banished Prince Yussupov to the Caucasus because he was having a love affair of which his mother did not approve; and when the daughter of a courtier was treated badly by her husband he had the marriage annulled and wrote majestically: 'This young person shall be considered a virgin.'

In the morning he worked at his desk; in the afternoon he visited the parade ground or rode through the capital in a carriage drawn by a magnificent Orlov trotter, pulling up unexpectedly at schools, barracks

On his numerous tours of inspection Nicholas liked to use a fast droshky or sleigh, because, as he wrote to the Empress: 'One sees everything and they never know when and where I am going to arrive.'

or hospitals as the fancy took him. If he noticed the slightest infraction of the rules the culprit would be given thirty days imprisonment or dismissed from his job. This last was the fate of a headmaster whose pupils in the sick-bay had the temerity to stare out of the window at Nicholas with unshaven faces. Occasionally he committed an act of kindness. Once, when he saw a poor unattended hearse making its desolate way through the streets, he walked behind it until he had collected a crowd of 8,000 people. And when he entered a building and found the porter asleep at his desk over a half-written letter – 'I am in despair. Who will pay my debts?' – he leaned over and wrote: 'I, Nicholas I.'

One of the most alarming features of the Emperor's character was his tendency to declare people insane if he did not agree with them. When Peter Chaadayev, the darling of the Moscow intellectuals, produced a *Philosophical Letter*, published in the *Telescope* in 1836, arguing that Russia floated in space, belonging neither to West nor East, he gave instructions that the writer must be kept under medical supervision as he was 'mentally unbalanced'. Later he grew even more stringent. He dispatched a young student, the grandson of a minister, to a lunatic asylum for organizing opposition inside the university, and he sent a professor of French, M. Rigaud, to the same institution for remaining seated during Divine Service in the Orthodox Church. He recalled Pushkin from exile but appointed himself the poet's censor and occasionally returned manuscripts to him triumphantly mutilated by the imperial hand.

Pushkin felt increasingly restricted under the reign of Nicholas. Shortly before his death, he wrote to his wife: 'Only the devil could have thought of having me born in Russia with a mind and talent.'

Despite the fact that Nicholas dealt personally with infringements that came to his notice he did not rely wholly on his own powers of observation. He streamlined the secret police and formed them into a new department known as 'The Third Section'. He placed his close friend, Count Benckendorff, in charge of the department, and explained that its function was to act as 'the nation's moral physician' in every town in Russia. Although the death penalty was not revived it was clearly understood that a man could be killed by the knout.

The Third Section became notorious for the close scrutiny it kept on intellectuals. Pushkin was frequently summoned by Benckendorff; on one occasion the latter reprimanded him for reciting a poem to a group of friends before it had been approved by the Emperor. The poet replied lamely that it had not occurred to him that his unpublished works must not even be read without the Emperor's consent. He then sent the first part of a play, originally entitled *The Comedy of Boris Godunov*, to Nicholas. A month later Benckendorff sent for Pushkin and triumphantly read out the Emperor's verdict. 'I consider that Pushkin's purpose would be attained if, with some necessary chastening, he turned his comedy into an historical tale or romance after the manner of Walter Scott.' Pushkin, however, declined the suggestion, saying regretfully that 'it is not in my power to transform what once has been written by me'. And in the end *Boris Godunov* appeared as the author intended.

This was one of Pushkin's rare victories. He slavishly followed the imperial lead when in November 1830 a full-scale rebellion broke out in the small, truncated Kingdom of Poland, vassal to the Russian crown and ruled by Nicholas's brother, the Grand Duke Constantine. A group of student cadets killed the Chief of Police and seized Constantine's viceregal Palace. The Grand Duke escaped through a concealed door; but soon thousands of Poles were flocking to the banner of freedom.

Constantine could have squashed the entire rebellion in a day if he had sent for the Lithuanian division outside the capital and occupied the Fortress of Moldine overlooking Warsaw. But he was so stunned by the insurrection of 'my own people' that he could do nothing but sob that sixteen years of hard work had been destroyed by irresponsible students and non-commissioned officers.

Within a week the whole country was aflame. The Russian Ambassador in Paris told Louis-Philippe (who had just snatched the crown of France from Charles X) that Polish insubordination touched the very question of Russian sovereignty in Europe. Unless the Poles were brought to heel the Emperor would be regarded as little more than an Asiatic sovereign.

Nicholas was quick to seize on this dramatic interpretation. He upbraided Constantine for his failure to act decisively. 'Which of the two must perish,' he wrote, 'Russia or Poland?' His query, of course, was the signal for a Russian invasion of Poland. The fighting lasted for nearly a

Nicholas's marriage to Louise Charlotte of Prussia, later known as Alexandra, was a love-match. Nicholas was only twenty-one when he married, and his bride seventeen. Their first child, Alexander, was born within a year.

НИКОЛАЙ ПАВЛОВИЧЬ.
Nicholas I
Emperor of all the Russias

АЛЕКСАНДРЪ НИКОЛАЕВИЧЬ.
Grand Duke Alexander
Heir to the Throne

АЛЕКСАНДРА ѲЕОДОРОВНА.
Alexandra
Empress of all the Russias

year, while England and France protested and offered to mediate, without success. European liberals were shocked to find that Pushkin, 'the poet of freedom', had joined the reactionaries in urging the break-up of the Polish state. 'Our ancient enemies will then be exterminated,' he exulted. Other intellectuals followed his example. 'We are not Frenchmen; everyone of us is ready to sacrifice his life for the Tsar,' declared Bakunin, the great anarchist of the future. 'There is not the slightest doubt that the Kingdom of Poland has never been so well governed as under Russian domination,' wrote one of the Decembrists, Bestuzhev, from his Siberian exile.

The Grand Duke Constantine died of cholera; and after ten months of bitter fighting the war came to an end in a blood bath of murder and anarchy. 'Warsaw is at the feet of Your Majesty,' the Russian general, Paskevich, wrote to Nicholas in August 1831. 'Ah! Why can I not flee to thee?' replied the Emperor. 'It is painful to be tied to a desk on days like these.'

He consoled himself by drinking champagne with his generals and smashing dozens of glasses after exuberant toasts.

Like many tyrants, Nicholas was a devoted family man. He adored his bird-like Prussian wife, Alexandra. He called her 'Mouffy' and she called him 'Nicks'. He showered her with so many precious stones that her room looked like a jewelry shop; and when he was parted from her, even for a day, he became so nostalgic that he sometimes burst into tears. Unlike his predecessors, as a young man he was prudish. When a woman accosted him at a ball and gasped: 'Sire, do you know you are the most beautiful man in Russia?' he replied in shocked tones: 'Madam, surely that is something that concerns my wife alone.'

What he liked best was to spend the evening in Mouffy's study in the Winter Palace, a large room hung with red damask with two windows overlooking the Neva, playing the cornet or listening to readings from his favourite author, Sir Walter Scott. Although German now replaced French as the language of the Imperial family, and Mouffy was eager to promote German culture, she could not impress Nicholas with the merits of Goethe or Schiller.

As the reign progressed quiet evenings became increasingly rare. Nicholas had the same grandiose ideas as his grandmother, Catherine the Great, and believed that power was best demonstrated by splendour. 'Let the people amuse themselves,' he would say, 'it keeps them out of mischief.' He thought nothing of employing thousands of workmen to transform gardens into oriental palaces or ballrooms into gardens complete with rockeries and fountains. At the annual fête at Peterhof there were so many candles in the park that it took eighteen hundred workmen thirty-five minutes to light them. The supper table in the Winter Palace could seat a thousand people; and although the temperature outside might be far below freezing, the galleries bloomed with so many exotic plants that the guests had the illusion of a summer day. The ballroom was a setting for the peacock uniforms designed by Nicholas;

ABOVE An eighteenth-century view of St Petersburg from the River Neva, with the Winter Palace and the Academy of Sciences.
BELOW The future Alexander II among his cadets at Peterhof.
Painting by Brülow.

A View of St Petersburg in coming down the River Neva, between Her Imperial Majesty's Winter Palace & ye Academy of Sciences. Проспектъ по низъ по Невъ ръкъ между зимнимъ

Vüe des bords de la Neva en descendant la rivière, entre le palais d'hyver de Sa Majesté Impériale & les batimens de l'Académie des Sciences. Ея Императорскаго Величества домомъ и Академіею Наукъ.

Printed for Rob.t Wilkinson N.o 58 Cornhill

mirrors reflected the flicker of candles, the flash of jewels. 'It was magnificent,' wrote the French artist, Horace Vernet. 'One could literally trample on diamonds . . . one walked on pearls and rubies; it has to be seen to be believed.'

The Empress was mad about dancing, and performed the mazurka more gracefully than any Polish woman; and as it was Nicholas's greatest pleasure to see Mouffy enjoying herself the parties never ended before dawn. As a young sovereign Nicholas spent most of the evening wandering through the vast supper-rooms talking, like a condescending deity, to guests who usually were too frightened to do anything but nod agreement. But as he approached middle age he began to show an interest in women. He flirted with Pushkin's beautiful wife, Natasha, and even forced the poet to become a Gentleman of the Bedchamber, a position usually held by 18-year-old fops, in order that he might see her more easily. When he was at a table he developed the playful habit of nudging with his foot the satin slipper of a pretty Maid of Honour. In 1844 he showed an attachment for Barbette Nelidova, a member of the same family from which the unfortunate Paul had drawn his mistress; and in his will he left her £200,000.

As the years passed other changes took place, the most important of which was Nicholas's increasing belief in his own omnipotence. If he could re-arrange literary works of art, there was nothing to prevent him from taking a hand in the design of new buildings. He built a new Hermitage Museum, a National Library, the Alexandrinsky Theatre, and half a dozen palaces for his sons and daughters. He loved peristyles, porticoes and colonnades and told his architects exactly what he expected of them. He turned Peterhof into a constellation of fanciful buildings, designing the Alexandra Palace especially for Mouffy.

In 1837 the Winter Palace caught fire and was so damaged that it had to be completely rebuilt. No one knows the cause of the conflagration but Nicholas was not dismayed. Although the edifice was the size of the Louvre and the Tuileries put together, he ordered a new one to be ready for occupation in a year. 'Unheard-of efforts were necessary,' wrote the French traveller, the Marquis de Custine. 'The interior works were continued during the great frosts; six thousand workmen were continually employed; of these a considerable number died daily, but the victims were instantly replaced by other champions brought forward to perish . . . the sole end of all these sacrifices was to gratify the caprice of one man!'[4]

What made the exercise all the more curious was the fact that Nicholas himself demanded the utmost simplicity. His bedroom was not very different from a monk's cell. He slept on a camp bed covered by a straw mattress and refused to have any ornaments on the wall except for a few geographical maps, a few pictures of brother sovereigns, and a holy icon.

The world, however, only saw the Emperor's grandeur. Foreigners found the lavishness of his court grotesque in the midst of so much squalor. The Marquis de Custine went still further and asserted that

Porch of the Little Hermitage supported by Atlantes, fifteen feet high, sculpted by Terebenev

The Alexandrinsky Theatre, designed
for Nicholas by Rossi

even among the upper classes civilization was only a veneer. He complained that the ladies never washed, and even the greatest noblemen
possessed beds merely as a status symbol, preferring to wrap themselves
in rugs and drop down on the floor. However, the princes of the realm
undoubtedly were right to avoid beds, for when Custine took a nap on his
sofa in the best hotel in St Petersburg he awoke to find his blanket
swarming with bugs. His servant advised him to avoid all padded
furniture, such as divans, as they were bound to be breeding grounds.
He solved the Marquis's immediate problem by procuring 'a light iron
bedstead, the mattress of which I had stuffed with the freshest straw
that could be obtained, and caused the four feet to be placed in as many
jars of water. . . .'[5]

168

Even the Winter Palace was not free of vermin; and Nicholas's doctor, Martin Mandt, reported that when the attic rooms were rebuilt after the fire it was discovered that cows had been kept in an apartment next to the Maids of Honour in order to provide milk for the kitchens. Custine believed that the country's slipshod methods were due to the absence of a middle class. Although Russia boasted three universities – Moscow, Petersburg and Kiev – the merchants, architects and engineers were German, French, English or Levantine. There was scarcely a Russian doctor, and not a single Russian apothecary, in the whole Empire; even the professors were foreigners. No railways existed until 1838, when Nicholas laid the first track, fourteen miles long, connecting St Petersburg with his estate at Tsarskoye Selo. The mass of the people rarely travelled, and eked out their lives in uncomplaining ignorance. Indeed, the peasants were so primitive many of them believed that the Emperor went to Heaven once a week to hold a consultation with God.

What dismayed tourists most of all, however, was the venality and inefficiency of the supposedly educated bureaucracy. It was impossible to get a passport or a travel permit without days and sometimes weeks of delay. The grandest officials were not above accepting a bribe, and lesser officials, impressive in velvet collars and gold buttons bearing the official crest, were so poor that their feet were wrapped in rags. 'They have a dexterity in lying, a natural proneness to deceit which is revolting,' wrote Custine. 'In Russia fear replaces, that is, paralyses thought . . . it is not order but the veil of chaos.'

Yet all this was lost on Nicholas. He spent weeks bumping over the appalling roads by carriage in order to visit remote corners of his Empire. He was impressed by the effusive welcome of his officials and believed the flattery poured upon him. On his return to St Petersburg he invariably remarked: 'What a happy country!'

Although Nicholas was relentless in forcing obedience from his subjects, he was surprisingly lenient as far as members of his own family were concerned. His younger brother, the foul-mouthed Grand Duke Michael, married a German princess from Württemberg, who was noted for her grace and intelligence. This lady, the Grand Duchess Elena, patronized music and the arts and ran the most *avant garde* salon in St Petersburg. Although she invited to her parties many intellectuals who were under supervision by the Third Section, Nicholas smiled at her caprices and referred to her proudly as 'the scholar of the family'. In her drawing-room the cleverest men in Russia could talk freely, as the police were not allowed to file reports on guests in royal houses.

The Grand Duchess was much taken by the work of a new writer, Gogol, and helped to persuade Nicholas to allow his play, *The Government Inspector*, to be produced at the Alexandrinsky Theatre in 1836. As the normal repertoire of the Russian theatre consisted of stylized drama translated from the French and German, the actors were puzzled by the strange way in which he wrote. 'Can it be a comedy?' they whispered when the play was read to them. 'The servant talks like a servant and the

Nicholas and his brother Michael (*right*) were very close. As boys they played soldiers, as men they drilled them.

BELOW Colonnade of the Anichkov Palace, home of the heir-apparent, overlooking the Fontanka River

locksmith's wife is no more than a common peasant woman, right out of the market place . . . What good can Pushkin and Zhukovsky possibly find in it?'[6]

The première was packed out. The whole of the Imperial family, flanked by courtiers and high officials, was present. But, much to Gogol's anguish, the play was acted as an uproarious and vulgar farce. Nicholas I enjoyed himself hugely. He laughed loudly many times and when the performance came to an end said: 'Well it was quite a play! Everyone has got his due, I most of all.' Gogol was utterly crushed that his message had been lost. 'I had made up my mind to collect all the evil things I knew, and then make fun of them . . . This was the first work I planned in order to produce a good influence on society.'[7]

The Grand Duchess Elena continued her efforts to encourage new talent, and in 1839 was presented with an unexpected ally. The Heir Apparent, the Grand Duke Alexander, whom Custine described as 'the finest model of a prince I have ever seen', fell madly in love with the 15-year-old Princess Marie of Hesse-Darmstadt, and married her two years later. Marie was not only a beauty with an oval face and huge eyes but 'alarmingly intelligent'. Alexander could not bear to be parted from her even for a moment, and spent his mornings sitting on her bed opening official documents and discussing state affairs with her. 'Those were the years of untroubled family happiness for the Grand Duke,' wrote the Russian historian Tatishchev. 'There were almost daily gatherings at the young court . . . Nothing was formal or forced . . . There would be readings aloud, music, cards . . . The host and hostess charmed everybody by their manners. . . .'[8]

Marie and Elena became close friends and frequently ran their salons as a joint adventure. They had plenty to talk about, for although the stifling 1840s were a monument to Nicholas's repressive zeal, they heralded the birth of Russia's greatest literature. No doubt the censorship was sufficient to ignite a flame; and the flame was fanned tirelessly by the literary critic, Belinsky, who believed that a great work of art could affect society as profoundly as any political tract. 'To deny art the right of serving public interests,' he declared, 'means debasing it . . . and would make it . . . a plaything of lazy idlers.'[9]

Marie and Alexander read together Lermontov's *A Hero of Our Time*, Gogol's *Dead Souls*, Dostoevsky's *Poor People*, and, later, Turgenev's *Sportsman's Sketches*. Almost all these works told of the terrible conditions of the serfs. Alexander and Marie were ardent abolitionists; so was Elena; and so, oddly enough, was Nicholas himself. Possibly that was why he raised no objection to the new school of writers; although it is more probable that his pedantic mind found it impossible to grasp that a work of fiction, no matter how moving its portrayal of life, could ever constitute a threat to the real world.

Nevertheless, Nicholas frequently expressed his paternal concern for the defenceless people who formed the bulk of his population. 'They know they have no other protector but me,' he once told a friend. Two

Nicholas believed in the divine right of kings.

years after his succession he appointed General Kiselev 'Minister of Imperial Domains'. 'You know the custom of serfdom cannot remain in its present state,' he said. 'My Ministers do not understand my feelings; in my own family my brothers are against my plans . . . I ask your help . . . God will inspire and guide us.'[10]

Although Kiselev set up directorates, redistributed land, re-apportioned taxes, and finally, in 1841, recommended that peasants no longer should be sold separately, which Nicholas accepted and made law, the basic problem seemed insoluble. How could any fundamental changes be made without destroying the whole economic system? Nicholas repeatedly asked the landowners for their co-operation, but instead they dug in their toes. 'All these plans of emancipation,' one of his ministers, Count Nesselrode, wrote in 1843, 'can only lead to peasant riots and the ruin of the nobility.' 'The peasants,' Nicholas countered, 'cannot be considered as property and still less as a thing. The nobility must help me to change gradually the state of the serf so as to forestall a radical upheaval.' But the landowners increased their opposition, other problems intervened, and at the close of his reign Nicholas said resignedly: 'Three times I attacked serfdom; three times I had to stop; it was the hand of Providence.'

Russian literature and peasant reform were absorbing; but the Grand Duchess Marie was even more fascinated by the fierce battle between 'Westerners' and 'Slavophiles' that divided the philosophical world. Was Russia part of the Western society? Or did she embody a unique civilization that must be preserved from contamination and encouraged to develop independently? The Slavophiles, led by Khomyakov, the two Aksakov brothers and the two Kireyevsky brothers, claimed that a youthful force rooted in the peasant commune and the Orthodox Church was destined to supersede the West and become the world civilization of the future.

The Westerners, on the other hand, led by Alexander Herzen, the brilliant publicist, Belinsky, Turgenev and Bakunin, believed that Russia could only be regenerated through Western science, and such Western values as free thought, rationalism and individual liberty.

'The mistake of the Slavophiles,' jeered Herzen, 'lies in their imagining that Russia once had an individual culture . . .' He even attacked their right to call themselves intellectuals. 'Slavism or Russianism,' he wrote, 'not as a theory, not as a doctrine, but as a wounded national feeling, as an obscure tradition and a true instinct, has existed ever since Peter the Great cut off the first beard.' Although he poked fun at them he thought their movement dangerous for he saw in it 'fresh oil for annointing the Czar, the new chains laid upon thought, new subordination of conscience to the slavish Byzantine Church.'[11]

Neither of the two Grand Duchesses were averse to anointing the Tsar and embraced the Slavophile cause with fervour. Although in its original conception Slavophile thought sprang from a detestation of Nicholas's régime, gradually the doctrine moved to the right, until

Louis-Philippe, regarded by
Nicholas as a usurper

finally it was able to support Nicholas's tyranny with the slogan: 'Autocracy, Orthodoxy and Nationalism'.

Academic discussion was silenced, however, by the tremendous events of 1848. The revolutionary tidal-wave which rolled across Europe threatened to bring an end to the monarchical principle. Louis-Philippe was swept off the throne of France by what was known as 'the revolution of contempt'. The Emperor of Austria had to flee twice from his capital, and his chief minister, Metternich, who for twenty-four years had served as the policeman of Europe, was unseated. Italy, united in a league of princes, revolted against Habsburg rule under the leadership of a liberal pope; Hungary broke away from Austria and declared itself independent.

In Prussia things were almost as bad. The Empress Alexandra's brother, King Frederick William IV, abandoned his capital in the face of mounting insurrection which spread to many of the smaller German states. 'You have heard about Berlin,' wrote Zhukovsky, the Grand Duke's tutor, from Baden. 'Poor, poor King of Prussia . . . To think that the Prussian monarchy should have been bested by such brigands . . . One's only hope lies in Russia. Let her turn away from the West and stand firmly behind her stout high walls . . . Here, all authority and power are in the hands of a tattered mob . . . They call it "the will of the people" . . . Baden is a volcano, Frankfurt a seething cauldron . . . The entire stage is occupied by brigands in tatters, drunkards, escaped prisoners, and Jews, and the rightful rulers of Germany dare not make their voices heard. . . .'[12]

Only the thrones of Russia and England remained steady. Nicholas I closed the frontier 'to stop the deadly virus' and intervened effectively to bolster the tottering thrones of his neighbours. He warned the German revolutionaries that if they declared a republic he would send troops to restore the old Prussia. And when a federation of German states was formed at Frankfurt and offered the throne to the King of Prussia he warned his brother-in-law against dealing with an 'illegal authority'. Consequently Frederick William IV declined the gift, explaining haughtily that he did not wish 'to pick up a crown from the gutter'. But it was to the Habsburgs that Nicholas rendered the greatest service. As the Austrian Emperor was powerless to bring Hungary back into the fold, Nicholas sent a Russian army under Paskevich to surround the Hungarian insurrectionists at Vilagos and forced them to surrender.

Meanwhile the Emperor Nicholas was taking no chances in Russia. Those who looked upon the early 1840s as oppressive found the late 1840s suffocating. Universities were placed under police supervision, and chairs of metaphysics and moral philosophy were withdrawn. Foreign travel was prohibited; public meetings banned; and the works of Gogol, Turgenev and even Pushkin placed upon the Index. The censorship became rigorous to the point of comedy. A commission was appointed to examine music for conspiratorial cyphers; even the rows of dots in arithmetic books were scrutinized with magnifying glasses.

A political meeting in St Petersburg
in the 1840s

All 'Westerners' were suspected of entertaining socialist theories and pursued doggedly by the Third Section. In 1849 a sensation was created by the arrest of Michael Petrashevsky, a junior member of the Foreign Office, and twenty youthful friends who were in the habit of holding Friday evening discussion groups. Among those picked up were two writers, M. E. Saltykov and Feodor Dostoevsky. None of the accused had done anything but talk, except for a young man named Durov who had bought a second-hand printing press which stood in his house, still in its pristine wrappings. But the talk was subversive. It ranged from criticism of serfdom and the censorship to arguments in favour of abolishing church, state and private property. Dostoevsky had committed the crime of reading aloud Belinsky's famous letter to Gogol which, of course, was prohibited.

174

After languishing for some time in the fortress of St Peter and St Paul the group was subjected to a mass trial. All twenty were sentenced to death. The execution was scheduled to take place in the Semenovsky Parade Ground. Not until the young men were waiting to go before the firing squad was 'a gracious reprieve' read out, commuting the sentences to imprisonment. This little drama had been planned by Nicholas I as part of the punishment. Years later Dostoevsky immortalized the terrible scene in *The Idiot*. The first group of three was ordered to don the traditional death garments, and hoods were placed over their heads. 'My friend was eighth on the list,' wrote Dostoevsky through the lips of Prince Myshkin, 'and he would therefore be in the third group to be marched to the posts. The priest went to each of them with the cross. It seemed to him that he had only five minutes to live. He told me that those five minutes were like an eternity to him, riches beyond the dreams of avarice . . .' Suddenly a retreat sounded, the men were led back from the posts and the pardon read out. All were condemned to Siberia. Petrashevsky received life imprisonment, Dostoevsky four years hard labour followed by four years in the army as a private.

Not only Westerners but also Slavophiles were looked upon as potential traitors. Nicholas I suspected the Slavophiles of trying to draw into their orbit the Slavs of other lands; and this was a crime against the monarchical principle. Foreign Slavs owed allegiance to foreign kings. No matter how tiresome those kings might be, Russians who inflamed subjects to rebel against their royal rulers were traitors. Indeed, Nicholas had experienced too much trouble with the Poles to encourage any form of insurrection.

In the end the pieces were glued together. Russia remained steady; and out of the European chaos Nicholas managed to re-establish the older order. The King of Prussia gradually regained control, and the democratic federation broke up; the 18-year-old Franz Joseph imposed his authority on the Austro-Hungarian Empire; and Louis Napoleon finally proclaimed himself Emperor of the French. Nicholas had defeated the first flow of Western liberalism and stood supreme.

Even Queen Victoria referred to Nicholas as 'a mighty potentate'. In 1853 he was at the height of his fame and prestige. Alone he had stretched out his arm and rolled back the liberal tide. His omnipotence was undisputed, and foreign diplomats in St Petersburg stirred uneasily as they seemed to detect a new arrogance in his majestic bearing. The French Minister referred to him as 'this great spoiled child' and pondered on what the future might bring.

Nicholas was also concerned with the future. All his life he had identified himself with Catherine the Great, the grandmother who had died when he was only a year old. He longed to cover himself with new glory; to make the heritage she had passed down to him as brilliant as her own. True glory, to a Russian Emperor, however, meant an extension of territory.

Although Nicholas's armies were moving forward steadily in the Caucasus he regarded Asian success as nothing more than the maintenance of order in his own backyard. His mind therefore began to turn on Catherine's unfulfilled dream; Constantinople and the Straits.

Russia had already fought seven wars against Turkey, one of which had been instigated by Nicholas himself in 1828. It was not difficult to pick a new quarrel, but war was not what Nicholas wanted. He was looking for a bloodless victory, and this meant gaining the backing of Britain and France.

The Emperor's aims had a noble ring. He sent an envoy to Constantinople demanding Orthodox rights in the holy places, and the recognition of Russia as the protectress of all the Sultan's Christian Slavs. It is scarcely surprising that England doubted the sincerity of Nicholas's religious fervour. Palmerston called him 'a great big humbug'; and the

British Ambassador in Constantinople advised the Sultan to accept the first of Russia's demands, but flatly to reject the second. Russia as a protectress, he said, could only be 'the thin end of the wedge'.

Nicholas was furious at Britain's attitude. Nevertheless he continued to try to win her over, this time by suggesting that Britain and Russia divide Turkey's European possessions. He coined the phrase 'the Sick Man' and spoke of the patient dying and 'being on our hands'.

But this plan also was rejected. Nicholas had no conception of the antagonism his high-handedness had aroused among his brother monarchs; no idea how hostile European opinion had become to him. The Austrian minister wrote to Vienna from Paris that many people saw the Russian sovereign as a despot devoured by ambition, 'ready to cover his plans of conquest and invasion with the mantle of religion'.

Nicholas thrashed about, toying first with one idea, then another, and heaping invective on all those who would not let him have his way. He referred to 'those Turkish dogs', 'that cad Palmerston', 'that adventurer Napoleon III'. But when he wrote to Queen Victoria he was the soul of politeness. He extolled his own Christian virtuousness, and received the cutting reply that 'the personal qualifications of a sovereign are not enough in international transactions'.

Nicholas began to realize that he had walked into a trap, but felt he had gone too far to draw back. He consoled himself with the thought that whatever Britain and France might do he could count on Austria as a loyal ally. In July 1853 he sent troops into Moldavia and Wallachia, provinces tributary to Turkey but under the protection of Russia. Turkey demanded Nicholas's immediate withdrawal, and, when he refused, declared war on Russia. Russia retaliated by sinking the Turkish fleet off Sinope.

Nicholas was not surprised when he received an ultimatum from Britain and France insisting on the evacuation of the Russian army. But he was stunned to find the signature of the Austrian Emperor alongside the other two. He could scarcely believe that a country whose monarchy he had saved in 1848 was capable of such treachery. 'Are you really intending to make common cause with the Turk?' he wrote. 'Does your conscience permit you, the Apostolic Emperor, to do so? If this proves to be the case Russia must march alone . . . under the sacred symbol of the Cross.' No matter how worrying Nicholas found the situation, the Slavophiles were overjoyed, and hailed the conflict as a turning-point in the world's history. 'What is beginning,' exulted Tyutchev, 'is not a war, not a policy: it is the birth pains of a new world . . . it is the decisive battle of the West and Russia.' Alexander Herzen, on the other hand, inveighed from Italy against Russian officialdom, 'a dumb unit without a flag and without a name, the cord of slavery around its neck . . . with the insolent pretensions of the Byzantine Empire. . . .'[13]

Britain and France declared war on Russia in March 1854; and although the Austrian Emperor did not join them he promised his diplomatic support. In September the Allies landed at Eupatoria to the

A British cartoonist's view of the Russo–Turkish relationship. Nicholas is reputed to have advised the Sultan, in his own best interest, to become Orthodox.

north of Sebastopol. They routed the Russians on the banks of the Alma and probably could have entered Sebastopol if they had pressed on. Their hesitation gave the Russian army time to strengthen its defences, and the siege lasted eleven months.

The Crimean War revealed the terrible cracks in Nicholas's glossy Empire. Although both the opposing armies operated in a sea of corruption and inefficiency, the Russian shortcomings proved decisive. First, there were no railways in the Crimea; indeed, there was only six hundred miles of track in the whole of Russia; the newly built line linking Moscow with St Petersburg and the older track running from St Petersburg to Tsarskoye Selo fourteen miles away. The Crimean roads were deep with mud and strewn with the carcasses of horses who had died from thirst and hunger, and whose rotting bodies spread a wave of epidemic. Medical supplies were almost non-existent; there was mould in the biscuits, weevil in the salted meat; the water was tainted; the soldiers' boots were falling to pieces. Yet everyone whispered of the great profits made by the Army Commissariat whose duty it was to feed the army. As war correspondent, Count Leo Tolstoy sent home despatches praising the dogged courage of the Russian soldier in face of frightful conditions. Yet everyone felt that things could never be the same again. The omnipotent bureaucracy had been shown to have feet of clay, and the mystique of Russian power exposed as a fraud.

In spite of the heroic defence of Sebastopol (*below*) the Crimean War revealed that Nicholas's military colossus had feet of clay.

Meanwhile Nicholas remained in St Petersburg, drilling the Palace Guard and inspecting their boots and buttons. Whatever confidence he imparted, he knew in his heart that his system had failed. In February 1855 he caught cold on parade and neglected to take ordinary precautions. Pneumonia developed, and his German doctor, Martin Mandt, began to fear the worst. The Emperor lay in his bedroom in the Winter Palace, on his iron camp bed, covered by two blankets and a military greatcoat. The only light in the room was a flickering candle. The wind howled in the chimney and snowflakes fluttered against the windowpanes. The Emperor's breathing was laboured. 'Tell me, Mandt,' he said, 'am I going to die?' Mandt took Nicholas's left hand, caressed it, and answered with brutal frankness, 'Yes, Your Majesty.' 'What is wrong?' 'The lung is beginning to collapse, Your Majesty.'

Mandt explains in his memoirs that many years earlier the Emperor had made him promise to let him know when the end was near. He also says that if the last sacrament had not been administered in time the Russian doctors would have held him responsible. Nevertheless it is not surprising to learn that Nicholas did not linger long after this depressing conversation. A courier arrived with despatches, but the Emperor waved them aside. 'This has nothing more to do with me. Henceforth I belong wholly to God.'

The funeral procession of Nicholas I in St Petersburg (*below*). Before he died the Tsar told his son: 'I hand over to you my command, but unfortunately not in such order as I would wish.'

CHAPTER VII

Alexander II

Alexander II and his eldest son walking through one of the halls in the Winter Palace

THE CORONATION of Alexander II in August 1856 threw a glittering cloak over the humiliation of the Crimean defeat. The new Emperor had worked hard to extract Russia from her unenviable position, and peace finally had been signed in Paris the previous February, eleven months after the death of Nicholas. Although the terms were not as severe as Alexander feared, he was indignant at having to cede Bessarabia to Turkey, and enraged to learn that the Black Sea could no longer be used as a base for Russian warships. But Prince Gorchakov, the Emperor's plenipotentiary, thought that Russia had not fared too badly. 'Sir,' he said consolingly, 'it is good the treaty is signed. We could not afford to go on . . .'

Those who attended the coronation would have found it difficult to believe that the Russian treasury was empty. Byzantine Moscow, with its hundreds of domes and cupolas, was gilded and painted until it blazed in the summer sun. Not only were the great palaces redecorated, but dozens of ornate pavilions were especially built by rich provincial landowners to house their families for the occasion. For weeks the roads leading to Moscow were crowded with coaches and carts mainly carrying food and bedding as a million people from all over Russia poured in.

The coronation procession entered the Kremlin through the Gate of the Redeemer and stretched for over a mile, a ribbon of high-stepping horses, glittering breastplates, marching feet. All the important dignitaries of the Empire rode past; then came the Imperial servants in a riot of fancy dress; Masters of Ceremony carrying silver wands with double-headed eagles; major-domos, valets and runners; huntsmen from Gatchina; boatmen from Peterhof; choristers from Tsarskoye Selo; even eight 'Court Arabs' who were, in fact, huge Negroes from Abyssinia. Finally came the thirty golden coaches of the Romanov family, the occupants dressed in velvets and blazing with jewels. Even the steps of the carriages and the harnesses of the horses were studded with precious stones. The Dowager Empress Alexandra, the widow of Nicholas I, passed first in a carriage lined in garnet velvet, her coachman and *piqueurs* in livery to match, and her horses sporting plumes of white ostrich feathers. The Empress Marie rode in a more modest carriage of silver and blue, preceded by four Cossacks of the Household, and followed by a hundred nobles wearing ancient boyar dress.

And then came Alexander II in a wonderful glass and silver coach drawn by eight white horses. He sat alone, his head bare. As he neared the cathedral eight thousand bells from Moscow's sixteen hundred churches began to peal. Crowds of onlookers fell to their knees, not only as an act of homage but in a sudden impulse of thanksgiving, for there was no doubt that a new era had begun. The Coronation Manifesto had set the tone: pardons were granted to the Decembrist mutineers of 1825,

Smolny Cathedral, designed by Rastrelli for Elizabeth, was not completed until the reign of Nicholas I.

and to the Petrashevsky 'conspirators', of whom Dostoevsky was one. Altogether thirty clauses of amnesties were read out and remissions of fines and taxes granted on a sweeping scale.

Although the coronation ceremony lasted five hours the spectators were not bored, for it was so ill-rehearsed they had plenty to gossip about. The singing was glorious, but Count Bludov and Prince Shakovsky allowed the cushion bearing the Order of St Andrew to fall just as they were about to hand it to the Emperor; and when the four court ladies tried to fix the crown on the Empress's head it nearly clattered to the ground, saved only by the folds of her cloak. That night the Emperor gave an outdoor banquet for three hundred thousand of the populace. The sky was illuminated by fireworks; the fountains flowed with wine; and three regiments of infantry served the food. Scarves and coronation medals were distributed by the thousand.

Alexander II fulfilled the popular conception of what a prince should be. Tall and distinguished, with brilliant blue eyes and features which might have served as the cast for a bronze medallion he dazzled the crowds. The foreign plenipotentiaries, however, had their reservations; at heart all Romanovs were tyrannical and ambitious; there was no reason to think that Alexander would prove an exception.

Yet the new Emperor was very unlike his despotic father. He hated war and did not consider that military training held the key to life. Sensitive and imaginative, educated by the liberal poet Zhukovsky, he believed that he had been placed upon the throne to alleviate the lot of his people. 'History will pass judgment on you before the whole world,' Zhukovsky had told him, 'and it will remain long after you and I have left the earth. . . .'

Queen Victoria's emissary, Lord Granville, admitted that Alexander's manner was 'singularly gentle and pleasing' but pointed out that he was not noted for his strength of character. It was up to the new Emperor to prove himself. Alexander surprised everyone by a flurry of activity. He lifted the ban on travel, watered down the censorship, withdrew police control from the universities. For the first time students were allowed to hold meetings, form committees, publish their own magazine. In St Petersburg and Moscow lectures were thrown open to the public and were crowded with middle-aged bureaucrats, women and priests.

Far more sensational was Alexander's determination to free the peasants. Echoing his father's words he told the Moscow nobility that serfdom must be destroyed from above, 'otherwise it may well start from below'. 'Gentlemen,' he said, 'I ask you to consider my words and carry them back to the country.' Alexander's salvo marked the first shot in a fierce battle that was to rage for five years, for the landowners were just as determined to block emancipation now as before. They reiterated the arguments that it would bankrupt the country and produce anarchy.

Nevertheless Alexander refused to be intimidated. Despite his autocratic powers it took five years of the whiplash and the velvet glove, five years of arguing, pleading and threatening before emancipation

became a reality. At times the problems seemed insoluble. Were the forty million serfs to be freed without land or with land? With land, Alexander ruled. Who was to compensate the landowners? The State was not rich enough to buy all the land in Russia and give it away. And how were the peasants to farm with no capital? and who would own the crops and animals and houses in the period of transition? The public body set up by the Emperor was floundering hopelessly; so, early in 1857, he supplemented it by a Secret Committee. But at the end of the year this, too, had failed to make progress. Alexander summoned the head of the Committee and handed him a Rescript for immediate publication. The Rescript dealt with peasant steading. Peasants were to have the right to buy an agreed amount of land, their huts and animals, by payments stretching over the years.

Things still moved at a snail's pace. 'The business of liberation,' the Empress Marie wrote to her brother in December 1858, 'goes on very slowly on account of the passive resistance of those in high places, and of the great prevailing ignorance. There has been a good deal of dispute in various local governments about it, and the majority is against it everywhere. The situation is serious, and the Tsar's position very difficult, since people show little or no sympathy with him. But thank God he is not losing courage.'[1]

The ignorance to which Marie referred was spread evenly between landowners and peasants. The peasants visualized themselves freed from all rentals, living a life of ease, while the gentry saw nothing but chaos ahead. The writer Saltykov depicted the fear and misunderstanding in his great work *The Golovlev Family*. The landowner, Arina Golovleva, complains to her son:

> Now I have got thirty sluts in the maids' workroom alone. How can I keep them when nothing will be mine any longer? Now we have bread and meat, cabbages and potatoes, why, everything . . . But once freedom is granted, will it not be my business to run to the market every day and to pay hard cash for everything? An onion would not grow unless it is planted . . . How am I going to keep all these folk? Do I have to send them right away from the estate? What would happen to them? And what about myself? I can neither prepare food nor cook it nor serve it . . . I have not been bred to it.[2]

The Emancipation Manifesto was published in March 1861 and Russian Liberals hailed Alexander as the Tsar-Liberator. On the Sunday that the proclamation was read in all the churches of the Empire Alexander was in St Petersburg. In his memoirs General Cherbachev wrote:

> At two in the afternoon the Tsarina meadow was crowded . . . Suddenly the Emperor came riding back to the Palace from St Michael's Riding School. At once caps and hats flew in the air . . . and it seemed as though the very ground under our feet was shaking – so thundering were the cheers and the hurrahs . . . No pen could describe the rapture of the people as the Czar rode past . . . I am happy to have witnessed such a moment . . . it beggars all description.[3]

The Fortress and Cathedral of Saint Peter and Saint Paul were designed by Tressini, the first foreign architect to come to St Petersburg

The Dowager Empress Alexandra
(*right*). An estate was valued, not by its
acreage, but by the number of 'souls' on
it, and the landowners (*below*) are shown
gambling for souls, not money.

When the Emperor reached the Palace he went to the room of his little daughter, the Grand Duchess Marie, kissed her and said: 'This is the happiest day of my life.'

The word liberal was on every lip and soon became the most over-worked adjective in Russia. The greatest change was the 'reduced circumstances' of the secret police. They still existed, but not in such large numbers, and their social status was definitely on the wane.

> A servant at Klee's Hotel, in St Petersburg, where I was staying [wrote *The Times* correspondent] informed me that the room next to mine had been taken by a police agent, who watched my going out and my coming in, and made notes as to the friends who visited me. One of the waiters told me that there was another spy who concealed himself under the principal staircase, and followed me whenever I went out. He spoke of this man with more pity than contempt. 'People of this class,' he said, 'are in a very sad position now, sir. I remember the day when that sort of work was done by perfect gentlemen, who dined at the *table d'hôte* and ordered their red wine and their champagne like the best in the land. Now they crouch under staircases and are glad to get a glass of vodka.'[4]

The Golden Age was regarded as a permanency. Yet under the melting Russian ice the currents were dangerous. The peasants did not understand the responsibilities of ownership. They believed that the Tsar had made them a gift; now they were told they had to pay their own taxes for the first time, and, even worse, to make annual payments to redeem the land, far higher than their former rents. Although they were free men, their poverty had increased. It could not be what the Tsar intended. They accused government clerks of trying to rob them; riots broke out in many parts of the country; and peasants murdered landowners and officials alike. Hundreds of arrests were made, and soon the rejoicing had given way to sullen disenchantment.

Even more disturbing was the revolutionary trend that began to develop in the universities. Russia possessed only eight universities, with a total enrolment somewhere in the region of five thousand. Moscow University was the largest, with nearly a thousand students. St Petersburg next with seven hundred. Most of the students were the sons of petty bureaucrats and impoverished landowners. Many were desperately poor, living in wretched conditions, with barely enough food to keep them alive. 'Steady progress' was a high-sounding phrase, but did it mean anything except a life-time of waiting? Emancipation was a case in point, a paper victory which had done nothing to improve the lot of the peasant.

Worried by a future that seemed to offer only frustration and penury, they began to campaign for a revolutionary change in the whole system. They distributed Golden Charters to the peasants, and printed fly-leafs attacking the monarchy. Alexander lost his head, and despite the protests of the Empress, appointed Admiral Putyatin as Minister of Education. Putyatin was so reactionary that he suspected subversive tendencies in anyone who drank a glass of milk during Lent. He forbade student gatherings without the permission of the authorities and abolished the rule that allowed poor students to study free of charge.

These restrictions produced the inevitable result. In the autumn of 1861 several hundred students staged riots, first in St Petersburg, then in Moscow. The police dealt brutally with them, and dozens were seriously wounded. Alexander hurried back to the capital. He sacked the Admiral and appointed in his place the lenient Golovnin who rescinded his predecessor's rulings. 'There is nothing but a growing desire to tease authority', wrote the Slavophile Yury Samarin. The trouble arose, he claimed, because the new middle-class intelligentsia had no roots in the land; atheism and materialism came naturally to such lost souls. 'Their shrill voices frighten the Government which goes on making one concession after another.'[5]

Nevertheless it was difficult to know how to deal with the new generation. No matter whether the reins were tightened or loosened, rebellion continued. A 19-year-old student, Zaichnevsky, wrote a pamphlet entitled *Young Russia* advocating wholesale nationalization and 'a bloody, ruthless revolution'; another young man, Pisarev, preached that 'everything that could be smashed must be smashed' on the theory that what could not be smashed must be good. His doctrine swept the universities and became a craze. Young men let their hair grow long and wore unconventional dress; women cut their hair short and practised free love. Only science could be tolerated; all else, from social institutions to moral values, must be razed to the ground. In 1862 Ivan Turgenev published *Fathers and Sons*, which gave the creed of total destruction a name which found its way into history.

> 'What is Bazarov?' smiled Arkady. 'Would you like me to tell you, uncle, what he is exactly?'
> 'Please do, nephew.'
> 'He is a nihilist . . . a nihilist is a person who does not take any principle for granted, however much that principle may be revered.'

Turgenev's novel created a storm, for the author was attacked by both wings of opinion: the radicals, who claimed that he was ridiculing their cause by making Bazarov a caricature; the reactionaries, who claimed that he was encouraging revolutionary tendencies by allowing Bazarov to be so glamorous. Soon after publication of the book mysterious fires broke out in St Petersburg and began to spread, devouring whole streets of wooden tenements. No one knew how they had started but everyone blamed the followers of 'Bazarov'. 'I returned to St Petersburg,' wrote Turgenev, 'on the very day when Apraxyn Market was set ablaze and the word "nihilism" was on everybody's lips. A friend I met on the Nevsky said to me – "Look what your nihilists are doing! There is arson all over St Petersburg!" '[6]

As though troubles at home were not enough, the Polish people made a second attempt to free themselves from Russian domination. The rising was the most violent in Poland's long and tragic history. For a brief moment it looked as though England and France might interfere on the side of Warsaw, but in the end the Russians put down the insurrection at terrible cost. The brutalities on both sides were horrifying. The Poles butchered scores of Russian peasants including women and children. The Russians erected gibbets in the streets of Polish cities and conducted public hangings by the hundred. No one knows how many people died, but it was estimated that a hundred thousand Poles made the long march to Siberia. Russian nationalist feeling was so strong that for a while radical voices were silenced. Alexander Herzen championed the cause of the Poles from London. His paper, *The Bell*, which up till then had enjoyed an impressive readership in Russia, dropped in circulation from three thousand to five hundred and never recovered.

Alexander II, meanwhile, maintained the same magnificent court as his father. The season began in early December and lasted until Lent.

The Jordan staircase in the Winter Palace was so called because the sovereign descended it every year for the Blessing of the Waters on the Feast of the Epiphany.

Alexander II, the Tsar-Liberator

Alexander II toyed with the idea of giving Russia a constitution in 1860. 'I give you my imperial word,' he said, 'that, this very minute, at this very table, I would sign any constitution you like, if I felt that this would be for the good of Russia.'

The endless balls and banquets were almost a necessity, for in a sub-zero temperature St Petersburg presented a mournful picture. There were only four hours of daylight and icy winds kept the broad avenues empty of pedestrians. Paint peeled off the damp house fronts, street lamps were dim and flickering, and shops dispensed with window displays and barricaded themselves against the cold. The only touches of colour came from the spires and domes of the churches; the red shirts of the doorkeepers which showed above their sheepskin coats; the occasional flash of a brightly decorated sleigh, pulled by fast trotting horses and driven by a bearded and padded coachman.

> I had pictured St Petersburg to myself as a second Paris [wrote a British diplomat, Lord Frederick Hamilton], a city glittering with light and colour, but conceived on an infinitely more grandiose scale than the French capital. The atrociously uneven pavements, the general untidiness, the broad thoroughfares empty except for a lumbering cart or two, the absence of foot passengers and the low cotton-wool sky all gave the effect of unutterable dreariness. And this was the golden city of my dreams! This place of leprous fronted houses, of vast open spaces full of drifting snow flakes, and of immense emptiness. I never was so disappointed in my life.[7]

Behind those sombre, flaking façades, ladies lived like hot-house plants, only poking their noses out of doors for an hour a day. They did not rise until two in the afternoon, received guests at four, dined at six; went to the opera or played cards at eight. Almost every night there was a ball which went on until the small hours of the morning, with the guests still eating supper when ordinary people were having their breakfast.

What people liked best, however, were the small, intimate parties the Emperor gave known as *les Bals des Palmiers*. On these occasions a hundred palm trees, specially grown at Tsarskoye Selo, were brought to the Winter Palace in huge, horse-drawn boxes. Around each palm in its tub supper tables were built seating fifteen people. English guests invariably had a guilty feeling walking into the warm lighted palace and leaving their poor coachmen to wait all night in the freezing temperature.

> That terrible cold! [wrote Sir Horace Rumbold]. . . . In the squares that adjoin the Winter Palace are iron pavilions, like great bandstands, where immense fires are kept up all night long for the coachmen and the sledge drivers. In their long caftans wadded some three inches thick, and their fur capes and collars, they are really able to brave the cold with impunity, though one hears now and then of some poor wretch, with an overdose of vodka, having been frozen on his box. But once the Imperial threshold has been passed, it is the contrast with the cruelly bleak scene without that beggars all description . . . The effect of the immense room is that of a tropical grove in some gorgeous fairy scene. . . .[8]

At the *Bals des Palmiers* it was Alexander's custom to make the rounds of the tables as soon as his guests were seated. As he approached, the occupants rose. He would say a few words to one or two of them, pick up a piece of bread or fruit and lift a glass of champagne to his lips.

This was done in order that his guests might say that he had eaten and drunk with them.

Alexander was not only noted for his graciousness as a host but was greatly admired for his elegance. At a Court Ball in 1865, when he was 47, the French writer, Théophile Gautier, described his appearance as nothing short of sensational. He 'wore a white tunic reaching half way down his thighs, frogged with gold and trimmed at the neck, wrists and hem with blue Siberian fox, the breast being plastered with orders. Clinging sky-blue trousers sheathed his legs, and ended in close-fitting top-boots.'[9]

Alexander certainly was the most glamorous of all the European sovereigns; and many people regarded him as the most interesting. Despite the savage reprisals of his army against the Polish mutineers he was still hailed as the Tsar-Liberator, the first true reforming ruler that Russia had produced. In 1863 he had introduced a new Education Act; and in 1864 he had given the country local self-government in the form of *zemstva*, an undertaking second in importance only to emancipation. That same year he had abolished corporal punishment, instituted public trials before juries, and approved the reconstruction of the judiciary. Recently he had instructed the War Ministry to work out a scheme which would allow privates to rise by merit to officer rank.

Innovations as well as reforms had been instituted. For the first time Russia had a national budget; thousands of miles of new railway track were being built; and permission had been granted for the opening of private banks. Even the arts had been given a tonic. The St Petersburg Conservatory of Music had been founded in 1862 by the Grand Duchess Elena, and a Moscow Conservatory was under construction.

The gods were smiling on Alexander II; yet, ironically, the Golden Age of Russian liberalism was almost at a close. The curtain began to drop in 1866 when a student, who had been dismissed from St Petersburg University, nearly succeeded in assassinating the Emperor. Alexander was returning to his carriage from a walk in the Winter Gardens. A small group of sightseers had collected, among them a peasant from Kostromo on the Volga, who was working in the capital as a hatter's apprentice. He was thrilled to see the Emperor at such close quarters but was disturbed by a youth who pushed roughly past him; a moment later the young man raised his arm and the apprentice saw the glint of a revolver. He struck at the man's hand, the bullet went wild and embedded itself in the pavement. After a moment of stunned silence spectators grabbed the would-be assassin, who made no attempt to escape, and handed him over to the police.

When word went round that a hatter's apprentice had saved the Emperor's life the crowd, which had swelled to some hundreds, lifted the hero shoulder-high. The nobility fêted him and the Emperor ennobled him, giving him a diamond ring and a pension large enough to keep him in luxury for the rest of his life. (The story had a disappointing end, however, for the apprentice took such a fancy to French brandy,

In 1867, while he was on a visit to Paris, yet another attempt was made on the Tsar's life.

which he had never drunk before, that he became an addict, and a few years later died of drink.)

The capital was stunned by the attempt on the Emperor's life. When the deed became known huge crowds lined the streets leading to the Winter Palace, and many people wept as Alexander passed. Although the police interrogated the Emperor's assailant for weeks, hoping to uncover a conspiracy, no accomplice came to light. The young man explained that he had tried to kill the Tsar in order to draw attention to the plight of the peasants; in the end this explanation had to be accepted and the verdict was 'unbalance of mind'.

Tragically, the student's bullet shattered Alexander's confidence in the path he was pursuing. He became convinced that something must be wrong with the educational system. A few weeks later he appointed as Minister of Education the hated reactionary, D. A. Tolstoy; and the following month he issued a Rescript making it clear that the curricula of schools and universities would be altered.

193

Providence has willed to reveal before the eyes of Russia what consequences we may expect from aspirations and ideas which arrogantly encroach upon everything sacred . . . My attention is now turned to the education of youth. I have given instructions that education must be directed to respect the spirit of religious truth, the right of property, the fundamental principles of public order; and that in all schools the open and secret teaching of those destructive conceptions which are hostile to the moral and material well-being of the people will be forbidden.[10]

The 'materialistic' approach thrown up by nihilism and other revolutionary creeds, it was believed, sprang from the popularization of natural science. Tolstoy decided therefore to use the classics to counteract the trend. Gradually the study of all subjects which stimulated independent thought, such as history, science, modern languages, and even Russian, were curtailed; instead the students were obliged to spend their time on Latin, Greek, pure mathematics and Church Slavonic. Discipline was the key-note.

The University of St Petersburg on the banks of the Neva

As a result thousands of frustrated undergraduates went abroad to Geneva and Zurich to sit at the feet of professional agitators. Some of them listened to Colonel Lavrov, a 40-year-old retired army officer who could scarcely be described as an extremist for he preached evolution rather than revolution. He encouraged the young to move into the villages and to try and win the confidence of the *muzhik*. This was easier said than done. Although many students dressed themselves in tattered clothes, ate nothing but black bread, and adopted the local idiom, the peasants regarded them as freaks. The young people called themselves *narodniki* (those who go to the people) and tried to explain that the future of Russia lay in the village commune; if the peasants would join the struggle one day the Empire would be ruled, not by a Tsar, but by the men who tilled the soil. The peasants listened with narrowed eyes, then denounced the students to the police. Hundreds of *narodniki* were brought to the trial in an area stretching over thirty-seven provinces.

Far more exciting was the teaching of the fiery, aristocratic anarchist, Michael Bakunin, who had moved to Geneva and now published a paper, *The Cause of the People*. Bakunin advocated straight revolution, preaching that all forms of compulsion were evil and that the chief abomination was the State. Like the Nihilists, he argued that sentiment had no place in the new world, and advocated the abolition of marriage, religion and maternal ties. The only things that mattered were those that were useful.

In 1871 Alexis Tolstoy wrote a ballad ridiculing this theme. A bride and groom are strolling in a lovely garden; the groom sighs and says:

> 'Soon the flowers will be uprooted for turnips and the nightingales driven away because of their uselessness.'
>
> 'But this place is ours,' protests the bride. 'What people are wicked enough to spoil what does not belong to them?'
>
> 'Ah, my love! they think that everything is theirs to destroy. They are out to ruin everything for the sake of the future, and they call such destruction progress.'
>
> 'You must be joking, my love, but if such people do exist, they should be shut up in a madhouse ...'
>
> The groom shakes his head, 'You would need too big an asylum for that, my dear one ...'

For a short while a new star in the revolutionary firmament eclipsed Bakunin. He was a 23-year-old schoolteacher named Nechayev whose dazzling personality had a hypnotic effect on people. He preached that the revolution could only be achieved by iron discipline and conspiracy based on a hitherto undreamed-of ruthlessness. He was, in fact, the first Bolshevik. His *Revolutionary Catechism*, which was studied by Lenin many years later, was a chilling document. 'The revolutionary is a dedicated man ... For him, morality is everything which contributes to the triumph of the revolution. Immoral and criminal is everything that stands in the way.'

Nechayev built up his movement on a system of cells. Groups of five were linked together by one person in each group. He created a cell at Moscow University, where he worked as a lecturer. He insisted on absolute obedience, and used any means to gain control over his fellow conspirators, even stealing their letters and blackmailing them. When a student named Ivanov, a cell member, refused to carry out one of his orders Nechayev was so enraged that he terrorized the other members into killing him.

The murder took place in a grotto in the college grounds. Five days later the corpse was discovered, and four of the accomplices arrested. One by one members of Nechayev's network, known as 'The Tribunal of the People', were picked up; but Nechayev himself escaped to Switzerland. The trial of the *Nechayevtsy*, 84 people in all, took place in July 1871. The *Revolutionary Catechism* was read in court, and people talked of the mysterious 'Nechayev monster'.

A year later Nechayev was arrested in Zurich and sent back to Russia. He was imprisoned in the fortress of St Peter and St Paul and died ten years later. He lives in Dostoevsky's novel, *The Possessed*.

Alexander's public anxieties were increased by the complexities of his private life. He had fallen desperately in love with the Princess Catherine Dolgoruky, a beauty with an ivory skin and chestnut hair, and a member of one of the most distinguished families in Russia. Alexander had been a close friend of Catherine's father; and when the latter died bankrupt he had undertaken the education of the Dolgoruky children. He had sent the boys to military academies and the girls to the Smolny Institute in St Petersburg, a finishing school founded by Catherine the Great.

When the 18-year-old Princess left the Smolny Institute in 1865 Alexander declared his passion for her. She resisted him for over a year, but when the attempt was made on his life she was shocked into the realization that she returned his love. Catherine was an unusual courtesan for she shunned society and refused to allow herself to be used by ambitious place-seekers. Alexander provided her with houses in St Petersburg, Peterhof, and Tsarskoye Selo.

Inevitably the Empress heard about the affair, but she did not attach any great importance to it, perhaps because infidelity was part of the Romanov tradition. Besides, she was not at all well, suffering from what the doctors described as a delicate chest. She took very little part in society and was forced to spend her winters abroad in a warm climate. Eventually Alexander built a palace for her at Livadia, near Yalta, in the Crimea. Marie's isolation was made all the more acute in 1865 when her favourite son, the heir to the throne, the Grand Duke Nicholas, suddenly died of tuberculosis of the spine. The new heir, Alexander, had none of his brother's charm or intellect, but Nicholas's fiancée, the Princess Dagmar of Denmark, a sister of the Princess of Wales, dutifully transferred her affection to him.

Not until 1872, when the Empress learned that the Princess Dolgoruky had given birth to a son, did she take her husband's infatuation

Smolny Cathedral (*right*), designed by Rastrelli for Elizabeth, was part of a monastic complex to which Catherine II added her 'Institute for Daughters of the Nobility' based on Madame de Maintenon's St Cyr.

BELOW The Tsarevich whose death in 1865 the Tsar felt bitterly as a 'dreadful blow from the Almighty'.

The Empress Marie (*opposite*) had to bear the humiliation of loving a husband who, as all the world knew, had transferred his affection to Princess Catherine Dolgoruky (*above*).

seriously. The story leaked out, and everyone in the capital from the highest noble to the lowest peddler speculated on the nuances of the family relationships. The following year the Princess had a second child, a daughter. The Emperor, very secretly, sent a *ukaz* to the Senate whereby the children were given the name and rank of Prince and Princess Yurievsky.

At last the Empress was forced to acknowledge that this was no ordinary liaison. She had lost not only a lover, but a confidante, for although Alexander treated her with consideration he no longer sought her advice. She still adored her husband and was bitterly hurt. She confided to her brother that she could forgive the insult to the Empress but not the cruelty to the wife.

Marie had always been religious, but now she embraced the Church with an almost frenzied fervour, attending mass twice, sometimes three times, a day. In 1872 her cup seemed to overflow, for her doctors told her that she was suffering from tuberculosis and had only a few years to live. Alexander was deeply solicitous, but nothing could diminish his love for Catherine; and nothing could mend Marie's broken heart.

The Empress's children were outraged by their father's callous behaviour. The five sons, led by the Grand Duke Alexander, refused to hide their disapproval and were cold and remote when the Emperor tried to talk to them. Only his daughter, the 16-year-old Marie, refused to take sides. She worshipped her father and could not find it in her heart to blame him for anything.

The Emperor became so dependent on this young girl that he could not bear the thought of her marrying and living far away from Russia. When in the winter of 1872 he received overtures from Queen Victoria, on behalf of her son, Alfred, Duke of Edinburgh, he dismissed them instantly. Victoria was furious, for although she did not relish the match herself she did not like to be snubbed. No English prince had ever married a Romanov, and the Queen saw drawbacks in the Orthodox religion and the Russian upbringing. On the other hand England regarded Russia as her most formidable enemy, and her ministers told her that the union might prove helpful in easing the tension, if only by putting the monarchs into correspondence with one another.

At that very moment the two countries were quarrelling over a frontier. Ever since the Crimean War Russian troops had been advancing in Central Asia. After completing the conquest of the Caucasus in 1859 they moved forward in the area between Siberia in the north and Persia, Afghanistan and India in the south. One by one they had subdued and annexed the decadent Turcoman and Tartar states. Turkestan was added to the Russian Empire in 1865; Bokhara fell in 1866; Khiva and Kokand in the 1870s.

In 1872 England and Russia were disputing the Afghan frontier and British newspapers were shrilly pointing out the dangers to India. Lord Augustus Loftus felt that Alexander II was not to blame.

Where an enormous standing army is maintained [he wrote] it is necessary to find employment for it. Every officer is anxious to gain the St George or some such decoration . . . When a system of conquests set in, as in Central Asia, one acquisition of territory leads to another and the difficulty is where to stop . . . Fresh conquests of territory are laid at the Czar's feet, gained by the prowess and blood of his troops. He cannot refuse them without offending his army; and troops so far distant . . . are difficult to restrain.[11]

Queen Victoria accepted this explanation with reservations, as she had always been suspicious of Russian ambition. Nevertheless, as the Duke of Edinburgh was eager to marry the Grand Duchess, and her ministers approved the match, she swallowed her pride and kept the offer open. Although the Russian Empress looked about for another husband for Marie she could not find one that her daughter would accept. Alexander protested that Britain was hostile to Russian aspirations, and that Marie would be unhappy in such a cold, unfriendly atmosphere. However, in July 1873 he finally gave his consent and the couple were married in January of the following year.

Alexander was right to be worried about the political situation. Within three years of his daughter's wedding a storm had blown up that nearly brought Britain and Russia to war.

It began in the early 1870s, when the gentle philosophy of the Slavophiles suddenly blossomed into the passion flower of Panslavism. The new creed had sprung into being with Bismarck's unification of Germany. If Prussia could forge all the German states and all the German peoples into a mighty Empire why should Russia not gather under her wing all the Slavs in European Turkey and the Balkans?

Two books appeared in 1870 and 1871 which not only put forward this thesis but triggered off a wave of militarism. One was a ninety-eight-page brochure written by General Fadeyev, the son of a former governor of Saratov; the other, *Russia and Europe*, a long treatise by Nicholas Danilevsky, a civil servant. Both books glorified war and held up as a goal 'a Slavic Federation with Russia at its head, with its capital in Constantinople'. The idea was dangerous, as it appealed to everyone. The Empress saw it as a religious crusade; a chance to alleviate the lot of the Balkan Christians; to bring back the great church of Santa Sophia to its rightful Orthodoxy and re-establish Constantinople as the greatest city in Christendom. The Heir Apparent, on the other hand, was mainly concerned with Russia's age-old dream of the opening of the Straits to Russian ships, and the acquisition of thousands of square miles of new territory.

A revolt in the Turkish province of Herzegovina in the summer of 1875 set the first sparks flying; a year later Serbia declared war on Turkey, and thousands of Russian volunteers poured into Belgrade. Alexander was appalled by the strength of the feeling among the nobility. Unless it was checked it would lead Russia to war; and war was something he abhorred.

Alexander and his only daughter Marie Alexandrovna (*above*). After the magnificent marriage ceremony in the Winter Palace, the Emperor sadly remarked: 'It is for her happiness, but the light of my life has gone out.'

'You ought to control your subjects,' the German Emperor bluntly told his nephew. Yet Alexander found himself unable to restrain even the activities of his own family. The Empress accepted the Presidency of the Red Cross and began to equip hospital trains at her own expense, and the Grand Duke Alexander was openly encouraging men in the Guards Regiments to volunteer by granting them long leave and assuring them of places upon their return. Court ladies were standing at street corners jingling money boxes, and in Moscow the Slav tricolour, red, white and blue, fluttered from many of the buildings. Altogether about eight hundred officers and five thousand men volunteered. Crowds collected at the stations and waved them off like heroes. But not everyone was caught in the frenzy. Prince Vyazemsky (whose father had helped to murder Paul I) regarded the frenzy as nothing short of madness. 'We have begun to imagine ourselves Slavs rather than Russians . . . We irritate Turkey, send first aid to "brother Serbs", beat the drum, drink champagne to speed off the volunteers, and shout ourselves hoarse about nothing . . . Please keep this letter. I would like future generations to know that there were a few sober Russian voices in an hour of drunkenness.'[12]

Soon after the outbreak of the Serbian war stories began to filter into the European press of an uprising in Bulgaria that had been put down by terrible Turkish reprisals. The British sent a diplomat to investigate, and on 19 September 1876 he described the retaliation of the Turks as 'the most heinous crime of the century', and spoke of 'a soil soaked and reeking with blood, an air tainted with every imaginable deed of crime and shame'. He put the number of villages destroyed at sixty, the number of people slaughtered at twelve thousand.

The British Leader of the Opposition, Mr Gladstone, took up the cause with furious vigour. He referred to 'the unspeakable Turk' and claimed that 'there is not a criminal in a European gaol, there is not a cannibal in the South Sea Islands, whose imagination would not arise

Alexander's brother, Grand Duke Constantine (*right*) was a radical reformer who incurred great odium in court circles by remarking that the Russian nobility were not even worth spitting upon.

and overboil at the recital of that which has been done.' He called for Europe to rise up and throw the Turks, bag and baggage, out of Bulgaria.

Although Disraeli, not Gladstone, was Prime Minister, the Russians took heart at the popular indignation. Britain was the only country they had to fear in their march to Constantinople. Perhaps a war against Turkey could remain an isolated affair; perhaps now was the time to strike.

Alexander meanwhile was at Livadia in the Crimea. Under a deep blue sky, surrounded by vineyards and orangeries, he listened to a ceaseless flow of Panslav talk. The Empress and her ladies fluttered about burning candles, referring tirelessly to Russia's holy mission. The Grand Duke Alexander and the Grand Duke Nicholas, the Emperor's brother, arrived from St Petersburg, and talked about Constantinople as Russia's rightful capital.

A post-war commission presided over by the Tsarevich revealed embezzlement on the part of the Grand Duke Nicholas (*right*) and the heir never spoke to his uncle again.

WORKING THE POINTS.

Alexander began to weaken. For two years he had swum against the currents; now he seemed to have no more strength. In November 1876 the Serbs were routed by the Turks, and the clamour became an uproar. The Six Powers agreed to a conference in Constantinople; and Lord Beaconsfield made a speech in London referring to the 'inviability of Turkish possessions'. But no one was in a mood to bother about Britain any more. The Emperor ordered partial mobilization.

No doubt Alexander hoped that the Constantinople Conference would provide a peaceful solution. The Powers delivered a Protocol to the Sultan on 9 April 1877, demanding autonomy for Bosnia, Herzegovina and Bulgaria; but the Sublime Porte politely turned it down. A fortnight later the Emperor announced that his patience was exhausted and declared war on Turkey.

The conflict lasted for nine months and took a terrible toll of life. In one battle alone the Russians lost twenty-five thousand men without gaining an inch of ground. 'We live among blood and corpses,' wrote the Emperor's nephew from the front, 'and see such horrible things that all our officers are disgusted with the war and would much rather go home.'

Although the Russian Commander-in-Chief, Alexander's brother, the Grand Duke Nicholas, was accused of hopeless inefficiency, although the Russian army seemed as badly organized and as corrupt as in the days of the Crimea, the Russians finally reached Adrianople, sixty miles from Constantinople. The British Foreign Office was not unduly alarmed as Alexander had assured the powers that geographical changes would be submitted to a European Congress.

But Queen Victoria became hysterical. For months she had been trying to instil into her Cabinet a sense of danger. Turkey was not the main issue, she insisted. 'It is the question of Russian or British supremacy in the world.' At one moment she became so angry that she threatened to abdicate. 'If England is to kiss Russia's feet,' she wrote to Mr Disraeli, 'the Queen will not be a party to the humiliation of England and will lay down the Crown.' Now she telegraphed to Alexander II urging him to stop the fighting; but he replied coldly: 'The Commander-in-Chief of my armies . . . knows the conditions on which a suspension of hostilities can be agreed.' 'Oh! If the Queen were a man,' she wrote to Lord Beaconsfield, 'she would like to go and give those horrid Russians whose word one cannot trust such a beating.' 'Oh! that Englishmen were now what they were,' she wrote to her daughter, adding with forced confidence, 'but we shall yet assert our rights – our position – and "Britons will never be slaves" will yet be our Motto.'[13]

The Queen knew her England, for suddenly the Cabinet took fright and instructed Admiral Hornby to take his six ironclads, stationed in Besika Bay, through the Dardanelles, to remind Russia that Britain wished to be consulted about an armistice. After some delay the ships steamed to the Island of Prinkipo in the Sea of Marmora and dropped anchor within sight of Constantinople.

The presence of the British Navy alarmed the Grand Duke Nicholas,

The Anglo-Russian confrontation, with Bismarck controlling the points.

for he knew that his army was in no condition to fight a war with England. Although Russian opinion clamoured for Constantinople he refused to occupy the city unless he was ordered categorically to do so by the Emperor. But the Emperor was also apprehensive and could not bring himself to give decisive commands. He sent several vague telegrams about capturing the heights or moving into the capital 'by some means or other'. The Grand Duke occupied San Stefano, six miles from Constantinople, and reported that it was 'a suburb of Constantinople'.

Meanwhile the Emperor's emissary, Count Ignatiev, had succeeded in wringing from Turkey a treaty triumphant for Russia. The agreement created a huge swollen Bulgaria that stretched from the Aegean Sea to Albania and virtually placed the whole of the Balkans under Russian control. Prince Gorchakov added fuel to the fire by saying airily that although Russia would attend a congress, she must 'reserve the liberty of accepting or not accepting a discussion of the questions raised'.

Suddenly Britain woke up. Votes of credit went whistling through Parliament; Indian troops were ordered to Malta; reservists called to the colours. Mr Gladstone was hooted in the streets and the music halls rang with the ditty:

> *We don't want to fight*
> *But by jingo if we do*
> *We've got the ships, we've got the men*
> *We've got the money too.*

The song was only too true. Russia, on the other hand, had an empty treasury and an exhausted army.

The Treaty that was hammered out at the Congress of Berlin was an accurate reflection of the relative strength of the two powers. Although Russia recovered the parts of Bessarabia lost after the Crimean War, although she was given indirect control of half of Bulgaria (the other part set up as an independent state), she had been denied access to the Mediterranean which she hoped to reach through Bulgaria's back door. And that, as Disraeli crowed to Queen Victoria, was the real object of the late war. 'Prince Gorchakov says,' he added, 'we have sacrificed 100,000 picked soldiers and 100 millions of money for nothing.'[14]

This view was shared by every Panslavist in Russia who had dreamed of the double-headed eagle spreading its wings to the Mediterranean.

Alexander received all the blame for Russia's humiliation. The upper class, the very prop of his throne, led by the Panslavists so insistent for war, accused him of weakness and indecision. He should have dismissed the Grand Duke Nicholas as Commander-in-Chief; he should have seized Constantinople from under the nose of the British; he should have sent more adroit diplomats to the Berlin Congress. Tired and haggard, and suffering from asthma, the Emperor looked far older than his 60 years. Catherine was his consolation, but even she came in for abuse. She had become such an accomplished *amoureuse*, people said, that she had sapped her lover of all vitality.

The revolutionaries were quick to take advantage of the general malaise. The shot that rang out early in 1878, fired by a young girl, Vera Zasulich, heralded a new age of terror. Vera walked into the office of Trepov, Governor-General of St Petersburg, took a revolver from her bag, and pulled the trigger. She was such a bad shot that the bullet wounded the Governor but did not kill him. Vera made no attempt to escape and when asked why she had committed the crime she replied that Trepov had ordered a political prisoner, Bogolubov, to be flogged; and flogging was no longer permitted.

The whole of St Petersburg society flocked to the trial. The verdict was believed to be a foregone conclusion; but the jury did not like Trepov, and to everyone's astonishment found Vera not guilty. The people waiting outside could scarcely believe their eyes when she walked into the sunshine. There was a scuffle; shots were fired; but Vera was spirited away and managed to escape to England.

Count Leo Tolstoy, whose *War and Peace* had made him the most celebrated author in Russia, was puzzled by the public's approval of lawlessness.

> It is open war [he wrote to his aunt on 6 April 1878]. Everyone of those who acquitted the assassin and everyone of those who approved her acquittal know full well that for their own personal safety a murderer must not be allowed to go unpunished; but in their eyes the question is not who is right but who in the long run, will prove the strongest . . . Since reading the account of the trial and all this commotion about it, I can think of nothing else.

The next day he wrote to a friend:

> The Zasulich business is no joking matter. This madness, this idiotic capriciousness that has suddenly seized hold of people is significant. These are the first signs of something not yet clear to us. But it is serious. The Slavophil madness was the precursor of war, and I am inclined to think that this madness is the precursor of revolution.[15]

Count Leo Tolstoy

Tolstoy was right, although the revolution took the form of a long and sporadic guerrilla warfare. General Mezentsev, the head of the St Petersburg police, was stabbed to death outside his office in broad daylight; and another attempt was made on the life of the Emperor. A schoolmaster fired four shots as Alexander was walking along the quai but missed each time. The Emperor brushed the incident aside and still refused to have a bodyguard; but when the Princess Dolgoruky received letters threatening herself and her children, he was thrown into such a panic he could neither sleep nor work until she consented to move into the safety of the Winter Palace. The Empress Marie was too ill to care. She was having such difficulty in breathing that her rooms were artificially impregnated with oxygen released from gas cylinders.

The Emperor's ministers begged him to appoint six governors with the power to put the country on an emergency footing. He agreed, and the new men were given the power to arrest on suspicion. All political cases would in future be tried by court martial; and those condemned to death would have no right of appeal. The sale of fire-arms was forbidden; houses could be searched without warrants; and all university towns were subject to strict regulations. Almost every one of Alexander's early reforms was suspended.

Nevertheless the terrorism grew. A small organization called 'Will of the People', an offshoot of 'Land and Liberty',* which once had contented itself with village propaganda, was formed for the express purpose of assassinating the Emperor. Although the young people who joined the group refused to call themselves nihilists their outlook was not wholly dissimilar. They had no plan for the future; their job was to destroy, and by destroying create a vacuum that could be filled by a new utopia. Yet they at least knew what they did not want. Constitutionalism, they declared, was old-fashioned. Only some form of socialism would do which allowed the peasants a direct voice in governing the nation. Some members favoured transforming the Empire into a 'Federation of Village Communes'.

'Will of the People' was led by an unsmiling fanatic, Zhelyabov, the son of a peasant, and a beautiful girl, Sophia Perovskaya, the daughter of an ex-Governor of St Petersburg, who eventually became his mistress. The group met in June 1879, under the very nose of the police, to plan their tactics. They voted to abjure such old-fashioned weapons as revolvers and knives and to make use of the military techniques of the Russo-Turkish war. Mines and bombs would be their means of destruction.

*Some members referred to Land and Liberty as the 'Social Revolutionary Party'.

The scene near Moscow after the attempt to blow up the Imperial train

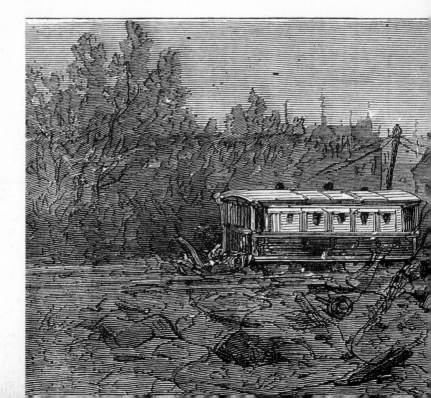

As Alexander was in the Crimea they worked out a scheme to blow up his train on its homeward journey. The staff work was excellent and when the Imperial train pulled into Kursky station at Moscow a terrific explosion blew the engine and three coaches off the track. Alexander, however, was safely in the Krèmlin. When the Imperial family travelled two trains were used; one for the personnel, the other for the baggage. On this occasion the baggage train, which usually preceded the one in which the Emperor travelled, had been delayed at Kharkov, owing to a fault in the engine, and had taken second place; and that was the train that had been mined. When the Emperor heard the news he said bitterly, 'Am I such a wild animal that I must be hounded to death?'

The terrorists' answer was unequivocal; and a few months later an even more daring attempt was made, this time on the Winter Palace itself. Sophia learned that repairs were being done in the basement of the palace; and one of the group, a trained carpenter, managed to enroll for the work. Each day he carried dynamite charges in his tool chest, placing them at a spot beneath the dining-room. The fact that there was an intervening floor, used as a guard room, did not worry anyone.

The Imperial family were unpunctual for dinner on the night of the attempt, as a guest from Berlin was late in arriving. Dinner, therefore, was delayed half an hour, something that had not happened for years. Just as the family was about to leave the drawing-room there was a deafening roar that could be heard all over the capital. The walls shook, and when the Emperor ran into the hall it was filled with smoke and dust. The dining-room was completely demolished; and in the room directly below eleven men of the Finnish Guard lay dead and thirty wounded. The Emperor rushed to Catherine's apartment but she was unscathed. He next went to Marie's apartment, but the Empress

had in fact been given sedatives and had not woken up.

The whole of Russia was horrified to learn that the terrorists were so all-pervasive that they even could penetrate the Winter Palace. Something had to be done; but Alexander II was too sick at heart to take matters into his own hands. Instead, he appointed General Loris-Melikov to take charge of the country and put it on a war footing.

The General was a happy choice. An Armenian by birth, he was both a liberal and a man of action. He called his régime 'a dictatorship of the heart' and immediately reversed many of the stringent and recently imposed regulations. He then seconded the cleverest intelligence officers in the army to serve in the police department. The terrorists were few in number but every one of them must be tracked to ground.

He sent the Emperor a paper analysing his ideas. The Emperor's reforms of the 1860s, he said, had coincided with the rise of Socialism, and this prompted Russian officials to withdraw the freedoms they had granted. If liberal concessions had been strengthened, not curtailed, '. . . new shoots would have thrust their roots . . . and the coming struggle with Socialism would have presented no danger to the state.' He then sacked three or four of the Tsar's most reactionary ministers, relaxed the censorship, and restored authority to the *zemstva*.

About this time the poor, abandoned Empress died; and a month later Alexander stunned his Court Chamberlain, Count Alderberg, by informing him that he planned to marry the Princess Dolgoruky the following week. The ceremony would take place at Tsarskoye Selo, in the utmost secrecy. Alderberg protested that the heir to the Throne was away, and asked if it would not be advisable to wait until his return. Alexander was adamant. 'I should certainly not have married again before the end of the year's mourning,' he explained to his sister Olga, 'if the times in which we live had not been so critical and if I had not every day to run the risk that a fresh attack would successfully put an end to my life. I am concerned therefore to secure as soon as possible the future of the being who has lived only for me during the past fourteen years, as well as the . . . children she has borne me.'[16]

The Emperor forced his sons and their wives to dine with himself and the Princess Yurievsky, as she was now called, but the ladies refused to respond to the beautiful Catherine, maintaining an icy reserve. On the way home the wife of the Emperor's brother, Michael, lashed out at her husband: 'No matter what you say or do,' she blazed, 'I shall never recognize that scheming adventuress. I hate her. She is despicable. Imagine her daring to call your brother "Sasha" in the presence of all the members of the Imperial family.'[17]

Meanwhile the terrorists had sprung to life again, stung into action, oddly enough, by the *zemstvo* of Tver, the most liberal organization in Russia. This group declared that Loris-Melikov had justified the hopes of the country by creating a new atmosphere between people and government and that 'a happy future was opening up for our beloved country'.

Such a prediction filled Sophia and her lover, Zhelyabov, with alarm, for if the Armenian dictator succeeded in winning the confidence of the Liberals it would make the revolutionaries' work almost impossible.

'Will of the People' now unleashed a storm of terrorist activities. They mined every street that the Emperor might travel over; and even theatres and shops that he occasionally visited. The capital was thrown into such a panic that when Alexander attended a gala performance of the opera before Christmas 1880, the house was nearly empty. In January 1881 Dostoevsky told the editor of the Russian *Times* that tragedy was in the air. 'You said that there had been some clairvoyance in my *Brothers Karamazov* . . . Wait till you have the sequel. I shall make my pure Aliosha join the terrorists and kill the Czar. . . .'[18]

For weeks Sophia Perovskaya stood outside the Winter Palace and watched the comings and goings of the Emperor. She discovered that on Sunday it was his habit to inspect the Guards on the Palace Ground at Michael Palace, and afterwards to call on his cousin, the daughter of the Grand Duchess Elena. 'Will of the People' therefore decided to mine one of the streets leading to the Ground. They managed to rent a shop on Little Garden Street, and turned it into a dairy. They dug a tunnel from the basement to the centre of the thoroughfare. Before their work was completed, however, Zhelyabov was picked up by the police in connection with another exploit. Sophia was distraught and for several days could think of nothing but how to free her lover. On Saturday she suddenly decided that the greatest gift she could bestow upon him was to continue with the plan to murder the Emperor. Hastily she collected four collaborators, two of whom were not even members of 'Will of the People'. As the land mine was not ready she informed them that hand-grenades would be used. The Emperor, when he left Michael Palace, could only take one of two routes. The conspirators were posted within sight of Sophia, who would wait at the corner and raise her handkerchief, to show which way he was coming.

Sophia Perovskaya (*above*), the driving force behind the terrorists dedicated to tsaricide

That same Saturday, 12 March 1881, Loris-Melikov called upon the Emperor and presented him with an official manifesto stating that all members of the *zemstva*, regardless of class or financial considerations, would be invited to participate in a Council of State. It was the first step toward parliamentary government. Alexander agreed to sign it and make it public the following day.

The dictator also begged the Emperor not to attend the Parade Ground the following day. An important terrorist, Zhelyabov, had been picked up by the police, others were still at large. Alexander replied that he had accepted a bodyguard with much reluctance; surely that was enough to ask of him. If he were not safe when surrounded by Cossacks he might as well abdicate.

The first explosion could be heard all over the capital. One of the terrorists had thrown a bomb which killed two Cossacks and three horses. But Alexander was not hurt. He dismounted from his carriage to see what could be done. 'Thank God Your Majesty is safe,' said one of

The assassination of Alexander II

the police officers. 'Rather too early to thank God,' shouted another terrorist. He raised his arm and threw what looked like a snowball at the Emperor's feet.

The second explosion shook the windows of the Winter Palace. By now the snow was crimson. The Emperor half-lay, half-sat, with his back to the canal railings. His face was streaming with blood, his abdomen torn open, his legs shattered. 'Quickly! Home to the Palace to die!' he murmured, and lost consciousness.

Everyone knew instinctively what had happened before the sledge arrived.

> We . . . started a mad race toward the Winter Palace [wrote the Grand Duke Alexander Mikhailovich], passing on our way the Preobrazhensky Regiment of the Guards doubling in the same direction with fixed bayonets. Thousands of people were already surrounding the palace . . . there was no need to ask questions; large drops of black blood showed us the way up the marble steps and then along a corridor into the Emperor's study . . . The Emperor lay on the couch near the desk. He was unconscious. Three doctors were fussing around, but science was obviously helpless . . . He presented a terrific sight, his right leg torn off, his left leg shattered, innumerable wounds all over his head and face. One eye was shut, the other expressionless . . . Princess Yurievsky burst in, half dressed. Something or perhaps some over-zealous guard had detained her. She fell flat on the couch over the body of the Tsar, kissing his hands and screaming, 'Sasha, Sasha!' A few minutes later the Emperor was dead. The Princess dropped to the floor 'like a felled tree'. Her pink négligée was soaked in blood.[19]

Russia was numbed by the horror of what had happened. Soon nearly every house, every balcony, every window, every lamp, was draped in black. 'Anguish, sorrow, shame – such are the feelings of every Russian heart,' wrote a former critic, Ivan Aksakov. 'What were his failings compared to his virtues?' asked another opponent, Sobolevsky. 'Let us not argue about him . . . He lived by his resolve to do good for his people.'

The funeral blazed with candles and glittering robes; and the wonderful singing reduced most of the mourners to tears. A young French diplomat, Maurice Paléologue, who happened to be a descendant of the last Byzantine Emperor, had just arrived in St Petersburg, and was counselled by the brilliant Eugène Melchior de Vogüé to take a good look at the dead sovereign; he was the man who emancipated the serfs, abolished corporal punishment, instituted the jury and established equality before the law.

> He brought the eagles of Muscovy to the shores of the Propontis, the very walls of Constantinople; he delivered the Bulgars; he established Russian domination in the very heart of Asia. Finally, on the very morning of his death he was working on a reform which . . . would have launched Russia irrevocably along the track of the modern world; the granting of a Parliamentary charter . . . And the Nihilists have killed him . . . Oh! a Liberator's is a dangerous job.[20]

CHAPTER VIII

Alexander III

1881–1894

Alexander III (*left*) was described by one of his ministers as 'just another Peter the Great with his cudgel' and by another as 'just the cudgel without Peter the Great'.

THE FIRST ACT of the new Emperor, Alexander III, was to tear up the unsigned manifesto lying on his father's desk, which made provision for a limited form of representative government at a national level. Next, he dismissed Loris-Melikov as Prime Minister and instructed the courts to deal with the regicides as speedily as possible. One of the terrorists had been killed in the explosion, and Sophia Perovskaya was still at large. She was picked up a week later and stood trial with five of her comrades. Besides Sophia, four were condemned to death: Zhelyabov, who had been in custody when the outrage took place; Kibalchich, the chemist who made the grenades; Rysakov who had volunteered at the last moment; and Mikhailovich who had attended early meetings at which the project had been discussed. Jessica Hellman, who had lent her flat to the conspirators, was spared the death penalty as she was pregnant. Instead, she was sentenced to penal servitude.

Count Leo Tolstoy, who had become deeply religious in his advancing age, was haunted by a spectre in which killing, and more killing, would dominate Russian thought. He awoke in the middle of the night and knew what should be done. Evil was destroying the structure of society; it was spreading everywhere, poisoning the minds of guilty and innocent alike. Alexander III must return to God's law, the Christian concept, and pardon his father's killers. His eyes brimming with tears he wrote to the Emperor:

> . . . it is true that it is presumption and folly on my part to demand that you, the Emperor of Russia and a loving son, should pardon your father's murderers in spite of the pressure of those around you, returning good for evil. It is folly, yet I cannot do otherwise than wish it . . . These young revolutionaries aspire to heaven knows what order, or rather none at all, and, by the basest, most inhumane method, fire and robbery and murder, they are destroying the structure of society . . . People have tried in the name of the State and for the welfare of the people, to oppress, deport and execute them; people have also tried, in the name of the same State and the same welfare of the people, to treat them humanely. The result has been the same in both cases. Why not try then, in the name of God, to carry out His law, thinking neither of the State nor the people? . . .[1]

Tolstoy persuaded the Emperor's brother, the Grand Duke Serge, to place his letter on Alexander III's desk. The autocrat read it but tossed it aside contemptuously. The regicides were hanged publicly in Semenovsky Square on 3 April 1881.

Thirty-six-year-old Alexander III was a giant of a man, and proud of his physical strength. He could tear a pack of cards in half, bend an iron poker over his knees and crush a silver rouble with his bare hands. His eyes were expressionless and he moved in a peculiarly ungainly way.

The assassins being taken to their public execution in St Petersburg (*above*)

Although almost every drop of blood in his veins was German, he had the stubborn, enigmatic look of a Russian peasant. Apparently this was how he liked to think of himself, for he grew a beard and wore the baggy trousers and checked blouses of the muzhiks.

Whereas Alexander II had refused to have plain-clothes men following him about, the new Emperor was only too glad of a bodyguard. When his advisers told him that it was impossible to make the Winter Palace completely secure, he willingly moved to Gatchina forty miles away. This vast palace, favourite home of Paul I, had six hundred bedrooms. It lay in a large park, complete with forests and lakes, and was surrounded by a moat. Its isolation made it easier to protect than any other palace, and every precaution was taken. An eye-witness reported:

Round the wall of the park is stationed a chain of sentries placed at distances of twenty-five metres, who are changed every hour, in order that the surveillance may be vigorously applied. Entry into the park and Castle is not permitted, even to the servants and to the employees of the Imperial Cabinet, without presentation of a special card which is changed every week. Besides this, all persons residing at the Castle, whatever their rank and station may be, are forbidden to lock their doors either by day or night. General Richter, General Inspector of the Imperial residence, and General Tcherevin [Cherevin], Chief of the Police, are entitled to make

216

investigations in the apartments of the Castle whenever they think proper. Gatchina is surrounded by a positively entrenched camp, and one would hardly believe, in passing it by on the railway, that a whole army was there simply to protect the life of one person.[2]

General Cherevin took his responsibilities so seriously that he lived in the house and frequently had meals with the family. The food put before the Emperor was prepared by a French chef who was under constant police supervision. And on the rare occasions when Alexander III left his fastness and visited his capital he rode to the station in an armour-plated carriage which had been bought from Napoleon III. The vehicle was so heavy that the horses which pulled it soon died of exhaustion.

Alexander had always been looked upon as the dullard of the family. His elder brother, the clever, liberal-minded Nicholas who had died of tuberculosis, had been educated for the throne, whereas Alexander had been relegated to the army. As a sovereign he was punctilious and conscientious. According to his daughter Olga:

[he] was up at seven every morning, washed in cold water, dressed himself in peasant clothes, made his own coffee in a glass percolator, filled a plate with cracknels, and, his breakfast eaten, went to his desk and settled to the day's work. There was an army of servants to wait on him. He disturbed none of them. There were bells in the study. He did not ring them. Sometime later his wife joined him, and a small table was brought by two servants. Husband and wife shared a breakfast of boiled eggs and rye bread and butter.[3]

He read every paper put before him.

Upon the margin of these documents [reported an anonymous contributor in the English *Contemporary Review*] he writes his decisions or his impressions with a frankness and abandon which laughs prudence and propriety to scorn . . . 'They are a set of hogs' is a phrase that recurs more frequently than most. 'What a beast he is!' is another. The account of a fire, of a failure of the crops, of a famine, or of some other calamity, is almost invariably commented upon in the one stereotyped word, 'discouraging'.[4]

As a youth Alexander had been tutored by Pobedonostsev, who later became Procurator of the Holy Synod. This man, known as the 'Black Tsar', had steely grey eyes and thin lips. Ascetic and intellectual, he possessed the most reactionary mind in the Empire, and had succeeded in passing on his fierce prejudices to his pupil. As a Panslavist, Alexander eagerly had embraced 'Orthodoxy, Autocracy and Nationalism'; and now, as Emperor, he coined a new, incisive slogan 'Russia for the Russians'.

The reign opened with a persecution of the Jews that was to be unequalled until the advent of Adolf Hitler fifty years later. Anti-semitism was endemic in Russia, and in the reign of Catherine the Great the Jews had been confined to territories which lay in the western and southern parts of the Empire, known as a Pale of Settlement. Under Alexander II,

however, they had been allowed to expand to all parts of Russia. Now Pobedonostsev proclaimed that one-third of the Jews of Russia must die, one-third emigrate, and one-third assimilate.

Death was easy to arrange. Government propaganda highlighted the fact that Jessica Hellman, at whose flat Alexander II's assassins had met, was a Jewess. This led to appalling pogroms which reached their climax in Kirovo and Kiev. There thousands of Jews were murdered and their property confiscated.

Alexander firmly believed that a gigantic plot was being organized by international Jewry to end the monarchical system. He never referred to 'Jews', but always to 'Yids'. The following year he published his 'May Laws' which became famous all over Europe. Only in exceptional circumstances could a Jew leave the Pale of Settlement; no Jew could hold an administrative post, or become a lawyer, or own land; no books were to be printed in Hebrew and all Jewish schools were to be closed; no Jew could marry a Christian unless he gave up his religion; no Jew could appeal against any sentence of any court; only a small proportion

Europe was shocked by the stories brought out of Russia by forcibly expelled Jews (*above*) of the savagery, pillage and pitiless persecution they experienced under Alexander III and his evil genius, Pobedonostsev.

of Jews could attend universities. During the six months following the publication of these laws it was estimated that 225,000 destitute Jewish families left Russia for Western Europe. The Emperor was delighted. 'Let them carry their poison where they will,' he said.

The persecution continued for the next decade. In 1892 the Emperor's brother, the Grand Duke Serge, a sadist and a homosexual, evicted thousands of Jewish artisans and petty traders from Moscow. Their quarter was surrounded by mounted Cossacks in the middle of the night while policeman ransacked every house. A contemporary observer, Harold Frederic, wrote:

> Of these unhappy people thus driven from their beds, and hauled off to prison in the wintry darkness, some were afterwards marched away by *etape*, that is, chained together with criminals and forced along the roads by Cossacks. A few were bribed out of confinement; the rest were summarily shipped to the Pale. Today they are scattered – who knows where? over the whole face of the earth . . . There was no charge of criminality or of leading an evil life against any of them.[5]

When Alexander III was given a report on this event he wrote on the margin: 'We must never forget that it was the Jews who crucified our Lord and spilled his priceless blood.'

Alexander's chauvinism did not stop at the Jews. He carried his russification policy into Finland and the Baltic states, depriving these countries of their hard-won autonomy, introducing a censorship, and making the Russian language compulsory in all the schools. Even the German families who had been settled in Russia since the time of Peter the Great did not escape his vigilant eye. A *ukaz* was issued, aimed at German manufacturers and merchants who had built up large businesses, prohibiting 'foreigners' from inheriting or acquiring property. Many were forced to close down their factories and leave.

A new military uniform was designed eliminating all Prussian details, and the German language was forbidden at Court. More important, every man with a German name who could be replaced by a Russian was dropped from government service. When the Chief

Before Alexander came to the throne he was irritated to discover that most of the officers in the famous Preobrazhensky Regiment had German names. As Tsar he ordered new uniforms so that his soldiers should at least look Russian.

Princess Dagmar, renamed Marie
Feodorovna. Alexander broke with
tradition by remaining faithful
to his wife. He maintained that 'an
autocrat's private behaviour should
stand above criticism'.

Astronomer of the Empire died, a man of German origin, Alexander ordered that the job should be filled by a Russian with a fully Russian name. Although the country was scoured for a Russian astronomer, the only man available was disqualified by the name of Kleber. The office finally was bestowed on a far from suitable Russian general.

Like his grandfather, Nicholas I, Alexander was devoted to his wife and five children. The Empress had none of the beauty of her sister, the Princess of Wales, but contemporary writers describe her as compelling; some even as radiant. She was badly educated, not at all clever, and echoed her husband's prejudices, frequently expressing surprise at the 'Jewish adventurers' in the Prince of Wales's entourage. She loved clothes and jewels, and particularly fancied herself in pearls, which she wore in great profusion.

Unfortunately her opportunities to dazzle were limited as the Emperor hated social life. When he was in St Petersburg he continued to live at the Anichkov Palace, using the Winter Palace only for official functions. On these occasions he wandered awkwardly through the vast supper-rooms, or played bridge in an ante-room. At two o'clock he began to look at his watch, although most Russian parties did not end until breakfast at six. He had a disconcerting habit of dismissing the orchestra one by one. When the band was reduced to a piano player and a violinist the most ardent reveller knew it was time to go home.

Alexander was frugal to the point of miserliness. Not only did he cut down on official entertaining, and make stringent economies in food and wine, but he examined the expenses of his many establishments down to the smallest items. He issued orders that soap and candles must be used up before they were thrown away, that table linen was not to be changed every day, and that lights were not to be left burning in empty rooms. He even decided that twenty people did not require an omelette made of one hundred eggs. Alexander's favourite food was cabbage and gruel, and although he did not inflict these dishes on his guests they frequently complained that the food at Gatchina was uneatable. Count Witte went even further. 'The Imperial table was always relatively poor,' he wrote, 'and the food served at the Court Marshal's board was sometimes such as to endanger health.'

The Emperor's son and heir, the 13-year-old Nicholas, once was so hungry that he opened the gold cross given to him at his baptism and ate the beeswax inside. This was an act of blasphemy, his sister Olga explained, for 'an infinitesimal relic of the True Cross was embedded in the wax'. Later he felt very ashamed of himself but admitted that it had tasted 'immorally good'. The reason for Nicholas's hunger, however, was not a lack of food but a lack of time in which to consume it. The children were the last to be served, as 'in those days it was considered very bad form either to hurry or to finish the food on your plate. By the time our turn came,' Olga explained, 'there was just time to have one or two bites.'[6]

Alexander III also was extremely economical with his clothes.

I had a curious proof of this [wrote Witte] when I accompanied the Emperor on one of his railway trips. Since I found it impossible, on account of my responsibility, to sleep of nights, I would often catch glimpses of His Majesty's valet mending the Emperor's trousers. On one occasion I asked him why he didn't give his master a new pair instead of mending the old so often. 'Well, I would rather have it that way,' he answered, 'but His Majesty won't let me. He insists on wearing his garments until they are threadbare. It is the same with his boots. Not only does he wear them as long as possible, but he refuses to put on expensive ones. If I should bring him patent leather boots, he would angrily throw them out of the window.[7]

Even at Gatchina the Emperor preferred rooms with shabby, well-worn sofas to those with brocades and expensive furniture. Lady Randolph Churchill, who visited Gatchina with her husband, recalled:

. . . a large hall worthy of an old English country house, full of comfortable arm chairs and writing tables, games and toys. I even spied a swing. In that room Their Majesties often dined, I was told, alone or when they had

222

For the most of his reign Alexander lived in seclusion at Gatchina (*above*), amid the strictest security. Roads leading to the castle were patrolled, and the park and adjoining forest were enclosed by a high wall.

guests, and after dinner the table would be removed, and they would spend the remainder of the evening there. This seemed strange to me when I thought of the many hundreds of rooms in the enormous building.[8]

The Empress, however, had as many as a hundred and fifty guests for the weekend, who travelled by special train from St Petersburg. On these occasions the State rooms were used and dancing went on until the small hours of the morning. The Emperor often scolded his wife for the large sums of money she spent on clothes, and was particularly indignant when she admitted paying £12,000 – in those days a fairly large sum of money – on a sable coat. The only extravagance Alexander permitted himself was buying jewelry. Every year he ordered an Easter egg from Peter Carl Fabergé, a Russian of French descent. Fabergé set up his workshops in St Petersburg about the time that Alexander came to the throne. Altogether he made fifty-six jewelled eggs for the Imperial family, each a masterpiece of ingenuity. Most of them had shells that opened; inside might be flowers or jewelled figures or enamelled birds that warbled and flapped their wings.

The only form of entertainment Alexander enjoyed was a beer evening. He liked to play the trombone, and sometimes gathered together as many fellow musicians as he could find at his court to form an orchestra. Everyone wore shabby clothes and drank beer from half-gallon mugs.

These economical evenings were in keeping with the Emperor's cuts in personal expenditure. He managed to reduce his Civil List by nearly two million pounds a year. He then issued a Family Statute proclaiming that in future only children and grandchildren of a sovereign were to be known as Grand Dukes and Duchesses. All others were to be styled Prince and Princess and their allowance reduced accordingly.

The courtiers with their centuries-old tradition of sycophancy were quick to take the new Emperor's measure, and, according to an eye-witness, 'emulated the appearance and aped the manners of the peasant' to please him. 'The gaieties and elegant amusements of the old régime were no more the fashion. A sort of medieval gloom fell over the capital . . . The Court was little more than a name.'[9]

St Petersburg society, however, refused to follow the lead of the Court, and as far as private entertainment was concerned, the season sparkled as brightly as ever. The stars of the fashionable world were two of the Emperor's four brothers, Vladimir and Alexis. These tall, handsome young men were so partial to wine, women and song, and spent money so freely, that they gave the title Grand Duke a notorious connotation of its own, especially in Paris, where coaches offered to take sightseers on a round of night-clubs known as *la tourneé des grands ducs*.

In St Petersburg, Vladimir and Alexis staged wild parties at Cubat's restaurant, which once ended in a brawl with a group of French actors and their lady friends. Furniture and mirrors were smashed, and both the Grand Dukes went home with black eyes. Vladimir was clever and artistic and eventually married a princess of Mecklenburg-Schwerin, who became the leading hostess in the capital. Alexis, however, remained a bachelor, establishing a *ménage à trois* with the beautiful Duchess of Leuchtenberg and her husband; the husband, so rumour had it, was persistently locked out of his bedroom and forced to sleep in the study.

Surprisingly enough, Alexander refused to be disconcerted by his brothers, and gave all of them important jobs. Vladimir was made President of the Academy of Fine Arts and Commander of the Imperial Guard; Alexis became a Grand Admiral of the Russian fleet, although according to his cousin, his knowledge of naval affairs 'could not have been more limited' and if he had been forced to spend a year at sea, away from Paris 'he would have resigned his post'. Even the third brother, Serge, the cold, arrogant pervert who had organized the expulsion of the Jews, was made Governor-General of Moscow, where he became more hated than ever. His wife, the beautiful Elizabeth of Hesse-Darmstadt, was an elder sister of Alix, who married Nicholas II. The only brother who provoked the Emperor's displeasure was the quiet, intelligent Paul

Alexander Nevsky Lavra was designed by Tressini and outstanding writers and composers such as Tchaikovsky and Rimsky Korsakov are buried here.

OVERLEAF The new Michael Palace, designed by Rossi for the younger brother of Alexander I, later became the Alexander III Museum.

who made the mistake of marrying a divorced commoner and immediately was banished from Russia.

The Grand Dukes were always present at the balls given in private houses, which took place nearly every night from Christmas to Lent. In the early hours of the morning they often visited the gypsy quarter outside the capital. This district was known as the Islands, for the canals of the Neva had turned it into an archipelago. The journey was always made in troikas, the fastest type of transport. The centre horse trotted in shafts while the outside horses, loose save for long traces, galloped. Driving a troika was a special art, for the driver had to stand. He wore a special badge – peacock feathers set in a round cap, he had a special name, *yamshchik*, and he charged a very special price.

The wild pace through the bitter cold forest, under a starlight sky, was an excitement in itself. Then the troika would draw up before a low building hidden among a clump of fir trees; everyone would jump out and bang loudly on the doors; and a few minutes later a sleepy-eyed Tartar would appear. Soon the bare whitewashed room was alive with waiters lighting candles, bringing champagne bottles, arranging seats and adjusting a samovar. The gypsy troupe usually numbered twenty or thirty. They sang in a curious metallic voice 'with a ring in it of something Eastern, barbaric and utterly strange to western ears, to the thrum of the guitars,' wrote Lord Frederick Hamilton. 'A tempest of wild, nasal melody arose, in the most perfect harmony . . . The un-European *timbre* of the voices conduced doubtless to the effect, but . . . it had about it something so novel and fresh – or was it something so immemorially old? – that the listeners felt absolutely intoxicated. On the Russians it acted like hypnotism.'[10]

These sophisticated pleasures did not tempt Alexander III, who was only happy at Gatchina. He loved country pursuits; cutting down a tree, mending a fence, cooking over an open fire. Frequently he took his two younger children, Michael and Olga, on exciting walks. 'My father always carried a big spade,' wrote Olga, 'Michael had a smaller one, and I had a tiny one of my own, each of us carried a big hatchet, a lantern, and an apple. If it was winter he taught us how to fell a dead tree. He taught Michael and me how to build up a fire. Finally we roasted the apples, damped down the fire, and the lanterns helped us to find our way home.'[11]

When Alexander travelled abroad, however, he maintained appropriate grandeur. Every summer the family set forth on the Imperial yacht and sailed to Denmark to stay with the Empress's father, King Christian IX. Over a hundred servants accompanied them, while twenty coaches carried their baggage to the port of embarkation; once a cow was taken aboard to supply the children with fresh milk.

This annual gathering at Fredensborg frequently included the Prince and Princess of Wales, King George and Queen Olga of Greece and their seven children, and relations from Germany, Austria and Sweden. Often there were so many guests that the children slept in huts in the park.

The red drawing-room in the Anichkov Palace

Tsaritsa of Russia   Tsar of Russia Alexander III   Prince of Denmark   Christian IX King of Denmark

Queen Louise of Denmark   Princess Alexandra

Duchess of Edinburgh

Fredensborg provided not only a holiday, but a sanctuary, the only place where the Imperial family could feel safe. In Russia the police rounded up hundreds of suspects, and mass trials took place every few months. Although all the major subversive organizations were broken up, and revolution, in the words of the revolutionaries themselves, became 'a cottage industry', individuals committed acts of terror that gave the public a false impression of their strength. In 1882 General Strelnikov, Public Prosecutor of Kiev, was assassinated while sitting on the boulevard in Odessa. A few weeks later a mine was discovered in the Kremlin where preparations were under way for the Tsar's coronation. At Easter the head of the Moscow police received a basketful of artificial eggs, several of which were charged with dynamite. These incidents did not soothe the Imperial nerves. 'The slightest rumours were believed,' wrote an eye-witness, 'assassins masked in Court livery, bombs hidden in the park, threatening letters found on the table – the most ordinary happenings were magnified to tales of horror.'

Alexander frequently took a nap in his study after lunch. One day the Empress heard a pistol shot and with her heart beating wildly rushed into the room to see what had happened. The Tsar sat, half-dazed, on the edge of his sofa, a gun in his hand. At his feet lay his aide-de-camp with a bullet through his head. Alexander had woken up to see the man standing over him with his fingers on his throat. He had snatched his revolver from under a cushion and fired. Apparently the aide-de-camp had come into the study with papers, and seeing the Emperor dozing, with a constricted look on his face, had attempted to unhook his military collar.

The tense atmosphere of the palace prompted Alexander's brother Vladimir to form a secret society of his own, called 'The Holy Band'. Its purpose was to preserve the life of the Emperor. The Empress became a patron; General Cherevin gave the organization his blessing; and almost all the 250 members of the ultra-exclusive St Petersburg Yacht Club (which had nothing to do with yachting) offered their services.

Unfortunately this society was so amateurish it soon developed into a comedy. Count Bobby Shuvalov was the President; Prince Belosselsky 'Minister of Foreign Affairs'; Demidov San Donate its 'Minister of the Interior'. All the members had bodyguards who accompanied them everywhere they went; and while the 'secret agent' paid a call, dined or supped, the bodyguard would sit in the kitchen entertaining the servants with his master's business.

One of the great hostesses of the day, Baroness Kleinmichel, had an uncle, Baron de Grote, who was Grand Marshal of the Court. One day he spoke harshly to his Lett valet and the latter told him reproachfully,

'You are very unjust, Excellency; yet I have refused to denounce you.'

'To denounce me? Who to? Why? How?'

'To the Holy League, and I could have had a lot of money for it.'

'Grote questioned the man,' wrote the Baroness, 'and learned that he had been offered so much per month if he reported faithfully all he

A traditional Russian troika

A family gathering at Fredensborg

heard at my uncle's table. M. de Grote thought the idea of suspecting him so funny that he ordered the servant to accept the offered increase in wage. By this means my uncle secured a valet all the more faithful as he was sure of double money as long as he remained at his post.'[12]

The society proved to be a bonanza to many of its members. Young nobles who left Russia on secret missions with thousands of roubles in their pockets were found sunning themselves in the south of France. Even more provocative, when an Imperial edict gave the Holy Band the right to make arrests, their members mistook the men of the Okhrana for revolutionaries, and jailed half the police force. Not surprisingly, people began to refer to the Holy Band as a league of madmen and the Minister of the Interior finally persuaded the Tsar to dissolve it.

Alexander's coronation took place without incident in 1883. But at the end of the year General Sudeiken, the Chief of the St Petersburg Police, was found battered to death in his flat, and the capital once again shivered with fear.

During the next three years, however, the killings decreased and the people began to say that terrorism was on the decline. Then came the winter of 1887. Three students, one of whom was carrying a bomb, were arrested on the Nevsky Prospekt. Another fifteen conspirators were rounded up, and after a brief trial five of them, including Alexander Ulyanov, a brother of Lenin, were found guilty of plotting to kill the Tsar. They were hanged on 20 May.

An eye-witness sketch of the train crash at Borki (*below*). The Imperial train had identical carriages, so that the public should not know where the Tsar was sitting.

232

Would Alexander III meet the same fate as his father? This question was uppermost in the public mind when the Imperial train, on its way home from the Caucasus in 1888, went off the rails near the town of Borki. Two engines were pulling twelve coaches when suddenly there was a violent lurch, the sound of splintering glass, the creak of breaking wood, followed by a thunderous noise as some of the carriages careered down the embankment. The Emperor and the Empress were having luncheon with their children in the dining-car. The roof caved in and the floor buckled as the carriage fell onto its side. For once the Emperor's Herculean strength proved of value for he freed himself from the broken timber and iron that was crushing him, and managed to hold up the roof of the coach so that his wife and children, servants and nannies could crawl out. The 6-year-old Grand Duchess Olga had been thrown through the window and had tumbled down the bank. Although she was unscathed she was screaming hysterically: 'Now they will come and kill us all!' Officials attributed the accident to the decrepitude of one of the engines, which had gone off the rails, pulling the carriages after it. Somehow that did not explain why the roof of the dining-car had caved in, and popular opinion continued to insist that bombs had exploded on the track.

Alexander III liked to play the part of a simple-minded muzhik, yet he had a streak of Asiatic cunning in his make-up. He locked up his revolutionaries at home, but astonishingly encouraged them abroad.

As a young man he had been a fervent Panslavist and one of the prime movers of the Russo-Turkish war. His views had not changed and he burned with indignation at the thought that Russia had failed in her mission to dominate the Balkans and to seize control of the Straits, either of which would have given her access to the Mediterranean. Stubbornly and surreptitiously he continued to pursue the same goal. As Bulgaria had been split into two sections by the Congress of Berlin he was determined not only to bring the half ruled by his first cousin, Prince Alexander of Battenberg, under Russian control, but to reunite the country. He was also determined to establish subservient governments in Serbia and Greece.

As the Emperor could not afford another war he kept his troops at home, which prompted the more naïve statesmen of Europe to refer to him as 'The Tsar Peacemaker'. Yet throughout his reign he waged the first, concerted 'cold war' in history. His Foreign Minister, de Giers, encouraged Russian revolutionaries to act as agents in stirring up trouble for the established régimes of the Balkans. Russian undercover men posing as icon sellers wandered through Serbia setting up subversive cells; Russian embassy officials paid crowds to stage riots; and Russian army officers in the Eastern Rumelian section of Bulgaria opened gymnasiums where they drilled boys and girls in guerrilla warfare. In 1882 one of the Russian agents conceived the brilliant idea of erecting a fortress under the very nose of the Turkish governors. The intention was to build a church to commemorate a Russian victory in the last war. But when the Russians submitted the plan to the authorities, the British minister reported that the building had 'walls of great thickness, cellars in which vast quantities of arms might be stored, and cells for monks which constituted a series of Block Houses, the cost of which edifice, it was estimated, would amount to three million francs.'[13]

The Emperor was not successful in winning control in Bulgaria, as Prince Alexander of Battenberg refused to act as a Russian puppet. Alexander III raged against his obdurate cousin, and referred to him as 'this man we have raised from the gu. . .'. But Queen Victoria supported 'darling Sandro'. 'Russia behaves and has behaved shamefully,' she snapped. 'Her anger against Prince Alexander is merely because her plan of deposing him and uniting the two countries under a Russian prince . . . failed.'[14]

In the end, Russia succeeded in breaking the Prince's morale. The Tsar approved a plan by which Russian agents stirred up a mutiny in the Bulgarian army. They kidnapped Prince Alexander and forced him to abdicate at the pistol point. He was taken by sea and deposited at the Russian port of Reni.

The outcry in Europe was stupendous. Queen Victoria raged that Russia's behaviour was 'without parallel in modern history'; and in a private letter to Sandro's father, Prince Alexander of Hesse, referred to the Russian Emperor as 'your barbaric, semi-asiatic, tyrannical cousin'. The uproar obliged Alexander III to return the Prince to the safety of Austria; but poor Sandro was so disillusioned by the treachery of the Bulgarian Army that he surrendered his throne. The Russian Emperor was elated, and thought he had won. To his chagrin, however, he soon discovered that the new régime in Bulgaria led by the staunch patriot Stambulov was just as hostile to Russia as had been the former government; so Russian agents now concentrated on murdering Stambulov. They did not succeed in killing him, however, until the next Tsar, Nicholas II, was on the throne.

Expansion abroad; repression at home. The Emperor's armies moved forward steadily in Asia, adding thousands of square miles to the Empire and nearly clashing with Britain over Afghanistan in 1885.

In 1892 Alexander III appointed the brilliant Sergius Witte to the post of Minister of Communications, and later in the year as Minister of Finance. Despite the stultifying intellectual atmosphere that hung over the country, industry began to leap forward. Witte negotiated huge foreign loans and started building the Trans-Siberian Railway. There was no shortage of labour as a terrible famine in the winter of 1890/91 had sent thousands of peasants to the towns looking for work. Hundreds of factories sprang into being, more than a third of them operating on loans from Britain and Germany, France and Belgium. In Moscow and St Petersburg textiles and engineering developed.

During the next few years coal production doubled, oil production increased fourteen times, and hundreds of new centres sprang up on the Donbas. Russians became increasingly boastful, and irritated foreigners

The kidnapping of Alexander of Battenberg (*above*) was a high-light in the cold war waged by Alexander III.

Sergius Witte (*right*) did not enjoy visiting the Tsar at Gatchina because of the austere hospitality. A connoisseur of good food, he complained that some of the dishes served at the Emperor's table were unfit to eat.

by their grandiose plans for the future. China and India and the Persian Gulf had always been part of the Grand Asian Scheme. And so had a path through the Balkans to the Mediterranean. But now Russians talked of pushing through Norway to the North Sea. Their goal seemed limitless: not sections of the globe, but the globe itself.

Germany's chancellor, Prince Otto von Bismarck, sensed the restlessness, and not wishing to be drawn into entanglements that might lead to war, persuaded Alexander III in 1887 to sign a secret pact known as the Re-insurance Treaty. In this document the two countries pledged neutrality in case the other went to war. This meant that Austria could not hope for German help if she found herself in a clash with Russia; but it also meant that France could not count on Russia in the event of a conflict with Germany.

Although Bismarck was well satisfied with his work, his achievement proved to be short-lived. A year later, in 1888, the 29-year-old Emperor William II mounted the German throne. Clever, impulsive, and exhaustingly energetic, the new Kaiser was eager to win applause. He

235

wanted, as a wit put it, to be the bride at every wedding, the corpse at every funeral. Annoyed by the fame of Prince Bismarck, in 1890 he found an excuse to drop the pilot and to grasp the helm himself. But his first major decision was a disaster. He allowed himself to be persuaded by his Foreign Office that the Re-insurance Treaty was not compatible with Germany's agreement with Austria, and he politely declined to renew it. Alexander III just as politely opened negotiations with France, and in 1894 a Russo-Franco military treaty was signed which split Europe into two camps. Germany and Austria faced France and Russia across a gulf which was destined to grow ever wider.

Sergius Witte was eager to interest the heir to the throne, Grand Duke Nicholas, now 25 years old, in Russia's industrial expansion. In 1892 he suggested to the Emperor that Nicholas should be made Chairman of the Committee dealing with the Trans-Siberian Railway.

Alexander III looked at Witte in astonishment. 'What? But you know the Tsarevich. Have you ever had a serious conversation with him?'

'No, Sire. I have never had the pleasure of having such a conversation with the Heir.'

'He is still a child, he has only infantile judgments, how would he be able to be president of a committee?'

'Nevertheless, Sire, if you do not begin to initiate him in affairs of state he will never understand them.'[15]

In the end Witte got his way, but Nicholas made no contribution. His apparent indifference was attributed to his youth and inexperience, but the truth was that he had no power of concentration.

Even as a child nothing had gripped his mind or imagination.

He never cried. He rarely laughed. He never played [wrote his first cousin, the Grand Duke Alexander Mikhailovich who had grown up with him as a boy]. He drew as his teachers a simple-minded Russian general, a sentimental Swiss tutor and a young Englishman who was extremely fond of outdoor life. None of the three had the remotest idea of the task facing the future Czar of Russia. They taught him all they knew, which proved to be little. At the end of his tuition and on the eve of getting his commission in the Hussar Guards, Nicholas II could have deceived an Oxford professor into mistaking him for an Englishman and possessed a similar command of German and French. But that was all. The rest of his knowledge consisted of loose bits of information never to be of any practical use in his life. . . .[16]

When Nicholas was 21 he had fallen in love with Princess Alix of Hesse who came to Russia to visit her sister, Ella, the wife of the Tsar's homosexual brother, the Grand Duke Serge. 'My dream,' he wrote in his diary several years later, 'is to marry Alix of Hesse.' Neither his father nor his mother approved of the match; not because she was a first cousin of the new German Emperor, William II; but because she was a granddaughter of Victoria of England, and very much under the Queen's influence.

In order to divert Nicholas the Grand Duke was sent on a tour around the world in 1891, accompanied by his cousin, Prince George of Greece.

The golden Romanov eagle in the Military Gallery of the Winter Palace above the portrait of Alexander I

But the lackadaisical heir found even this adventure dull. 'My trip is senseless,' he told the Grand Duke Alexander when they met at Colombo. 'Palaces and generals are the same all the world over and that is all I am permitted to see. I could just as well have stayed at home.'[17]

Japan, however, provided excitement, although not of a particularly welcome nature. Here Nicholas was almost murdered. It happened when the two royal visitors reached Ossu, near Kyoto, and rode through the town in a rickshaw.

> We passed through a narrow street [wrote Prince George] decorated with flags and filled with crowds of people on both sides of the thoroughfare. I was looking toward the left when I heard suddenly something like a shriek in front of me, and saw a policeman hitting Nicky a blow on the head with his sword, which he held with both hands.
>
> Nicky jumped out of the cart, and the man ran after him, Nicky with the blood streaming down his face. When I saw this, I too jumped out, with my stick in my hand, and ran after the man, who was about fifteen paces in front of me. Nicky ran into a shop but came out again immediately, which enabled the man to overtake him; but I thank God that I was there the same moment, and while the policeman still had the sword high in the air I gave him a blow straight on the head, a blow so hard that he had probably never experienced a similar one before. He now turned against me but fainted and fell on the ground; then two of our rickshaw pullers appeared on the scene; one got hold of his legs, while the other took the sword and gave him a wound in the back of the head. . . .[18]

When the news of the attack reached Europe, newspapers jumped to the conclusion that the policeman was a Nihilist. After an investigation, however, it was revealed that the man was a religious fanatic, enraged at some imaginary breach of etiquette on the part of the visitors.

Nicholas cut his trip short; but soon after he returned to Russia, his head still in bandages, he was sent to Denmark for a visit; and in June 1893 he was packed off to London to represent his father at the wedding of the Duke of York, the future George V, to Princess Mary of Teck.

The Prince of Wales was greatly distressed by the Grand Duke's appearance. 'Uncle Bertie of course sent me at once a tailor, a bootmaker and a hatter,' he wrote to his mother. He visited the House of Commons, where many MPs were struck by his resemblance to the Duke of York. One of the members, T. P. O'Connor, found the Grand Duke's presence curiously depressing.

> The Czarevitch certainly did not give the impression of either mental or physical vigour. It was hard to realize that this slim, not very tall and decidedly delicate looking stripling was the son of the giant who could twist tin plates in the hollow of one of his brawny hands. There was something singular, and even a little sinister and foreboding in the manner in which the Czarevitch entered the gallery . . . He seemed shy, uncertain, indecisive, looked back as if to get a hint; and altogether went to his place with much awkwardness and shamefacedness. . . .[19]

ABOVE Katalnaya Gorka at Oranienbaum originally had a wooden switch-back, hence the name 'sliding hill'.
BELOW Anichkov Palace, home of Alexander III when he was heir-apparent

Princess Alix of Hesse (*above*) was betrothed to Nicholas at Livadia on the day after Alexander's death.

This description perfectly described Nicholas's character. But there was one thing about which he was not indecisive; and that was his wish to marry Princess Alix of Hesse. His mother mentioned a possible match with Princess Hélène, daughter of the Comte de Paris, saying that it might help to strengthen the Franco-Russian pact. 'Two roads seem to be opening before me,' he wrote in his diary. 'I myself want to go in one direction, while it is evident that Mama wants me to choose the other. What will happen?' The question resolved itself, as the Princess Hélène flatly refused to change her religion.

The same problem faced Princess Alix. Would she be willing to give up her Protestantism for the Greek Orthodox faith? Most of her relations believed not, but Nicholas was determined at least to ask her. In the early winter of 1894 the Emperor was taken ill and as a result became increasingly eager to see his son married. When Nicholas, in a rare moment of resolve, told his parents that he would court Alix, or no one at all, they finally gave their consent.

The occasion for the proposal was provided by the wedding of the Grand Duke of Hesse, Alix's brother, to Princess Victoria, the daughter of the Duke of Edinburgh. Coburg was the scene of a large family gathering which included Queen Victoria and William II of Germany. Everyone seemed to know what was on the mind of the Grand Duke Nicholas, who found an unexpected ally in the German Kaiser. The truth was that the temperamental William was deeply distressed by the Franco-Russian pact. If his cousin Nicky married his cousin Alix perhaps the ties linking the two dynasties would prove strong enough to modify the effects of the obnoxious treaty.

The Kaiser wasted no time before taking Nicky in hand. The Grand Duke was terrified lest Alix prove so adamant as to deprive him of all

Queen Victoria presiding over the wedding-breakfast at Coburg, in the Throne Room of Ehrenburg Castle

hope. William tried to raise his morale, and finally, 'in his cheery impulsive way took Nicholas by the arm, led him to his room, made him buckle on his sword and carry his fur cap in his hand, stuck some roses in his hand and said: "Now we will go and ask for Alix." '[20]

As most of the guests had prophesied, Nicholas was not successful. 'I had a long and very difficult talk with Alix,' he wrote to his mother, 'in which I tried to explain to her that there was no other way for her than to give her consent, and that she simply could not withhold it. She cried the whole time, and only whispered now and then "No, I cannot!" Still I went on, repeating and insisting on what I had said before. And though this talk went on for two hours it came to nothing because neither she nor I would give in. . . .'[21]

Everyone at Coburg was fascinated by the drama. The relations, wrote Nicky, 'were very touching in their solicitude'. The Kaiser, however, was determined to bring the matter to a triumphant conclusion, and had another long talk with Alix himself. His eloquence proved decisive for on 8 April he drove Alix to the house where Nicholas was staying and pushed them into a room together. 'We were left alone,' Nicholas wrote to his mother, 'and with her very first words she consented! The Almighty only knows what happened to me then. I cried like a child, and she did too; but her expression had changed; her face was lit by a quiet content . . . The whole world is changed for me; nature, mankind, everything; and all seemed to be good and lovable and happy. I couldn't write, my hand trembled so. . . .'[22]

In the summer of 1894 the doctors told Alexander III that he was suffering from dropsy, which had come as a result of the damage to his kidneys sustained at the time of the Borki train disaster. In October the Imperial yacht, *Polar Star*, dropped anchor at Yalta. Although the physicians knew that the end was only a matter of weeks they had recommended the soft air of the Crimea. Alexander had never liked the lovely palace at Livadia, with its orangeries and oleanders, built for his ailing mother, but he was too ill to ignore the doctors' advice. The crowds that gathered at the port were shocked by his appearance. The giant frame was all bones, and the ghostly skin and sunken cheeks wore the look of death.

On 1 November the Grand Duke Alexander Mikhailovich arrived at Livadia. 'Nicky and I stood on the verandah of the beautiful palace . . . armed with bags of oxygen and watching the end of the Colossus . . . Alexander died as he had lived, a bitter enemy of resounding phrases, a confirmed hater of melodrama. He just muttered a short prayer and kissed his wife.'[23]

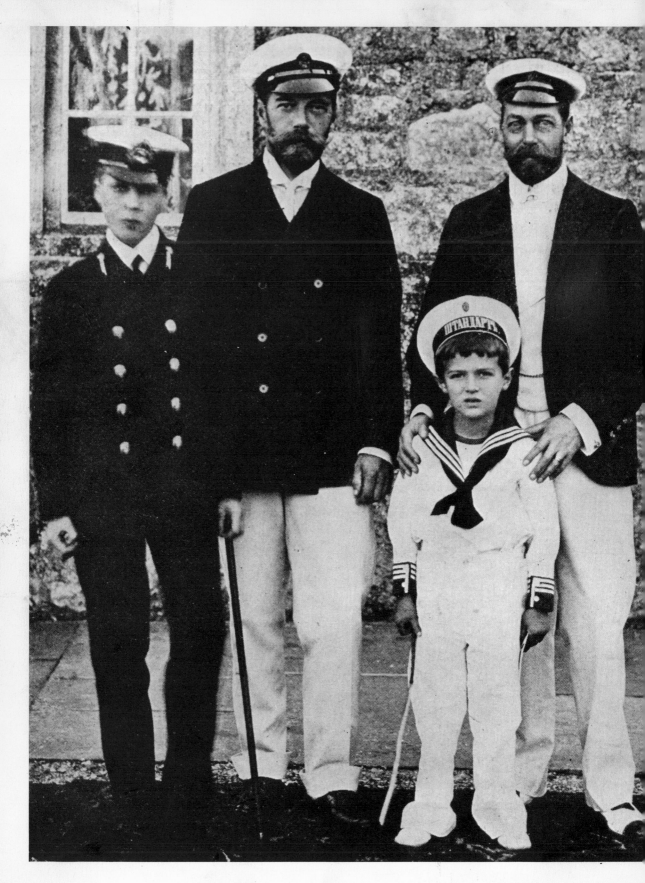

CHAPTER IX

Nicholas II

1894–1917

I AM NOT READY FOR IT. I don't even know how to talk to my ministers,' wept the 26-year-old Emperor, Nicholas II, to his cousin, the Grand Duke Alexander. 'Even Alicky his fiancée could not help him,' Nicholas's younger sister, Olga, told a journalist many years later. 'He was in despair. He kept saying that he did not know what would become of us all, that he was wholly unfit to reign . . . Nicky had been trained as a soldier. He should have been taught statesmanship and he was not. It was my father's fault. I can't tell you why . . .'[1]

For years Alexander III had been grumbling about his son's lack of maturity; the boy never seemed to grow into a man. The Empress, on the other hand, adored Nicky, and accepted him as he was. Even in his middle twenties she continued to treat him like an adolescent. When Alexander lay dying, it did not occur to her to consult Nicholas about future arrangements, despite the fact that at any hour he would be Emperor of all the Russias. Dagmar simply continued issuing orders and exacting obedience. Princess Alix of Hesse, who arrived at Livadia to be at her fiancé's side, was astonished and angry to see how completely everyone ignored him. The force of her own character is revealed by the fact that without a moment's hesitation she tried to drive a wedge between the Empress and her son. 'If the doctor has any wishes and needs anything,' she wrote in Nicholas's diary, 'make him come *direct to you*. Don't let others be put first and you left out. You are Father's dear son and must be told all and be asked about everything. Show your own mind and don't let others forget *who you are*. Forgive me, lovey.'[2]

Poor Nicholas's emotions were in such a turmoil that he was not sure himself who he was. 'It was the death of a saint!' he wrote. 'Oh! God help us during these dreadful days! Poor dear Mama! In the evening at half past nine we had prayers – in the room where he died! I feel as if I were dead myself! My darling Alix's feet have again begun to hurt her!'[3]

The funeral took place in St Petersburg. The Prince of Wales, accompanied by Lord Carrington, did the official honours for Britain, while the Princess of Wales tried to comfort the widow, her sister. The open coffin lay in state for two weeks in the Cathedral of St Peter and St Paul; and the royal mourners had to undergo the ordeal of kissing the dead Emperor's lips.

'As he lay uncovered in his coffin,' wrote Lord Carrington, 'his face looked dreadful and the smell was awful. He was not embalmed until three days after his death.'

The Prince of Wales was surprised at the ascendancy of the Dowager Empress over Nicholas. Ten days after the funeral court mourning was suspended for a day so that he could marry his princess, who became known in the capital as 'the funeral bride'. Yet his mother refused to let

Nicholas II and his cousin, the future George V, with their sons at Cowes

Nicholas II, by Ferov

him retreat to Tsarskoye Selo after the ceremony, saying somewhat fancifully that she did not wish to be left alone. Dutifully Nicholas brought his bride back to the Anichkov Palace and moved into the rooms that he and his brother had shared as bachelors. The Prince of Wales told Lord Carrington that the couple came down to breakfast 'as though nothing had happened'.

Not surprisingly the Prince came to the conclusion that Nicholas II was 'as weak as water'. The new sovereign did not try to conceal his apprehension at the thought of ruling 133,000,000 people, twice the population in his grandfather's day, and he talked about his accession as 'the task I have always feared'. In 1894 Russia was enjoying a mild industrial boom, thanks to Witte's policies. But the world price of grain had dropped and the discontent among the peasantry was growing. Political controversy bubbled dangerously beneath the surface, and people in all parts of the country were calling for parliamentary government and a free press.

Many members of the intelligentsia were hopeful that Nicholas II would follow the liberal path of Alexander II, but the Prince of Wales told Lord Carrington that he was disturbed by the young man's slavish adherence to his father's autocratic ideas and fierce prejudices, and his total lack of worldly sense. Carrington replied gloomily that a revolution was inevitable. The Prince snapped back that nothing was inevitable if the Tsar would move with the times. Unfortunately Nicky's only concern was to behave in the way that 'dear saintly Papa' would have approved. When he received the dignitaries of the Empire at the Winter Palace he made a pronouncement that broke upon the assembly like a clap of thunder. He rejected the mildest form of representative government as 'a senseless dream', and declared that he would 'maintain for the good of the whole nation the principle of absolute autocracy as firmly and strongly as his late lamented father.'

From that moment onward every liberal element in the country joined battle against him.

The Dowager Empress did not permit Nicholas and Alix, who took the Russian name Alexandra, to set up their own household until six months after the death of Alexander III. In May 1895 she went to Copenhagen, and this gave Nicholas and Alexandra the opportunity of moving into a small palace at Peterhof, then into the Alexander Palace at Tsarskoye Selo, which became their permanent home. Alexandra, who at first was lavish in her praise of 'mother dear', had grown to resent this fitful, selfish woman who treated the Emperor as though he still was a boy under parental control. Alexandra's tight lips and unsmiling face had not gone unnoticed by the Dowager, who found her daughter-in-law strangely unsympathetic.

The wives of Nicholas's four uncles also were aware of the unspoken disapproval; and they, in turn, began to criticize the bride for her cold nature, her tasteless clothes, her bad Russian and total absence of humour.

Alexandra was shocked by the gay, loose society of St Petersburg. 'The heads of the young ladies,' she wrote, 'are filled with nothing but thoughts of young officers.'

Only when Alexandra was alone with Nicholas could she unbend. Far from being cold, she had an impulsive, passionate nature and returned the fervent love he had for her with a blazing ardour. 'Thank God for having granted me such happiness, complete beyond words,' he wrote in his diary. 'At last united, bound for life, and when this life is ended, we meet again in the other world and remain together for eternity,' rejoined Alexandra on the day of their wedding, 'Yours, yours.'

Yet this couple so deeply in love, this funeral bride and groom, seemed fated for horrific experiences, the first of which came the day after the coronation. According to custom, every newly crowned Tsar presented gifts to the populace; and on this occasion Khodinka field, on the outskirts of Moscow, was chosen as a suitable place where the distribution could take place. The choice seems questionable, as the field was normally used as a military training ground and was criss-crossed with ditches. Nevertheless the Governor-General, the Grand Duke Serge, approved the plans. Although a crowd of nearly half a million was expected from all over Russia, the Grand Duke sent only one squadron of Cossacks and a small detachment of police to maintain order.

Early in the morning families began to gather outside the frail wooden fence that protected the field, watching carts laden with beer, and more carts bearing the eagerly sought gifts – enamel mugs stamped with the double-headed eagle – lumber on to the grounds, while helpers arranged the stalls.

Suddenly a rumour swept through the mass that there would not be enough cups to go round, and before anyone knew what was happening a stampede had begun. The field was transformed into a mass of stumbling, screaming, suffocating, kicking humanity. Over four thousand people were trampled to death.

The Imperial party was not due to make its appearance for several hours, and when it finally arrived, according to Princess Radziwill, officials tried to hold back the full details of the disaster. 'A frantic effort was made to conceal every sign of the catastrophe. Peasant carts were requisitioned and the dead bodies carried away in all haste. Finally, when it was realized that it would be quite impossible to dispose of the innumerable corpses in time, the floor of the Imperial pavilion, from which the Emperor with his guests were to view the festival, was removed and piles of dead men, women and children were thrust under it.'[4] The Grand Duke Alexander, one of the Imperial visitors, speaks of passing wagons laden with dead bodies. 'The cowardly chief of Police,' he wrote, 'tried to distract the attention of the Czar by asking him to acknowledge the cheers of the populace. Each "hurrah" sounded to me like a slap in the face.'[5]

Despite the disaster, Nicholas and Alexandra were urged by their uncles, the Grand Dukes, to attend a ball that night given by the French Ambassador, the Comte de Montebello. The French Government had gone to great trouble to furnish the Comte's house with works of art from Paris and might take exception if the Emperor absented himself at the last moment. It seems incredible that Nicholas and Alexandra could have accepted such advice. Nevertheless they appeared at the embassy and led the first quadrille. Apparently this was a feat in itself, as two hours earlier dozens of police minions had swarmed into the residence saying that a bomb was concealed in one of the flower pots. They had un-potted over two thousand plants, and the ballroom looked, according to a British guest, like a ploughed field. Not only the public but many members of the Imperial family were deeply shocked when they learned that the Emperor had danced at the French Embassy. 'Cold and heartless' was the verdict.

Unfortunately Alexandra continued to confirm this unfavourable impression. The first Court ball that she attended was a dismal failure. 'The awkward, shy, and silent young woman ... did not seem to possess the talent of drawing people to her,' wrote Princess Radziwill. 'She knew no one and she did not seem to wish to know anyone; she danced badly, not caring for dancing; and she certainly was not a brilliant conversationalist.' Apparently even her beauty went unnoticed, as it was spoiled by a bad complexion. 'She had red arms, red shoulders and a red face which always gave one the impression that she was about to burst into tears ... Everything about her was hieratic, to the very way she dressed in the heavy brocade of which she was so fond, and with diamonds scattered all over her, in defiance of good taste and common sense.'[6]

If Alexandra disappointed Court circles, she, in turn, viewed the Establishment with deepest suspicion. 'I feel that all who surround my husband are insincere,' she wrote during the first years of her marriage, 'and no one is doing his duty for Russia. They are all serving him for their career and personal advantage, and I worry myself and cry for days on end as I feel that my husband is very young and inexperienced, of which they are all taking advantage.'[7]

This beautiful, humourless, censorious princess despised St Petersburg society, forgetting that the nobility, whose ramifications stretched across the whole of Russia, was the most important prop on which the monarchy rested. Gradually the balls at the Winter Palace came to an end, and in their place came theatricals, which no one enjoyed, at the Hermitage. Then the theatricals ceased and the lights went out in the Imperial drawing-rooms of St Petersburg. Nicholas and Alexandra spent most of their time quietly at Tsarskoye Selo, living as much like a private family as possible, forgetting the duties expected of an Emperor and Empress.

During the first six years of their marriage Alexandra presented her husband with four daughters; and finally, in 1904, she gave birth to a boy, Alexis. Six weeks after this momentous event the baby bled at the navel. The awful spectre of haemophilia presented itself; but it was not until the boy was two that the hereditary disease was confirmed. It was, of course, incurable.

Alexandra and her two-year-old son. 'The Empress refused to surrender to fate,' wrote Grand Duke Alexander. 'She talked incessantly of the ignorance of the physicians. . . . She turned towards religion and her prayers were tinged with a certain hysteria.'

Meanwhile the new Emperor ruled by sudden and often contradictory urges. 'Nicholas II was almost entirely deficient in will,' wrote the British historian, Sir Bernard Pares, who lived in Russia for many years of the reign. 'Alexander had been his own Prime Minister. Nicholas had no Prime Minister at all. He was by no means deficient in personal courage, but it was the courage of a fatalist.' Nicholas's officials were less flattering. 'Mark my words, he will be a modern Paul I,' warned the Minister of the Interior, M. Durnovo. 'He is nothing but a rag that one cannot launder,' exclaimed General Cherevin. 'A ruler who cannot be trusted, who approves today what he will reject tomorrow, is incapable of steering the Ship of State,' wrote Sergius Witte.

Yet the dreamy Nicholas was not without ambition. Although his mind swung, like a pendulum between one impulse and the next he liked to imagine the Ship of State setting forth on a voyage of high adventure. 'I told Witte,' wrote General Kuropatkin in 1896, 'that our Czar had grandiose plans in his head: to capture Manchuria for Russia and to annex Korea. He is dreaming also of bringing Tibet under his dominion. He desires to take Persia, and to seize not only the Bosphorus but the Dardanelles.'[8]

The question of the Bosphorus arose when the Russian Ambassador to Constantinople, M. Nelidov, presented Nicholas with an incredibly hare-brained scheme which the latter seized upon with boyish excitement. As the Turks once again had outraged European feeling by carrying out massacres – this time against the Armenians – the Ambassador argued that the time was ripe for Russia to seize the heights of the Bosphorus above Constantinople. His proposal envisaged a bold *coup de main*, a sort of lightning commando operation, which would be an accomplished fact before Britain or any of the other great powers realized what was happening. The Emperor would dispatch thirty thousand troops on warships and transports from Odessa to the Upper Bosphorus and land them on both sides of the Straits.

The arrangements were amazingly amateurish. Nelidov would return to Constantinople; and when he deemed that the right moment had arrived he would give the signal for the descent of the Russian landing-force by a telegram: 'Long without news.' Nicholas held a secret ministerial council at which he won the support of the President and the Ministers of War and the Navy, but luckily Witte managed to convince him that the result would not be a localized conflict but a European war, with Britain and Austria allied with Turkey.

Three years later Nicholas had put the idea of force out of his mind and proposed a peace conference to be held at The Hague, at which the limitation of arms would be discussed. Apparently Russia was engaged in re-organizing her infantry and could not afford the increases in artillery being planned in Austria-Hungary. Twenty European powers accepted the invitation, as none wished to be branded as war-mongers, but privately they denounced the conference and agreed with the Prince of Wales when he described it as 'the greatest nonsense and rubbish I ever heard of'.

The Hague idea soon gave way to another impulse. A treaty signed with China in 1896 had accorded Russia the right to extend the Trans-Siberia Railway across the north of Manchuria. However, the Boxer Rebellion of 1900 presented Nicholas with a pretext for occupying the whole of Manchuria, which he did against the advice of his ministers. This upset the Japanese, who had their eyes on Korea. Nicholas could have reached an agreement with Tokyo by promising to remain within the confines of Manchuria and recognizing Japan's preponderance in Korea. But he had designs on Korea himself and in 1903 personally sanctioned the infiltration of Russian troops into Northern Korea and the exploitation of a timber concession near the Yalu River. By 1904 Russia and Japan were at war.

As usual, everybody thought that Russia would win, and as usual everybody was wrong. The Japanese inflicted heavy losses upon the Russian army, and once again Russian disorganization and corruption

Bloody Sunday

became glaringly apparent. 'This country has no real government,' lamented the British Chargé d'Affaires in St Petersburg in 1904, who continued:

> Each Minister acts on his own, doing as much damage as possible to the other Ministers . . . It is a curious state of things. There is an Emperor, a religious madman almost – without a statesman, or even a council – surrounded by a legion of Grand Dukes – thirty-five of them and not one of them at war at this moment, with a few priests and priestly women behind them. No middle class; an aristocracy ruined and absolutely without influence, an underpaid bureaucracy living, of necessity, on corruption. Beneath this, about 100 million of people gradually becoming poorer and poorer as they bear all the burden of taxation, drafted into the army in thousands. . . .[9]

Meanwhile the terrorists had sprung to life again. In 1902 they assassinated the Minister of the Interior, Sipyagin, and two years later his successor, Plehve. Terrorism no longer was a cottage industry; nor was the new generation of revolutionaries unsure of the path ahead. Two large and determined parties dominated the scene. The Social Democrats, or S.D.s, embraced Marxism and concentrated their propaganda on the factory workers in the urban centres. In 1903 their leader, Plenkhanov, quarrelled with one of his lieutenants, Lenin, and the party split into two groups, Mensheviks and Bolsheviks.

The second party, the Social Revolutionaries, or S.R.s, came into being in 1900 and worked to provoke an uprising among the peasants, advocating a socialist society based on the village commune. The S.R.s claimed to wear the mantle of 'Land and Liberty', and set up a terrorist Battle Organization to carry on the work of 'Will of the People', the group that had murdered Alexander II. The S.R.s were responsible for most of the murders from 1900 to 1909.

Although the propaganda of the S.D.s and the S.R.s set the stage for the miniature revolution of 1905, it was sparked off by a man who belonged to neither organization. In January a strike broke out in the Putilov engineering works in St Petersburg and spread rapidly to other factories. Father Gapon, a woolly-minded priest, who led a labour union authorized by the police, was faced with the choice of relinquishing his job or taking positive action. He decided to lead a peaceful demonstration of workers to the Winter Palace and present a petition to the Tsar. The paper called for a constituent assembly, an eight-hour day, freedom of speech and religion, an amnesty for political prisoners, etc. He had prepared the petition with the help of the S.R.s and had collected 135,000 signatures.

Nicholas was informed of the demonstration the night before, but it never crossed his mind to travel the fourteen miles to St Petersburg and to receive the document in person. Apparently none of his ministers thought of it either.

Instead, the maintenance of order was left to the St Petersburg police, who called in the army. As the vast crowd moved towards the

Nicholas was advised by his ministers to dissociate himself from the massacre. Instead, he decided to receive a small delegation of workers whom he lectured on the dangers of listening to the advice of treacherous revolutionaries.

Palace, carrying icons and religious banners, the troops opened fire, and between two and four thousand people were killed and wounded; when it was over the huge square was dotted with shapeless Russian bundles and the snow was stained an angry red.*

Bloody Sunday sent a shock-wave of anger and horror across the whole country. But the Empress Alexandra did her best to defend the action of the authorities.

Yes, the troops, alas, were obliged to fire [she wrote to her sister from Tsarskoye Selo]. Repeatedly the crowd was told to retreat and that Nicky was not in town (as we are living here this winter) and that one would be forced to shoot, but they would not heed and so blood was shed . . . Petersburg is a rotten town and not one atom Russian. The Russian people are deeply and truly devoted to their Sovereign and the revolutionaries use his name for provoking them against the landlords etc. but I don't know how. . . .[10]

*No one knows the exact number. The Empress, in a letter to her sister, claimed that only 92 people had been killed and between two and three hundred wounded; but most historians put the figure much higher.

Alexandra's flood-tide of emotion engulfed her husband and children. Far from diminishing her love, Nicholas's irresolute character called forth an untapped reservoir of maternal feeling. She worshipped him as a sweet-natured child who must be protected from the scheming world. She had a deep respect for the autocracy, imbibed from her early visits to Russia as the guest of her sister and brother-in-law, the Grand Duke Serge. Her task was to remind her beloved Nicky that his will was all that mattered.

Now she had a second axiom of faith, a view held by Nicholas himself. The great mass of the people, the peasants, worshipped the Tsar. If it were not for the intelligentsia, many of them Jews, the country would be free of disaster. Apparently it did not occur to Alexandra that Nicholas's own anti-semitism, inherited from his father, was not conducive to winning Jewish hearts and minds for the Tsar.

The Empress became convinced that if Nicholas could find the right man – a wise minister – to carry out his policies, internal difficulties would subside. Conversely, when things went wrong it was the fault of bad advisers. 'Poor Nicky . . . tries so hard,' she wrote to her sister, 'works with such perseverence but the lack of what I call "real" men is great . . . on my knees I pray God to give me wisdom to find a man and cannot; it is a desperate feeling. . . .'[11]

Although the Tsar hoped for military victories which would restore the prestige of the throne, in the middle of April 1904 Russian troops were defeated at Turenchen; in August, after an unsuccessful engagement near Miao-Yang, the army fell back on Mukden; and in December Port Arthur fell to the enemy. By this time even the occupation army in Manchuria was demoralized; but a worse blow was still to come. The Emperor despatched the Baltic Fleet to the Far East; and in May 1905 it was annihilated in the Battle of Tsushima. There was no alternative but to sue for peace. Nicholas II sent for Sergius Witte, who had resigned two years earlier in protest at the penetration of Korea, and asked him to negotiate terms with Japan.

By this time the whole Empire was disaffected. In February Nicholas's uncle, the hated Grand Duke Serge, had been assassinated; and as the months rolled by violence spread to every corner of the Empire. 'It makes me sick to read the news,' wrote Nicholas to his brother, 'strikes in schools and factories, murdered policemen, Cossacks, riots. But the ministers, instead of acting with quick decision, only assemble in councils like a lot of frightened hens and cackle about providing united ministerial action.'[12]

By the middle of October conditions had worsened and the country was in the grip of a general strike. Factories closed down, trains came to a halt, and in St Petersburg the electric lights went out and deliveries of food ceased. In the country peasants raided estates, burning the houses and stealing the cattle. In the Black Sea the crew of the *Potemkin* mutinied. Barricades sprang up in the streets of Odessa, Kharkov and Ekaterinoslav.

A revolutionary view of the icing on the cake. Above the oppressed workers are the rich capitalists: 'We do the eating'; then the army, 'We shoot you'; the clergy, 'We mislead you'; and finally the Imperial family, 'We rule you'.

As the court prepared to celebrate the Romanov tercentenary, unrest among the workers continued to grow. At the Lena gold mines, a drunken police officer ordered his men to fire at demonstrators, and two hundred people were killed.

253

Overnight a new leader emerged. Leon Trotsky, a member of the Menshevik branch of the Marxist S.D.s, announced the formation of a *soviet* or council, with each member representing a thousand workers. The council threatened to wreck every factory which did not shut, causing Nicholas to retaliate by sending troops into the big centres. Civil war was imminent. Sergius Witte, who had been made a Count as a reward for his skilful peace negotiations, implored the Emperor to give Russia a constitution. This, and this alone, was the only concession that would rally the liberal elements, now in danger of swinging to the extremists. After anguished soul-searching, Nicholas II agreed to the momentous step. Witte was invited to accept the Presidency of the Council.

The Imperial Manifesto of October 1905 transformed Russia from an autocracy into a semi-constitutional monarchy. It promised 'freedom of conscience, speech, assembly and association'; it granted an elected Parliament, the Duma, and pledged that 'no law may go into force without the consent of the State Duma'. Yet this announcement did not quieten things as Witte had hoped. The extremists of the left were furious as they saw the revolution slipping from their grasp, and they doubled their activities, while the extremists of the right turned against the Jews and instigated terrible pogroms.

Nicholas and Alexandra did what they always did on such occasions; blamed Witte for their misfortunes. In one breath Nicholas told his mother that he was trying to force Witte to act 'more energetically'; in the next that he had never seen 'such a chameleon of a man'. 'Now he wants to hang and shoot everybody.' Instead of backing Witte's policy and giving it time to work, Nicholas encouraged him to draft a series of Fundamental Laws designed to reduce the powers so recently given to the Duma. Law One read: 'To the Emperor of All the Russias belongs the supreme autocratic power.' Then he asked for Witte's resignation and appointed a hopeless old gentleman, Goremykin, in his place.

The first Duma lasted only two months. Apart from the two revolutionary parties, the S.D.s and the S.R.s, two liberal parties had sprung up, the Cadets and the Octobrists. When the Duma met in May 1906 its 524 members represented all four parties.

Nicholas, however, was appalled by the Address to the Throne, which demanded universal suffrage, land reforms, the release of political prisoners, and the pledge only to appoint ministers with the approval of the Duma. In the opening session the speakers delivered stinging attacks on the Government; and when, in July 1906, Goremykin resigned and Stolypin became Prime Minister, the Tsar urged him to shut down the Parliament, which he did.

Stolypin, a tall man with a dead white face and a jet black beard, was the most able Prime Minister the Russians ever had. 'I cannot tell you how much I have come to like and respect this man,' Nicholas wrote to his mother.

Stolypin was no time-server. Although the Emperor would have

The Winter Palace, St Petersburg, now the State Hermitage Museum, Leningrad

liked to have kept the Duma in permanent suspension, Stolypin insisted that the October Manifesto be honoured. A second Duma met later in the year, but ended with thirty S.D.s being sent to Siberia, and other members of the revolutionary parties being put under surveillance. Stolypin then published a new electoral law which abolished universal suffrage and concentrated the elective power largely in the hands of the country gentry. The Third Duma met at the end of 1907 and lasted until 1912.

Under Stolypin's stern leadership and imaginative reforms the country gradually quietened down. Once again the great palaces of St Petersburg blazed with lights; once again guests made their way home as dawn was breaking over the ice-bound capital, or climbed into troikas and flew over the snow to the Islands to listen to the melancholy gypsy songs.

The Grand Duke Vladimir and his clever wife, Marie Pavlovna, made up for the darkened windows of the Winter Palace by providing an alternative court. In their vast drawing-rooms the world of rank and riches mingled with dancers and writers and musicians. The sharp tongue of the Grand Duchess did not spare the Empress Alexandra, whom she held responsible for Nicholas's failure to carry out his social duties. When Marie Pavlovna visited Bulgaria and was congratulated by an official on her impeccable memory she replied tersely: 'One ought to know one's job. You may pass that on to the Grand Court.'

The Grand Duke Vladimir was President of the Academy of Arts and took a special interest in the ballet. In 1907 he made friends with an impresario, Diaghilev, who complained that the management of the Imperial Theatre – the Maryinsky – was too conservative. Diaghilev had a dream: to collect a troupe of artists from the Maryinsky and take them abroad from May to September when the Russian theatre was shut. He would provide them with new dances and new music.

Vladimir backed Diaghilev with his own money. Between 1909 and 1914 his brilliant protégé thrilled the capitals of the West by blending music, poetry, painting and dancing in a way that had never been done before. Sometimes Diaghilev created new ballets; sometimes he took the Maryinsky's staid productions – *Le Pavillon, Prince Igor, Carnaval* – and cast his magic over them. He employed artists such as Benois and Bakst to design his sets; encouraged great choreographers such as Fokine to strike out on new lines; and finally commissioned the great Stravinsky to write music for ballet rather than adapting ballet to existing music.

Not everyone liked Diaghilev's break with the past. When *Le Sacré du Printemps* was shown in Paris in the spring of 1913 it was greeted with catcalls that nearly stopped the performance. In London the critic of the *Daily Mail* described Nijinsky's steps as 'comic' and Stravinsky's music as 'sheer anarchy'. 'I am accused of a "crime against grace,"' the dancer retorted. '. . . . Really I have a horror of the very word. "Grace" and "Charm" make me feel sea-sick . . . I detest conventional "nightingale

Romanov Tercentenary Egg made by Fabergé. It bears the portraits of thirteen Romanov rulers.

The Tsar and his friends bathing (*right*). Nicholas enjoyed the water so much and considered it so healthy that he had a large indoor pool constructed and filled with warm salt water, so that he and his family could swim daily.

'Our constitution – please don't blow!'

and rose" poetry; my own inclinations are "primitive". I eat my meat without Sauce Béarnaise.'

While Diaghilev tantalized and dismayed foreign audiences, the fashionable world of Russia was engrossed in stock market speculation. Aristocratic officers of the Guards, who formerly gambled at cards, now gambled on steel and wool. The Grand Duchess delighted her guests by introducing them to promoters – 'a genius from Odessa, darling, who has made a terrific killing in tobacco'.

Money, easily won, was easily spent, and the imposing building with the granite pillars on the Morskaya, where Fabergé presented his wonderful jewelry, was crowded with opulent buyers. The great craftsman had reached the zenith of his fame in 1900, when he had created a Great Siberian Easter Egg, in commemoration of Nicholas II's one-time presidency. Inside the egg was a scale model of the locomotive and five cars of the Siberian express. 'Driving wheels, double trucks under carriages, and other moving parts were precision made to work so that, given a few turns with a gold key . . . the gold and platinum locomotive, with a ruby gleaming from its headlight, could actually pull the train.'[13]

If the Emperor had found the man he needed in Stolypin, the Empress, at almost the same time, had found another man, not only needed, but worshipped, deified. He was to prove fateful to both their existences. By the middle of 1905 there was not the shadow of a doubt that Alexis was suffering from haemophilia, a hereditary malady stemming from the weakness of the finer blood vessels, carried by females and only transmitted to males. Queen Victoria was the carrier. Her son, Prince Leopold, was afflicted by the disease; and two of her granddaughters, Princess Henry of Prussia and Empress Alexandra transmitted it in turn to their sons. The slightest bruise could lead to haemorrhages and swellings as the blood would not clot; and this caused the sufferer days, sometimes weeks, of excruciating pain.

Queen Victoria (*centre*) who was grandmother to most European royalty, had a mutant gene which made her a carrier of haemophilia. The Romanovs were tragically affected through the queen's daughter Alice (*seated far right with baby*), mother of Alexandra.

Although Alexis's condition was a closely guarded secret, the sight of a Cossack carrying the heir caused great consternation. One eye-witness wrote, 'I clearly heard exclamations of sorrow at the sight of this poor helpless child. . . .'

The knowledge that her wonderful son, the heir to a great throne, was doomed to a life of seclusion and suffering caused the Empress such anguish that she flung herself into the arms of the Church with the same frenzied abandon as had another Princess of Hesse-Darmstadt – Marie, the wife of Alexander II. Alexandra refused to accept the fact that the disease was incurable. Where the doctors failed, God would protect. It was only a matter of faith.

This was Alexandra's mood when the superstitious Montenegrin princesses, married to Russian Grand Dukes, brought an illiterate, *farouche* holy man, or *starets*, into the imperial family. On 1 November 1905 the Emperor wrote in his diary: 'We have got to know a man of God – Gregory – from the Tobolsk province.' Gregory Rasputin was tall and dark with a thick black beard and a sensuous mouth. But 'the full expression of his personality,' wrote the French Ambassador, Maurice Paléologue, 'seemed concentrated in his eyes. They were pale blue, of exceptional brilliance, depth and attraction. His gaze was at once piercing and caressing, naïve and cunning, far-off and intent. When he is in earnest conversations his pupils seem to radiate magnetism. He carried with him a strong animal smell, like the smell of a goat.'[14]

From the very first, this astonishing man seemed able to soothe the child, to banish a headache, to put him to sleep. As Alexis grew older he was not allowed to run about, to play games and ride bicycles like other boys. But the bumps and bruises came anyway, and only Rasputin could bring relief. 'Call it what you will,' said Alexis's nurse, Teglova, 'he could really promise her [the Empress] her boy's life . . .'

The 'holy man' was not only dirty and foul-smelling, but drunken and lascivious. Ladies who visited him looking for salvation usually found themselves in bed with him. He staged orgies that came to the attention of the police, and before long his link with the Imperial family had be-become a subject of anxious speculation among the Tsar's ministers. No one, however, knew the reason for the Empress's dependence upon Rasputin, as Alexis's disease was a closely guarded secret. The parents feared that the boy might be unacceptable as heir if his condition were known. Most people believed that Rasputin had won the Imperial favour through the Empress's religious fanaticism.

Surprisingly enough, Rasputin did not often visit Alexis in person. As long as the Empress kept in touch with him, which she did through her friend Anna Virubova, he was able to exert his powers from afar. Nevertheless he was not one to hide his connection with the Emperor and Empress. He called them 'papa' and 'mama' in peasant fashion, and boasted widely of the esteem in which he was held.

Early in 1911 the Prime Minister, Stolypin, ordered a police investigation of Rasputin's debaucheries, and sent a shocking and detailed report to Nicholas. The Emperor refused to take any action and the Empress indignantly dismissed the charges as a tissue of lies. 'Saints are always calumniated,' she told a friend. 'He is hated because we love him.'

Stolypin was so disgusted by Rasputin's licentiousness, however, that

Rasputin recognized that the strength of his position lay in his patrons' autocracy, and that if the Duma (*below*) were to be given more power, he would be the first to go.

on his own authority he ordered him out of St Petersburg. Although Alexandra raged, Nicholas was afraid to overrule the Prime Minister. From that day onwards the Empress hated Stolypin with every fibre of her body. She did not have to tolerate him for long, however, as he was shot by a terrorist later in the year while attending an opera in Kiev, at which Nicholas and Alexandra were also present. The Prime Minister was taken to a nursing home and lived for three days. His friend and Cabinet colleague, Kokovtsov, who spent most of his time at the hospital, claims in his memoirs that the Imperial family did not visit the dying man or send any condolences. Only when Stolypin was dead did they pay their respects. His widow was so angry she refused to see them.

Kokovtsov succeeded Stolypin as Nicholas's Chief Minister and was shocked by the coldness with which the Empress alluded to his predecessor. 'Find your support in the confidence of the Tsar,' she told him. '. . . The Lord will help you. I am sure that Stolypin died to make room for you, and this is all for the good of Russia.'

Despite the fact that the Empress alienated almost everyone with whom she came in contact, as 1913 drew closer the St Petersburg nobility hoped that Alexandra would make an effort to win popularity with the public: 1913 was the year of the Romanov Tercentenary. Three hundred years earlier the boyars had searched for Michael Romanov and found him living quietly at Ipatiev Abbey near Kostromo. They had escorted him back to Moscow and crowned him King of Muscovy. His descendant, Nicholas II, was not only Tsar of Muscovy but ruler of a vast Empire. Although Turgenev had evoked the picture of Holy Russia in a drunken stupor, with 'her forehead at the Pole and her feet in the Caucasus', no one could deny that the size of the giantess was ever-expanding.

For this reason alone the celebrations should have been triumphant. Instead, even the Te Deum at Kazan Cathedral on 6 March, which marked the opening of the ceremonies, aroused little enthusiasm. It was raining hard and the crowd that lined the Imperial route was embarrassingly thin. All the famous Guards regiments, carrying their standards, led the procession; then came an open victoria in which sat the Emperor and his 8-year-old son. He was followed by two state coaches, the first carrying the Empress Alexandra and the Dowager Empress, and the second the four daughters.

The Cathedral was filled with the highest dignitaries of the State, and when the Imperial family entered a hush fell over the assembly. Alexis, looking painfully thin and pale, was carried by a Cossack. What was wrong with the boy? Nobody knew. The Empress, on the other hand, appeared as remote and disdainful as ever. It was a fairy-story setting, yet there was no feeling of warmth in the vast assembly, only irritation.

Nicholas II refused to give a ball at the Winter Palace, and the Empress failed to appear at the two receptions held by the Tsar. The only real glimpse the public had of her was at the Maryinsky Theatre where Glinka's *Life for the Tsar* was sung.

Her lovely tragic face was expressionless, almost austere as she stood by her husband's side during the playing of the National Anthem . . . [wrote Meriel Buchanan, the daughter of the British Ambassador]. Not once did a smile break the immobile sombreness . . . The Diplomatic Body had been given places all along the first tier and our box happened to be next to the Imperial one, and, sitting so close, we could see that the fan of white eagles' feathers the Empress was holding was trembling convulsively, we could see how a dull, unbecoming flush was stealing over her pallor, could almost hear the belaboured breathing which made the diamonds which covered her bodice rise and fall, flashing and trembling with a thousand uneasy sparks of light.[15]

A few minutes later the Empress left the box and a wave of resentment rippled across the theatre. Was it not always the same story?

No one except the Imperial family knew that the Empress's anxiety over her son, Alexis, had unbalanced her nervous system; that she suffered from psychosomatic hysteria which produced dizziness and heart palpitations. At Tsarskoye Selo she in fact lived the life of a semi-invalid, spending half her day reclining on a chaise-longue in her mauve boudoir.

In the year of the tercentenary, Alexandra looked back to the time when she had arrived in St Petersburg as a bride. 'I was so happy then, so well and strong. Now I am a wreck.'

Both the aristocracy and the general public were unaware of the fact that the heir was suffering from haemophilia. Six months earlier, in the autumn of 1912, Alexis had nearly died. Bulletins were issued and the press had speculated wildly as to the nature of his illness. Some journalists claimed that he had been born with too few layers of skin; others that he suffered from an incurable bone disease. Alexis had bumped his leg climbing out of a boat at Spala, the Tsar's shooting lodge in Poland. Internal bleeding had started, causing a tumour to form in his groin. The pain was excruciating. The swelling pressed on the inflamed nerves of his leg and his temperature rose alarmingly. For eleven days the Empress never undressed, never went to bed, never lay down for more than an hour at a time. She sat soothing the brow of the child who lay huddled on one side, moaning with pain, his left leg drawn up so sharply that for nearly a year afterwards he could not straighten it out. No one thought the boy could live.

After dinner when we were sitting very quietly in the Empress's boudoir [wrote Anna Virubova, the Empress Alexandra's confidante] Princess Henry of Prussia, who had come to be with her sister in her trouble, appeared in the doorway very white and agitated and begged members of the suite to retire as the child's condition was desperate. At eleven o'clock the Emperor and Empress entered the room, despair written on their faces. Still the Empress declared that she could not believe that God had abandoned them and she asked me to telegraph Rasputin for his prayers. His reply came quickly. 'The little one will not die,' it said. 'Do not allow the doctors to bother him too much.' As a matter of fact the turning came a few days later, the pain subsided, and the boy lay wasted and utterly spent, but alive.[16]

It is not surprising that the Empress felt Rasputin to be indispensable.

TILL FURTHER NOTICE.

Both Britain and Russia were highly suspicious of each other's moves in the Far East. After the Japanese fiasco, Russian nationalists talked wildly of attacking India, and Nicholas himself referred to the British as 'our mangy enemies'.

After Spala she believed utterly that he was a man of God. And she not only turned to him to ease the pain of her son but to instruct the Emperor on how to run his Empire.

With his Far Eastern venture at an end, Nicholas once again began to dream of Constantinople – or the domination of the Balkans, which could lead to the same thing. The stumbling block of course, was Austria-Hungary.

Nicholas II was persuaded that there were ways of circumventing this barrier. He played a dangerous game by allowing his officials to use Serbia to stir up trouble in the Austrian Empire, particularly in Bosnia and Herzegovina which became honeycombed with subversive societies. He also allowed the formation of a Balkan League which, as Poincaré, the French President, pointed out, contained 'the germ not only of war against Turkey but ... Austria' and established further 'the hegemony of Russia over the Slav Kingdoms. ...'

The Balkan League declared war on Turkey and their unexpected victories were hailed in Moscow and St Petersburg. Serbia's increase in territory and growing arrogance worried the British Ambassador in Vienna, Sir Fairfax Cartwright, who wrote to London in January 1913: 'Serbia may some day set Europe by the ears and bring about a universal conflict on the Continent. I cannot tell you how exasperated people are getting here at the continual worry that little country causes Austria under encouragement from Russia. ...'

Many of Nicholas's advisers were disappointed that the Emperor had not taken Russia into the Balkan War. He nearly succumbed, but Rasputin intervened with the Empress. 'Fear, fear war,' he said; and the Empress managed to dissuade her husband. This story became common knowledge. In December 1913 the Holy Synod paper referred sarcastically to Rasputin's political rôle. 'That we escaped a war last year is due to the holy *starets* who directs our foreign policy for which we should be profoundly grateful. ...'

There were others, besides the Panslavists, who were bitterly disappointed that peace had been maintained. 'A war between Austria and Russia,' wrote Lenin in the spring of 1913, to his friend Maxim Gorky (who ran a school for revolutionaries on the unlikely island of Capri), 'would be a very useful thing for the revolution ... but it is not likely that Franz Joseph [the Austrian Emperor] or Nikolasha [the Tsar] will oblige.'

Things were not going well for the Bolshevik revolutionaries in 1913, for Russian industry was enjoying a boom. Production was increasing, foreign trade was expanding, gold reserves were swelling. Strikes were also multiplying, but optimistic employers dismissed them as normal growing pains. 'Russia was rapidly moving ahead along the capitalist lines of development, catching up with the older capitalist countries ... ,' a Soviet historian tells us in *Outlines of History of the October Revolution*.

Even agriculture was expanding due to the change in Government policy. Formerly the Government had tried by all kinds of artificial means to preserve the landlords' holdings. Now it had seriously begun to encourage the transfer of these lands into the hands of the peasants. Between 1906 and 1913 the State Peasant Land Bank had bought up from the landlords and resold to the peasants over twenty million acres of land. Even Trotsky admitted that the pre-war years saw giant strides. 'Agriculture entered upon a state of indubitable capitalistic boom,' he wrote. 'The export of agricultural products from Russia rose between 1908 and 1912 from one billion roubles to one and a half billion roubles.'[17]

In 1912 the Fourth Duma was elected. It contained only a handful of Marxist extremists – eight Mensheviks, and six Bolsheviks directed by Lenin from his refuge in Austria. The Mensheviks were now the majority party and Lenin was so poor that he found it hard to survive. 'His chief means of livelihood was the meagre salary the party was able to pay him, which at times was far from sufficient, so that in 1913 he even considered having to give up his work in Austria, emigrate to England and find some means of earning a living.' 'These were terrible moments,' one of the Duma Deputies records. 'What if the party cannot find any means? Then Ilyich will have to leave the movement, for he never gets his work into either bourgeois journals or newspapers.'[18]

Lenin's man in St Petersburg was Joseph Stalin who, in 1912, launched the newspaper *Pravda*. Although the newspaper flourished for two years and achieved a circulation of 40,000, Stalin was picked up by the police in 1914 and sent to Siberia.

The ranks were thinning out. According to Alexander Kerensky, a newly-elected Labour Deputy in the Fourth Duma, there no longer was any need for secret underground activity. 'The public was now accustomed to a free press,' he wrote, 'to political meetings, to political parties and clubs. [The Duma] could . . . give expression to the feeling of every class since freedom of speech for the deputies was absolute . . . The old secretive underground conspiratorial methods of revolutionary activity had passed to the limbo of history.'[19]

Yet industrial unrest once again was growing. In 1910 there had been 222 strikes; in 1914, between the months of January and July, over 4000.

In the early months of 1914 many European statesmen believed that the danger of a world war had passed. 'Never,' said David Lloyd George on New Year's Day, 'has the sky been more perfectly blue.' Six months later a group of revolutionaries from Bosnia, Austria's controversial province, trained and encouraged by the Serbian Chief of Intelligence, who in turn was encouraged by the Russian military attaché in Belgrade, acting on orders from the Imperial General Staff in St Petersburg, threw a bomb at the Archduke Franz Ferdinand, heir to the Austrian throne. Both the Archduke and his wife were killed.

An outraged Austria, well aware that the Serbian Panslavist organizations engaged in terrorist activities in the Habsburg Empire were subsidized by Russia, decided to strike at the root of the trouble by occupying Belgrade. Russia immediately countered by setting herself up as the 'protectress of the Slavs', a rôle that she had always been eager to assume but which, until now, had been strenuously denied her by the Western Powers. Once again Russia and Austria faced each other as the main protagonists in a quarrel that had been simmering ever since the Crimean War.

> Austria, in acting against Serbia, was taking the only step by which she believed that she could preserve her very existence as a state [wrote the American historian, Sidney Fay]. Russia however, in claiming to protect Serbia and to exercise a kind of protection over the Balkan Slavs, did not have any such vital interest at stake; her existence as a state was not in jeopardy; her interest was more to preserve and increase her prestige. Austria's action aimed at a localized war. Russia's action made inevitable a European War.[20]

Germany had no choice but to support her ally, Austria, and France no choice but to join Russia. For a few days Britain sat on the side-lines, but when Germany invaded Belgium aligned herself with France. The most fearful holocaust in history had begun.

During the feverish five weeks of diplomatic activity before the declaration of war Rasputin had done everything in his power to prevent the conflict. He was in his native village of Pokrovski in Siberia, recovering from a stab wound given him by a jealous woman. He telegraphed to the Tsar: 'Let Papa not plan war for with war will come the end of Russia and yourselves and you will lose to the last man.'

The Empress regarded his pronouncement as prophetic; and Anna Virubova tells us in her memoirs that she implored Nicholas to resist his militarists. When she learned that the die had been cast she gave way to a paroxysm of tears, declaring passionately: 'This is the end of everything!' The next day, when the Imperial pair travelled to St Petersburg to be present at the reading of the Manifesto in the Winter Palace, Alexandra's distress was apparent, and unjustly attributed to her German sympathies.

But the fickle crowd outside the Winter Palace had forgotten its grievances. The enthusiasm for war was so tremendous that it had closed the chasm between ruler and ruled, just as in the days of the Napoleonic invasion. When the Emperor and Empress stepped onto the balcony of the Winter Palace thousands fell on their knees. Nicholas raised his hand and tried to speak, but someone began singing the National Anthem and soon it had swelled into a thunderous refrain. 'To those thousands on their knees,' wrote Paléologue, 'at that moment the Czar was really the Autocrat, the military, political and religious director of his people, the absolute master of their bodies and souls.'[21]

Eighteen months earlier, in 1912, the War Minister Sukhomlinov had written an article for the St Petersburg army manual flamboyantly entitled: 'We are Ready', but ready was the one thing the army was not, at least against the relentless and meticulous German machine. The Russian artillery ran out of shells within a few months of the opening of

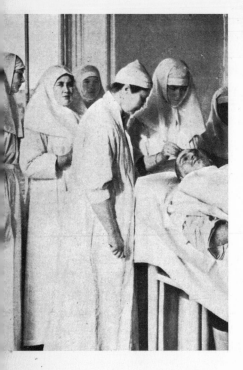

The Empress (*centre*) nursing, with her daughters Tatiana and Olga on her left

hostilities; at one moment gunners were threatened with a court-martial if they fired more than three rounds a day. Yet the Russian débâcle cannot be blamed on an ammunition shortage. It was a Romanov tradition to go to war in a hopeless sea of inefficiency and corruption, to spill oceans of blood, to endure the humiliation of defeat, yet to remain, through sheer size, massively intact.

In 1914 the Russian Army was crushed in Eastern Prussia; in 1915 it lost Poland, Lithuania and Courland; and before the year was over it suffered disasters in Galicia on an unprecedented scale. During the first twelve months of the war the number of casualties – dead, wounded and prisoner – came to the staggering figure of 3,800,000 men.

For much of this terrible year the Emperor lived at Army headquarters, where his cousin, the six-foot-six Grand Duke Nicholas Nicholayevich, with trim white beard and blazing blue eyes, commanded the army. The Empress and her daughters put on Red Cross uniforms and spent their time at the hospitals nursing the wounded.

At the end of 1914 Rasputin returned to Petrograd, as the capital was now called, and a few months later he performed a 'miracle'. Anna Virubova lay dying as the result of a train accident. Her skull and spine had been badly injured and her legs crushed by a steel girder. The surgeon had given up all hope, but when Rasputin strode into her bedroom and commanded her to open her eyes and speak she responded. 'She will recover but she will remain a cripple,' he pronounced. The prognosis proved correct; soon she was well, but walking on crutches. If Alexandra needed any more proof that Rasputin was a man of God, possessed of supernatural power, this episode provided it. From that moment onwards she placed her whole faith in his hands.

This marked the beginning of one of the most bizarre, pathetic, grotesque, tragi-comedies in history. Alexandra and Nicholas exchanged passionate love-letters every day that they were parted; but now Alexandra's letters contained more than endearments. She referred to Rasputin as 'our Friend' and judged everyone's goodness and capacity by their attitude toward the *starets*. Those who snubbed or criticized him aroused her implacable enmity. Unfortunately, Rasputin asked permission of the Grand Duke Nicholas to visit Army headquarters. 'Yes, do come,' was the reply. 'I'll hang you.'

Alexandra blazed with anger, and immediately set about the business of persuading Nicholas to sack his cousin as Commander-in-Chief. 'I have absolutely no faith in N – know him to be far from clever,' she wrote to her husband on 16 July 1915, 'and having gone against a man of God, his work can't be blessed or his advice good . . .'; on 17 June: 'Nobody knows who is Emperor now . . . It is as though N settles all'; on 24 June: 'Ah, my Nicky things are not as they ought to be and therefore N keeps you near to have a hold over you.'[22] This barrage of criticism was maintained until, in August, the Emperor decided to relieve the Grand Duke of his functions and take over command of the army himself.

Nicholas's Council of State was aghast. Eight of his thirteen ministers signed a joint letter tendering their resignations, but the Emperor merely ordered them to remain at their posts. 'The behaviour of some of my ministers amazes me . . .' he wrote plaintively to Alexandra.

But now the ministers no longer belonged to the Emperor. To all intents and purposes they had become the servants of the Empress, for with Nicholas II living permanently at Army headquarters, Alexandra was Regent of Russia in all but name. Her mind was filled with the over-riding determination to get rid of the eight ministers who had dared to challenge the Autocrat's authority. She succeeded completely. 'Forgive me, but I don't like the choice of Minister of War, Polivanov. Is he not our Friend's enemy?' '. . . long-nosed Sazonov . . . Sazonov is such a pancake. . . .'

The Empress's zeal did not end with the demise of the eight defiant ministers. She continued to put forward and champion 'our Friend's' recommendations, which came with bewildering rapidity. Rasputin held his own court, demoting anyone who offended, rewarding anyone who pleased. During the next eighteen months Russia had four different Prime Ministers, five ministers of the interior, four ministers of agriculture, and three ministers of war. Occasionally Nicholas II protested. 'You must agree that our Friend's ideas are sometimes odd . . . Com-

Alexandra's letters to Nicholas reveal glimpses of the private life of their children (*below*). 'Baby (Alexis) improves playing the balalaika. Tatiana too . . . Marie stands at the door and, alas! picks her nose. . . .'

plaints come from everywhere'; 'Our Friend's opinions of people are sometimes very strange . . . One must be careful . . . All these changes are not good for the country.' But in the end he always bowed to his wife's will. 'After the middle of 1915,' wrote the historian Michael Florinsky, 'the fairly honourable and efficient group who formed the top of the bureaucratic pyramid degenerated into a rapidly changing succession of the appointees of Rasputin. It was an amazing and extravagant and pitiful spectacle, and one without parallel. . . .'[23]

It was not Alexandra's ailing son who had turned her into an autocrat, as some writers suggest. Queen Victoria's eldest daughter had written to her mother, long before Alexandra's marriage, that 'Alix is very imperious and will always insist on having her own way; she will never yield one iota of the power she will imagine she wields. . . .'[24] Alexandra had always resented the Duma, and Rasputin encouraged her antipathy until she could speak of the institution only with a burning contempt. 'Now that members of the Duma want to meet in Moscow . . . Lovie, have that assembly . . . forbidden . . . You are lord and master of Russia, autocrat, remember that.' And again: 'We are not a constitutional country, and dare not be; our people are not educated for it, thank God, our Emperor is an autocrat, and must stick to this as you do – only you must show more power and decision. I should have cleared out quickly those I did not care for.'[25]

The letters became progressively more lunatic. She advises Nicholas to keep an image in his hand, and several times to comb his hair with Rasputin's comb before seeing his ministers. She tells him that 'our Friend sends his blessing to the whole Orthodox army. He begs that we should not strongly advance in the north, because he says if our successes continue good in the south they will themselves retreat in the north . . .'[26] She lashes out against the Dowager Empress. 'When you see poor, dear Mother, you must rather sharply tell her how pained you are that she listens to slander and does not stop it, as it causes mischief and others would be delighted, I am sure, to turn her against me, people are so mean. . . .'

With worsening conditions even members of the Imperial family could sense the growing unpopularity of the autocracy. One by one Nicholas II's relations came to him and begged him to grant Russia a constitutional government. They even told him that his wife was hated. Each time Alexandra responded with the ferocity of a wounded lioness. 'Show everyone that you are master . . . Why do people hate me? Because they know I have a strong will and that when I am convinced a thing is right (when, besides, blessed by Gregory) I do not change my mind . . .' And again: 'Be master, and all will bow down to you. We have been placed by God on a throne, and we must keep it firm and give it to our son intact. . . .'[27]

This last letter was written in December 1916. By this time the Russian army was facing total collapse. In the two and a half years since the outbreak of war 15,000,000 men had been called to the colours.

The casualties, including dead, wounded and prisoners, came to nearly 8,000,000 – over half the total. The corruption, incompetence, and abyssmal lack of leadership was responsible for a large proportion of these figures.

The paralysing shortage of equipment meant that many soldiers had no weapons at all and were obliged to rummage through mounds of corpses for rifles and bayonets. Shells were still rationed, and hospitals so scarce that the wounded often were not picked up from the battle-fields. The peasants, who provided the cannon fodder, had lost all faith in the Tsar, their Little Father, who, as Commander-in-Chief, had identified himself wholly with the disasters of the army. 'When ten or fifteen generals are on the gallows we shall begin to win,' was a remark frequently heard in the villages.

The situation in the big cities was not much better. Rising prices, a scarcity of food, and a fall in real wages was producing widespread demoralization. 'The proletariat of the capital is on the verge of despair,' a Police Department report stated. '. . . The mass of industrial workers are quite ready to let themselves go to the wildest excesses of a hunger riot.'

Rasputin's connection with the Palace was common knowledge. Everyone knew that the drunken, boisterous *starets* enjoyed the Empress's confidence, and the ordinary man in the street assumed that she was his mistress. Even more sinister, rumours were circulating that the Holy Man was a German agent. His opposition to the war was well known; and the fact that he dined every week with a Petrograd banker, Manus, seemed to strengthen the accusation. Rasputin was not noted for his discretion, and his tongue was loosened still further by the pretty women and abundant drink with which Manus provided him.

Even the Imperial family believed that information from Rasputin was falling into enemy hands. Indeed, the affair was becoming such a scandal that people were whispering that the Empress should be de-ported – some even said, murdered. On 2 December 1916 a right-wing deputy, Purishkevich, an ardent supporter of the dynasty, stood up in the Duma and for two hours denounced the 'dark forces' which were destroying the monarchy. It required only the recommendation of Rasputin to raise the most abject citizen to high office, he cried in ringing tones. Then, turning to the Ministers, he begged them to have the courage to tell the Emperor the truth. 'Have the courage to tell him that the multitude is threatening in its wrath . . . Revolution threatens and an obscure muzhik shall govern Russia no longer.'[28]

A rich young nobleman, Prince Felix Yusupov, heard the speech and next day called on Purishkevich. He knew by experience, he said, that the Emperor would not listen to criticism of Rasputin; therefore he had decided to kill the *starets*, but he needed assistance. Purishkevich agreed to help, and three others were found: the 26-year-old Grand Duke Dimitry, a cousin of the Tsar; an army officer, Sukhotin; and a doctor, Lazovert.

The proletarian hammer smashes the old to make way for the new. Sketch by Ischeremunch.

The scheme was simple enough: Yusupov would invite Rasputin to his house – the fabulous Moika Palace – and feed him poison. The others would have the task of disposing of the body. Everything went according to plan except that Rasputin would not die. Yusupov led him to the luxurious salon in the basement, where late-night revellers often gathered in order not to wake up other occupants in the house, and offered him refreshment. Rasputin drank two glasses of poisoned wine and devoured two poisoned cakes, and began to sing. Yusupov then went upstairs to get a pistol. When he returned he drew Rasputin's attention to an icon on the wall, and while the *starets* was examining it, shot him in the back. The victim fell down, apparently dead. Yusupov started up the stairs and suddenly heard a roar. Rasputin was on his feet lurching towards him.

The Prince, who had always feared the *starets'* supernatural powers, was convinced that he was facing a devil. Terror-stricken, he ran screaming to his friends. Rasputin reached the front hall and walked out of the door into the courtyard. Purishkevich, who saw his prey slipping away, ran after him brandishing his pistol. He fired at the man's back four times, hitting him twice. Once again, Rasputin fell to the ground. This time his assassins bound him hand and foot and took him to the Neva. They made a hole in the ice and dumped him in.

The Empress knew from Anna Virubova that Rasputin had accepted an invitation from Felix Yusupov, and had not been seen since. She fought against fears of foul play, but at the same time wrote urgently to Nicholas to return to Tsarskoye Selo. 'I cannot and won't believe that he has been killed. God have mercy. Such utter anguish (am calm and can't believe it) ... Come quickly....'[29]

The corpse was found three days later. It was buried in the Imperial Park at Tsarskoye Selo. The Empress, ashy white, her blue eyes tragic in their tearlessness, placed a letter on the Holy Man's breast before the coffin lid was fastened: 'My dear martyr give me thy blessing that it may follow me always on the sad and dreary path I have yet to follow here below. And remember us from on high in your holy prayers. Alexandra.'[30]

Although thousands of people rejoiced at the death of Rasputin, even kissing each other in the streets, the passing of 'the Beast' brought no relief to the fortunes of Russia. By the end of February 1917 the shortage of food and fuel in Petrograd was acute. The army had taken fifteen million men off the farms; the railway system had never been more than barely adequate; and now in a month of bitter cold, twelve hundred locomotives froze and burst. The inadequate supplies of flour, coal and wood dwindled to nothing. On 8 March the long silent food queues suddenly ignited. People smashed their way into shops and helped themselves. The revolution had begun.

Two days later most of Petrograd went on strike. People paraded through the streets with banners: 'Give us Bread' and 'Down with the German Woman'. Nicholas's ministers telegraphed frantically to the Emperor, who was on a train travelling to Army headquarters, imploring

The Tauride Palace, which housed
the Duma

him to return, and begging him to appoint a Government acceptable to
the Duma. He refused both requests. Instead, he ordered the Petrograd
garrison to restore order. The army, however, refused to fire on the
people, and began to fraternize with the rebels. On 11 March Nicholas
telegraphed dissolving the Duma. But the Duma also refused to obey.
The following day the Assembly formed its own Provisional Government, appointing the Social Revolutionary, Alexander Kerensky, to the
key post of Minister of Justice.

Even this did not calm the crowds. Later in the day thousands of
troops, who by this time had mutinied, gathered together and marched
toward the Duma. 'Their movement was completely unorganized and . . .
anarchical,' wrote Kerensky, 'The need for some kind of centre for
the mass movement was recognized by everybody . . . A Soviet? The
memory of 1905 prompted this cry . . .' Before evening fell, the Duma
and the Soviet sat in the two wings of the Tauride Palace, the great
residence that Catherine the Great had given to her lover, Gregory
Potemkin.

Two days later, on 14 March, Nicholas II abdicated. The former
President of the Duma, Rodzianko, talked over the telephone to
General Alexeyev at Headquarters, and asked him to sound opinion
among the generals commanding the different fronts. Their verdict was
unanimous. The only hope of saving the dynasty and continuing the
war was the voluntary resignation of Nicholas. .

Nicholas resigned. 'In agreement with the State Duma we have deemed it good to abdicate the crown. Not wishing to be separated from our beloved son, we leave our heritage to our brother. . . .'

At first Nicholas abdicated in favour of his son, Alexis. But when it was pointed out to him that this would mean the separation of the boy from his parents, he asked for a new sheet of paper and abdicated in favour of his brother, Michael.

When Kerensky learned that Russia still had a Tsar, he was aghast. As Kerensky was not only Minister of Justice but Vice-Chairman of the Soviet, he was a key figure. Michael travelled from Gatchina to Petrograd and went straight to a house where the new Provisional Government was meeting. Kerensky told him that if the news of his accession was communicated to the Soviet he could not guarantee his life. What might have been possible a month ago had been swept away by revolutionary fervour. After a brief discussion, Michael signed a hastily typed statement announcing his abdication. The rule of the Romanovs had come to an end.

The sixteen months that followed the overthrow of the monarchy revealed a new and noble Nicholas and Alexandra. These lamentable rulers, these tragic, misguided autocrats, who possessed not an inkling of understanding of the swift currents swirling around them, endured the trial and humiliation to which they were submitted with such rare dignity and courage that none but the coldest heart can fail to admire them. Their love for each other, their unquestioning faith in God, gave them a nobility that shines through the mists of time. The vacillating monarch became a man of strength; the censorious consort a woman of

Nicholas and his family at Tobolsk. 'I am so sad,' wrote Alexandra, 'because they are allowed no walks except before the house and behind a high fence. But at least they have fresh air and we are grateful for anything.'

compassion. On 13 March, not long before her death, Alexandra wrote to Anna Virubova:

> How I love my country with all its faults! It grows dearer and dearer to me, and I thank God daily that He allowed us to remain here, and did not send us further away. Believe in the people, darling. The nation is strong and young, and as soft as wax. Just now it is in bad hands, and darkness and anarchy reign. But the King of Glory will come and will save, strengthen and give wisdom to the people who are now deceived.[31]

Although the Imperial family were under house arrest at Tsarskoye Selo, at first they were treated with courtesy and allowed to lead their restricted lives unmolested. But as the extremists began to return to Russia, first Trotsky, then Lenin, their conditions deteriorated. In

July 1917 an abortive Bolshevik uprising prompted Kerensky to move the family to Tobolsk in Siberia, where, he hoped, they would not fall into violent hands.

Here they lived in closely-guarded seclusion and reasonable comfort. They still had retainers, and were allowed to write letters to the outside world. But when the Provisional Government fell in November 1917, and the Bolsheviks attained full power, the scene changed. New guards were brought in, young men burning with revolutionary fervour. These youths amused themselves by subjecting the family to jeers and insults, and by drawing lewd pictures on the walls. 'The strange thing about the Russian character,' wrote Alexandra, 'is that it can so suddenly change to evil, cruelty and unreason, and as suddenly change back again.'

During the months of April and May 1918 the family, accompanied by a doctor, and three servants, were moved to Ipatiev House in Ekaterinburg on the eastern slope of the Urals. Here they were subjected to insults and indecencies. The doors were taken away from bedrooms and lavatories, and they were forced to dress and undress and perform the most intimate functions with their jailers grinning at them.

Shortly after midnight on 16 July the guards awoke Nicholas, Alexandra, their son, four daughters, the doctor and three servants, and instructed them to dress. The White Army was approaching and they must be moved immediately. They were led to a small room in the basement, with an iron grille, and told to wait until the motors arrived.

But no cars ever appeared. Instead, a Cheka squad, carrying revolvers, pushed their way into the small room. The leader stepped forward. 'Your relations have tried to save you. They have failed and now we must shoot you.' The murder perhaps took place by the personal order of the new ruler of Russia, Lenin.

'The atmosphere around us is fairly electrified,' Alexandra had written to Anna Virubova, a few days before leaving Tobolsk for Ekaterinburg. 'We feel that a storm is approaching, but we know that God is merciful . . . our souls are at peace. Whatever happens will be through God's will.'

Bibliographical References

The full title of book and name of author is repeated in each chapter where subsequent references occur.
The name of publisher and date of publication are given only once, however: the first time that a work is mentioned.

Chapter I
THE FIRST ROMANOVS

1. Samuel Collins,
The Present State of Russia,
LONDON, 1671, ch. XV.

2. R. Nisbet Bain,
The First Romanovs,
LONDON, 1905, p. 30.

3. Adrien de la Neuville,
Zapisski: Relation curieuse et nouvelle de la Moscovie, PARIS, 1698.

Chapter II
PETER THE GREAT

1. Eugene Schuyler,
Peter the Great, vol. I,
LONDON, 1884, pp. 350–1.

2. W. Bray (ed.),
The Diary of John Evelyn,
LONDON, 1890, p. 571.

3. Schuyler,
Peter the Great, vol. I, p. 386.

4. Zinaida Schakovskoy,
Precursors of Peter the Great,
transl. J. Maxwell Brownjohn,
Jonathan Cape, LONDON, 1964, p. 300.

5. Lionel Kochan,
The Making of Modern Russia,
Jonathan Cape,
LONDON, 1962, p. 111.

6. Walter Kelly,
History of Russia, vol. I,
LONDON, 1854, pp. 378–9.

7. Sloane Papers,
British Museum,
Additional Mss 4164, 43–6.

8. Ibid.

9. Ibid.

10. Thomas Carlyle,
History of Frederick the Great,
ed. J. Clive, University of Chicago Press,
1969, pp. 84–5.

11. B. H. Sumner,
Peter the Great,
E.U.P., LONDON, 1950, p. 85.

12. Schuyler,
Peter the Great, vol. II,
pp. 543–4.

Chapter III
ANNA, ELIZABETH AND
PETER III

1. V. O. Kluchevsky,
A History of Russia, vol. IV,
transl. C. J. Hogarth, Dent,
LONDON, 1926, p. 307.

2. Mrs Ward (formerly Lady Rondeau),
Letters from a Lady in Russia,
LONDON, 1775, p. 93–4.

3. R. Nisbet Bain,
The Pupils of Peter the Great,
LONDON, 1897, pp. 196–7.

4. Ward,
Letters from a Lady in Russia,
p. 73.

5. Kluchevsky,
A History of Russia, vol. IV,
p. 356.

6. Dominique Maroger (ed.),
The Memoirs of Catherine the Great,
Hamish Hamilton,
LONDON, 1955, p. 62.

7. R. Nisbet Bain,
The Daughter of Peter the Great,
LONDON, 1899, p. 140.

8. Maroger (ed.),
The Memoirs of Catherine the Great,
p. 99.

9. Ibid., p. 13.

10. Alexander Herzen (ed.),
Mémoires de l'Impératrice Catherine II,
Trübner, LONDON, 1859, p. 102.

11. Maroger (ed.),
The Memoirs of Catherine the Great,
pp. 118–9.

12. Ibid., p. 13.

13. R. Nisbet Bain,
Peter III,
LONDON, 1902, pp. 69–70.

14. Ibid., p. 130.

15. Ibid., p. 171.

Chapter IV
CATHERINE THE GREAT

1. Zoë Oldenbourg,
Catherine the Great,
Heinemann, LONDON, 1965, p. 216.

2. William Coxe,
Travels into Poland, Russia, Sweden,
vol. II, LONDON, 1792, p. 281.

3. Ibid., p. 288.

4. The Marchioness of Londonderry
and H. M. Hyde (eds),
The Russian Journals of Martha and Catherine Wilmot,
Macmillan, LONDON, 1934, p. 275.

5. Ibid., p. 56.

6. C. F. P. Masson,
Secret Memoirs of the Court of St Petersburg,
LONDON, 1895, p. 318.

7. Oldenbourg,
Catherine the Great, p. 248.

8. Maroger (ed.),
Memoirs of Catherine the Great, p. 356.

9. Katherine Anthony,
Catherine the Great,
Jonathan Cape,
LONDON, 1931, p. 227.

10. Maroger (ed.),
Memoirs of Catherine the Great, p. 356.

11. G. P. Gooch,
Catherine the Great and other studies,
Longmans, LONDON, 1954, p. 25.

12. G. Oudard (ed.),
Lettres d'amour de Catherine II à Potemkin,
Nouvelle Collection Historique,
PARIS, 1934, pp. 36–7.

13. Ibid., p. 159.

14. Gooch,
Catherine the Great, p. 35.

15. Masson,
Secret Memoirs of the Court of St Petersburg, p. 83.

16. Comte de Ségur,
Mémoires, PARIS, 1826.

17. Ibid.

18. Maroger (ed.),
Memoirs of Catherine the Great, p. 377.

19. Miriam Kochan,
Life in Russia under Catherine the Great,
Batsford, LONDON, 1969, p. 32.

Chapter v
PAUL I AND ALEXANDER I

1. E. M. Almedingen,
The Romanovs,
Bodley Head, LONDON, 1966, p. 189.

2. Francis Gribble,
Emperor and Mystic,
Nash & Grayson,
LONDON, 1931, p. 45.

3. C. Joyneville,
Life and Times of Alexander I, vol. I,
LONDON, 1875, p. 201.

4. Londonderry and Hyde (eds),
*The Russian Journal of Martha and
Catherine Wilmot*, p. 216.

5. P. Putnam (ed.),
*Seven Britons in Imperial Russia,
1698–1812*,
Princeton University Press, 1952,
p. 361.

6. Leonid Strakhovsky,
Alexander I of Russia,
Williams & Norgate,
LONDON, 1949, p. 127–8.

7. Robert Wilson,
Private Diary of Travels,
ed. Rev. H. R. J. Murray,
LONDON, 1860, pp. 172.

8. Ibid., p. 178.

9. Ibid., pp. 179–180.

10. Ibid.

11. Ibid., pp. 213–14.

12. E. M. Almedingen,
The Emperor Alexander I,
Bodley Head, LONDON, 1964, p. 150.

13. Gribble,
Emperor and Mystic, p. 62.

14. Ibid., p. 181.

15. Ibid., p. 187.

16. Ibid., p. 217.

17. Almedingen,
The Emperor Alexander I, p. 196.

18. Thomas Riha (ed.),
*Readings in Russian Civilization:
The Decembrists*,
University of Chicago Press, 1964,
p. 299.

19. Una Pope-Hennessey (transl.),
A Czarina's Story,
Nicholson & Watson,
LONDON, 1948, p. 14.

20. Ibid., pp. 44–5.

Chapter vi
NICHOLAS I

1. Constantine de Grunwald,
Tsar Nicholas I (quoted from the diary
of the Empress Alexandra Feodorovna),
Douglas Saunders with MacGibbon &
Kee, LONDON, 1954, p. 39.

2. Ibid., pp. 7–8.

3. *The Letters of Queen Victoria*,
First Series, vol. II, John Murray,
LONDON, 1911, p. 14.

4. Marquis de Custine, *Russia*,
LONDON, 1854, p. 50.

5. Ibid., p. 58.

6. Riha (ed.),
Readings in Russian Civilization, p. 317.

7. Ibid., pp. 318–19.

8. E. M. Almedingen,
The Emperor Alexander II,
Bodley Head, LONDON, 1962, p. 63.

9. Kochan,
The Making of Modern Russia, p. 50.

10. Grunwald,
Tsar Nicholas I, p. 169.

11. Alexander Herzen,
My Past and Thoughts, vol. II,
transl. Constance Garnett,
Chatto & Windus,
LONDON, 1924–7, pp. 257, 254.

12. Almedingen,
The Emperor Alexander II, p. 85..

13. Grunwald,
Tsar Nicholas I, pp. 268–75.

Chapter vii
ALEXANDER II

1. Count Egon Corti,
The Downfall of Three Dynasties,
Methuen, LONDON, 1934, p. 103.

2. M. E. Saltykov,
Selected Works,
MOSCOW, 1946, pp. 132–3.

3. Almedingen,
Alexander II, p. 166.

4. E. Sutherland Edwards,
The Romanoffs,
W. H. Allen, LONDON, 1890, p. 247.

5. S. S. Tatichev,
The Emperor Alexander II, vol. II,
ST PETERSBURG, 1903, p. 401.

6. D. Margaschack (transl.),
Turgenev's Literary Reminiscences, vol. I,
Faber, LONDON, 1959, p. 107.

7. Lord Frederick Hamilton,
The Vanished Pomps of Yesterday,
Hodder & Stoughton,
LONDON, 1920, p. 88.

8. Sir Horace Rumbold,
Recollections of a Diplomatist, vol. II,
Edward Arnold,
LONDON, 1902, p. 254.

9. Maurice Paléologue,
The Tragic Romance of Alexander II,
Hutchinson, LONDON, 1926, p. 47.

10. Alexander Kornilov,
Modern Russian History, vol. II,
Skeffington,
LONDON, 1916, pp. 112–13.

11. Lord Augustus Loftus,
Diplomatic Reminiscences, vol. II,
Cassell, LONDON, 1894, p. 210.

12. Almedingen,
The Emperor Alexander II, pp. 280–1.

13. Monypenny and Buckle,
The Life of Benjamin Disraeli,
John Murray,
LONDON, 1920, pp. 132–3.

14. Ibid., p. 325.

15. Henri Troyat,
Tolstoy, Doubleday,
NEW YORK, 1967, p. 385.

16. Corti,
The Downfall of Three Dynasties,
p. 272.

17. The Grand Duke
Alexander Mikhailovich,
Once a Grand Duke,
Cassell, LONDON, 1908, p. 63.

18. Almedingen,
The Emperor Alexander II, p. 338.

19. Mikhailovich,
Once a Grand Duke, p. 72.

20. Paléologue,
The Tragic Romance of Alexander II,
pp. 28–9.

Chapter viii
ALEXANDER III

1. Troyat, *Tolstoy*, p. 406.

2. Charles Lowe,
Alexander III of Russia,
Heinemann,
LONDON, 1895, pp. 253–4.

3. Ian Vorres,
The Last Grand Duchess,
Hutchinson,
LONDON, 1964, pp. 26–7.

4. *The Contemporary Review*, January 1893.

5. Harold Frederic, *The New Exodus*, Heinemann, LONDON, 1892, p. 200.

6. Vorres, *The Last Grand Duchess*, p. 37.

7. Count Sergius Witte, *Memoirs*, p. 39.

8. Lady Randolph Churchill, *Reminiscences*, Edward Arnold, LONDON, 1908, p. 169.

9. E. A. Brayley Hodgett, *The Court of Russia in the 19th Century*, Methuen, LONDON, 1908, p. 239.

10. Hamilton, *The Vanished Pomps of Yesterday*, p. 157.

11. Vorres, *The Last Grand Duchess*, p. 39.

12. Baroness Kleinmichel, *Memories of a Shipwrecked World*, transl. V. Le Grand, Brentano, LONDON, 1923, p. 116.

13. Wyndham & Greville, F.O. 78/3393.

14. *The Letters of Queen Victoria*, Second Series, vol. III, John Murray, LONDON, 1932, p. 699.

15. Tsar Nicholas II, *Journal Intime*, transl. A. Pierre, Payot, PARIS, 1925, p. 45.

16. Mikhailovich, *Once a Grand Duke*, p. 186.

17. Ibid., p. 75.

18. Lowe, *Alexander III*, p. 348.

19. Ibid., p. 355.

20. Prince von Bülow, *Memoirs*, vol. I, Putnam, LONDON, p. 98.

21. E. Bing (ed.), *The Letters of Tsar Nicholas and The Empress Marie*, Ivor, Nicholson & Watson, LONDON, 1937, pp. 75–6.

22. Ibid., pp. 75–6.

23. Mikhailovich, *Once a Grand Duke*, p. 189.

Chapter IX
NICHOLAS II

1. Vorres, *The Last Grand Duchess*, p. 67.

2. Princess Catherine Radziwill, *The Intimate Life of the Last Czarina*, Cassell, LONDON, 1929, pp. 36–7.

3. Ibid., p. 37.

4. Princess Catherine Radziwill, *Nicholas II : The Last of the Czars*, Cassell, LONDON, 1931, p. 17.

5. Mikhailovich, *Once a Grand Duke*, p. 193.

6. Radziwill, *The Intimate Life of the Last Czarina*, pp. 75–6.

7. Anna Virubova, *Memories of the Russian Court*, Macmillan, NEW YORK, 1923, pp. 21–2.

8. *Krasny Arkhiv*, vol. II, p. 31.

9. *The Letters and Friendships of Sir Cecil Spring Rice*, Constable, LONDON, 1929, p. 425.

10. Radziwill, *Nicholas II*, pp. 158–9.

11. Ibid., pp. 158–9.

12. Bing (ed.), *The Letters of Tsar Nicholas and the Empress Marie*, p. 183.

13. Harmon Tupper, *To the Great Ocean*, Little, Brown, Boston, 1965, p. 269.

14. Maurice Paléologue, *An Ambassador's Memoirs*, vol. I, transl. F. A. Holt, Hutchinson, LONDON, 1923–5, p. 292.

15. Meriel Buchanan, *Dissolution of an Empire*, John Murray, LONDON, 1932, pp. 36–7.

16. Virubova, *Memories of the Russian Court*, pp. 93–4.

17. Alexander Kerensky, *The Crucifixion of Liberty*, Day, NEW YORK, 1934, p. 125.

18. Ralph Fox, *Lenin*, Gollancz, LONDON, 1933, p. 189.

19. Kerensky, *The Crucifixion of Liberty*, p. 172.

20. Sidney Fay, *The Origins of the First World War*, Macmillan, NEW YORK, 1959, p. 569.

21. Paléologue, *An Ambassador's Memoirs*, vol. I, p. 52.

22. *The Letters of the Tsaritsa to the Tsar*, *1914–17*.

23. Michael Florinsky, *The End of the Russian Empire*, Collier Books, NEW YORK, 1961, p. 67.

24. Radziwill, *The Intimate Life of the Last Czarina*, p. 18.

25. *The Letters of the Tsaritsa to the Tsar*, p. 145.

26. Ibid., pp. 346–56.

27. Ibid.

28. Bernard Pares, *The Downfall of the Russian Monarchy*, Jonathan Cape, LONDON, 1939, pp. 396–7.

29. *The Letters of the Tsaritsa to the Tsar*, p. 461.

30. Paléologue, *An Ambassador's Memoirs*, vol. III, p. 136.

31. Virubova, *Memories of the Russian Court*, p. 336.

List and sources of black and white illustrations

Page numbers printed in *italics* indicate illustrations.